BECAUSE WE CAN - WE MUST

Achieving the Human Developmental
Potential in Five Generations

ALEXANDER T. POLGAR Ph.D.

Sandriam Publications Inc.
Hamilton, Ontario, Canada

BECAUSE WE CAN – WE MUST: ACHIEVING THE HUMAN
DEVELOPMENTAL POTENTIAL IN FIVE GENERATIONS
BY ALEXANDER T. POLGAR PH.D.

©2009 Sandriam Publications Inc.
Hamilton, Ontario. Canada

atpolgar@sympatico.ca
www.atpolgar.com/sandriam-publications

All rights reserved.
No part of this book may be reproduced, stored in a retrieval system or transmitted in any form or by any means, electronic, mechanical, microfilming, recording, or otherwise without written permission from the Publisher.

ISBN: 978-0-9730389-8-9

Printed and bound in Canada
3rd Printing 2019

Cover: Workhorse Design Studio

This work is dedicated to all those who, after reading it,
say to themselves and to others:
"Why aren't we doing something like this?"

ACKNOWLEDGEMENTS

The ideas in this book and the courage to write them are the product of many processes which began and continued with emphatically encouraging and gracious mentoring. Key individuals are forever in my mind starting with one particular elementary school teacher, Jim Hughes, and culminating in post secondary teachers, Dan Yarmey, Erv Zentner, John Eisenberg, Kim Lambert, and those who became life long friends such as John Gandy and Francis Joseph Turner. These and other educators played a key role in my development. They were the invaluable and timely environmental influences on the evolution and synthesis of my notions. To them and all the others, in my life, who took their teaching responsibilities seriously, I am eternally grateful.

The development of my ideas and their relevance to real life, also are the result of fortunate happenstance. When I was most troubled by knowing that I did not know how to resolve, competently, competing claims among staff and residents and between staff and residents on a treatment unit, of which I was manager, there was Reg Reynolds who introduced me to the domain of cognitive moral development. He helped me to see the value of this framework for making fair and just decisions as well as for helping offenders to reason and behave in pro-social ways. This experience marked the beginning of my life long interest in the ideas of Lawrence Kohlberg and, more importantly, the application of what he and others in the field had to say about enhancing and improving the human condition.

The production of this work could not have been possible without the patient toil of my typist, Karen Rachner, who endured several revisions and a seemingly never ending collage of notes to add, delete, and move around paragraphs, sometimes several pages of text. I also benefited greatly from discussing and debating ideas, which become the content of this book, with friends and colleagues, whose wisdom and insights I very much value. I am especially grateful to David Lloyd Angles who volunteered to proof read and edit the text after I could no longer see the most obvious typo, grammatical error or awkward sentence structure. Ultimately, however, I am responsible for how and what is written. Whatever offense is taken to what I wrote, no offense was unintended. My sole purpose was and is to convey optimism even about the worst maligned factions and conditions in our world.

After this experience, I now fully understand the almost predictable acknowledgement, by most authors, of the support and encouragement of their spouse and family. I truly cannot imagine how any accomplishment, let alone writing a book, could be possible without the support of significant others. It is surely an axiom of life, that any task is made only better when a significant other is involved. Because of this I am literally lost for words to express the gratitude I have for the love and support of my wife, Drina Omazic. Not only did she simply accept, as fact, that I was going to abandon my revenue generating work, as long as it took to write this but she also read the drafts, offering invaluable commentary each time. Whatever positive comes of this effort she rightfully is entitled to share it. The unintended, albeit inevitable negative, that also is visited upon all good intentions, however, belongs entirely to me.

CONTENTS

Acknowledgements v
Introduction 1

PART ONE
WHAT ARE THEY SAYING?

Part One Preamble 15
Chapter One The Environment 25
Chapter Two Corruption 53
Chapter Three Misbehaviour... 93

PART TWO
WHAT IT ALL MEANS!

Part Two Preamble 159
Chapter Four Defining The Method of Interpretation 165
Chapter Five The Activity of "Ethicing" 219
Chapter Six Status Quo 263

PART THREE
THIS IS WHAT WE NEED TO DO!

Part Three Preamble 285
Chapter Seven The Anatomy of Change 295
Chapter Eight Who Will Be the Agents of Change 341
Chapter Nine The Critical Path To Achieving Our Vision ... 363
Epilogue 389
References 395
About The Author 405

INTRODUCTION

*"From the state of a man's heart proceed
the conditions of his life; his thoughts blossom
into deeds, and his deeds bear the fruitage of
character and destiny."*

James Allen
As a Man Thinketh 1864-1912

This book is all about the need and how to promote fully the development of all our children so that they can blossom optimally. The focus is first remedial and then preventive. First we must address what is and then prevent it from happening, ever again.

The quote from James Allen sums up the foundation upon which what is proposed is built. Unfortunately the sentiment conveyed by Allen is difficult to explain especially using language to which we can all relate. Nevertheless, intuitively, at some level of awareness, we all recognize that there is much truth in what Allen says. That, "As a man thinketh in his heart, so is he". Moreover, there are many who are inspired to act upon what Allen and others with similar views postulate as axiomatic of the human condition. I count myself to be among those who are constantly seeking the behavioural imperatives embedded in the wisdom and insights of others. This work represents such an ambition, one which, at the very least, I hope will serve as an impetus for dialogue about what we ought to do to change the human condition, starting with changing how we raise our children.

I believe James Allen articulates that every human being is shaped, indeed determined, physically and psychologically by two factors. That with which we are born and that which we experience. While the debate about nature and nurture continues, the debate has subsided considerably, at least partly, because of the technology now available to study physical development. While undeniably we are all born with unique innate propensities, invariably it is our environment which shapes the activation of our innate propensities, indeed our development as individuals. Because of the greater influence of environment on our development it is not surprising that our determining influences are intergenerational legacies perpetuated by the conditions created by parents and, in some parts of the world, by extended families. The importance of environment is a fundamental premise of this book. As such, the 'to do' part prescribes environmental interventions with which to finally actualize, on mass, the potential of which we are all capable. The challenge is not nearly as grandiose as it seems.

Insofar as, in part, this is 'a how to book' I will speak to innate propensities such as genetics or temperament mostly in passing.

Until we can manipulate directly the innate propensities with which we are born, there is not much value in examining this aspect of our makeup. Apart from academic researchers, for the rest of us, placing emphasis on the innate propensities almost always serves to justify abdicating personal and social responsibility for the conditions we have created and through which the dysfunctionalities of each generation are perpetuated.

The premise of this book is that our intergenerational, collective maladaptive patterns, start with how we care for our children prenatally and during the most crucial, formative stage of life, which constitutes the first two years. Insofar as dysfunctionalities start there they must also be stopped there. This will take five generations to accomplish as is the sage edict of many aboriginal elders. In fact, according to the elders, to achieve a significant change takes five hundred years. I am more optimistic. I am betting on five generations, approximately a hundred years, hopefully less. In the process of change, with each successive better developed generation, also it will be possible to reverse much of the harm we have perpetrated on each other and our world. For example, scientists such as James Hansen, director of NASA's Goodard Space Flight Centre in New York, studying climate change, is spearheading a campaign to have 350 parts per million carbon in the atmosphere recognized as the long term target for reversing global warming. He believes a hundred years may be sufficient time to achieve this.

Given the goal of this book to precipitate a significant change in the human condition, this book is not another litany of complaints or descriptions of what has been and continues to be. I do not mean to imply, however, that professional activists, historians, and social commentators do not serve a vitally important role. They raise our consciousness and make us painfully aware of the dismal condition of our world; they alert us to the forces responsible for robbing us of a quality of life we all have the potential to achieve. Tragically, most professional activists, historians, and social commentators offer few remedies. Some advocate and rely on being in compliance with rules, laws or international accords such as those formulated in Kyoto. Most, however, have unwarranted, grand expectations of people analogous to that of Freudian psychoanalysts. Specifically, that becoming aware, raising consciousness, will lead to marked changes in thought patterns, emotions, and behaviour. Unfortunately, precipitating positive and sustainable action is a complex enterprise, made more so because of the unavoidable human developmental element. Moreover, contrary to the belief of some, almost everyone agrees with the professional activists who state, for example, that we are exponentially destroying our environment. Similarly, almost everyone knows what constitutes acceptable and unacceptable behaviour. It is acting on what we know that is the problem! How to get people to do the right thing in a predictably consistent pattern is the challenge. When this is accomplished the world will cease to exist as we know it now. It will be completely different. It will be a world as the prophets envisioned before their messages were distorted by lesser people than they were.

Sustainable and significant change of the type prescribed in this book cannot happen spontaneously. Such change requires the implementation of processes. Fortunately, the processes do not have to be invented. Fortunately, many are familiar and comfortable with the processes. Unfortunately, the processes have been best applied to technological pursuits and/or the amassment of wealth. For example, to accomplish the goal of the Apollo Space Program, to land on the moon and then return the astronauts to earth, some two million tasks had to be completed. For one million of these tasks the prerequisite knowledge and skills did not exist at the outset. The fact that people walked on the moon, not once but several times, and then returned to earth speaks of what we are capable when we commit ourselves to a task. This and many other achievements give much cause for optimism about the goal of this book.

The fact that probably it will take five generations to achieve a drastic change in the human condition, as encouraged by the prophets, simply requires that we respond as the French General Lyautey when he was admonished, as he set out to plant a certain sapling. When he was told that the tree would take one hundred years to reach full maturity, he responded, "Why then we must begin this very afternoon". Along a similar vein, Franz Kafka said, "There is hope, but not for us". Perhaps Kafka is not entirely correct. I am certainly counting on this since each generation will need encouragement to continue and build upon the accomplishments of former generations. Hence change will be incremental, and the benefits accrued will bear witness to the axiom of life: "Nothing succeeds like success".

In order to achieve the goal of this book, I adopt the familiar problem solving process including creating a strategic plan. In essence, this book is a vivid illustration of the methodology. Problem solving on which a strategic plan is based begins with defining operationally that which is being experienced as objectionable. An operational definition entails translating all the concepts, in a statement of the problem, into observable and measurable (qualitatively and/or quantitatively) indicators. In Part One this activity will be illustrated abundantly albeit not exhaustively. The formulation of a problem in this context is really a delineation of symptoms. A symptom, for example, is a child's fever or skin rash or in this context global warming. A problem formulation also is a statement of what constitutes a solution. At the risk of sounding pedestrian, a solution in the case of the sick child is for the fever to subside by fixing what ever caused it to occur in the first place. In the context of this book, a solution entails fixing the conditions associated with global warming. It is terribly important the we differentiate between simply addressing the symptom, fever, global warming, and the processes that caused the symptoms. Sometimes it is imperative to address immediately the symptom but invariably, sooner than later, the cause also must be resolved.

Addressing the underlying cause of any symptom requires attributing meaning to it. Often a fever is indicative of a child's immune system fighting an infection, ie., an invasion of the child's body by some foreign organism. Similarly, the misbehaviour of people, as a symptom, has numerous meanings attributed to it. The meanings have evolved over time from being possessed by the devil to an individual acting out systemic oppression caused by poverty. Regardless of the meaning, or more accurately the theory, there are specific interventions indicated by the explanation to which we subscribe. Not that long ago, bleeding a fevered patient was the standard comparable to today's prescription of antibiotics.

Part Two explains the underlying cause of the symptoms that characterize the human malaise described in Part One. Without the explanations, the proposed interventions in Part Three would make no sense. Without the explanations, the proposed interventions would amount to an exercise based on some requirement to act on an authority that is void of reasoned elaboration. Such authority seldom, if ever, accomplishes much.

This book begins, therefore, with a review of the writings of mostly contemporary commentators/activists and historians about world events and the people in them. Admittedly, the temptation was great to stay at this level.

In fact, this project was originally conceived and started with this focus in mind. It then occurred to me that, regardless of how clever my exposé of past and current malfeasance, it would still amount to just another complaint. It also dawned on me that such critics as Michael Moore, David Suzuki, Al Gore and Noam Chomsky, while making extremely valid points, do not really threaten the status quo. Consequently, instead of being assassinated they are marginalised, ridiculed or exposed for doing not that which they preach. Reportedly Michael Moore has two hot tubs and refuses to be interviewed, by at least some, members of the media, and Al Gore lives in a home that consumes a lot of electrical energy.

It also occurred to me that the activists and social commentators are probably recognized by the protectors of the status quo as serving a useful function, one which invariably leads to little or no action. By concentrating on the various tragedies, such as, global warming, corporate fraud, and the like, activists are no more than "rubberneckers" who gawk at gruesome scenes on the peril ridden roads of life. "Rubberneckers" seldom do anything besides back up traffic, only to speed up once the scene of an accident is out of sight. Most never reflect upon what could have caused the accident and, more importantly, how it could be prevented from occurring in the future.

The fate of those who did little exposing or critiquing but actually began to initiate change to the status quo bare some reflection and for the recklessly adventurous should serve as an impetus for considerable emulation. Some were assassinated for the threat they posed to the status quo. Nevertheless, their impact lives on ideologically and in the actual changes they created . Assassination has not silenced or reversed the accomplishments of Martin Luther King Junior or Mahatma Ghandi, although the message and changes precipitated by Jesus and Mohammed have been distorted over time, in every which way.

Citing a small sampling of changers and their demise is intended to be inspirational and to illustrate that change has been accomplished and the potential continues to exist, however, to change the status quo, to propose a five generation strategic plan and then critical path the entire process, will be a formidable undertaking. In recognition of this reality, I decided not to distract you with extensive reviews or heroic efforts at being scholarly. I certainly do not want this work to be viewed as a complaint about the complainers. Quite to the contrary, I implore you, if you have not already done so, to read in full at least some of the references I provide. See for yourself the wonderful scholarly ways in which each author provides the background, often from a historical perspective to that about which they are writing. See for yourself how the human condition has only changed in content (what is done) and has remained in structure (organization of reasoning) the same. We no longer go to the Roman Coliseum to see mayhem we now have CNN to provide us with the gore, albeit without the stench that accompanies it. Even sanitized gore is still gore in which we continue to have a morbid interest. More importantly, by reviewing the references, see for yourself the absence of meaningful solutions, let alone an action plan, to remedy the problems being described. The edict to "get involved", simply does not suffice.

The plan by which to achieve the goal I am proposing is deliberately advanced in a very particular way. I came upon this strategy after a delightful lunch on an extremely cold January day, with a personally admired scholar, Professor Dwight Boyd. Dwight was a star pupil of another personally admired scholar, Lawrence Kohlberg, who taught at Harvard University in Cambridge, Massachusetts. Obviously, they shared a particularly meaningful bond as was evident in the warmth with which Dwight related a story told to him by Professor Kohlberg.

Prior to being appointed to The Centre For Moral Development and Moral Education at Harvard University, Professor Kohlberg was invited to address an audience of campus scholars. In his physical, intellectual, and academic prime, Professor Kohlberg reportedly applied all of his capabilities to crafting and delivering the best possible and most thorough presentation. Those who knew him personally and those who know of his work will have no difficulty in imagining how superb his presentation was. In fact, it was so well done that when the moderator invited comments, after each and every effort to stimulate discussion, there was silence. Professor Kohlberg had covered all of the bases; the scholars had nothing to discuss let alone challenge. Instead of creating an exciting buzz and discussion about himself and more importantly, about his ideas, Professor Kohlberg's arrival on campus fizzled. Subsequently Dwight Boyd, who was about to go through a similar process was advised by Professor Kohlberg: "Some things worth doing are not worth doing well!"

I certainly do not want this work to fizzle out. My intent is to generate much discourse, and I am willing to endure whatever it takes to give life to the critical path in Part Three. From the buzz, I hope variations on my proposed plan will evolve and that, sooner than later, the five generation long critical path will become disassociated from its origins. To achieve the goal I have set will require unleashing the creativity of others as well as fostering their ownership of both the vision and the process for its actualization.

I also do not want to bore you with so much detail as to dissuade all but the most tenacious from engaging in a critical discussion of the message and the strategies with which to end the human condition as we have known it so far. In this spirit I have selected very carefully the references and, with equal care, the extent to which I summarized what the various sources say.

I anticipate that the types of response to its book will be twofold in nature. The greatest and most pervasive response, I fully anticipate, will be a negative one; it will come mostly from the establishment, the status quo, and from those who aspire to it. Status quo is synonymous with power and wealth, privileges enjoyed by people whose number has changed little over the centuries, although the membership of this small group does change from time to time. For example, while the names change occasionally, still only five percent of Americans control nearly half of their country's wealth.

Those who are the status quo want to protect their position but then so do many who aspire to it. The Western capitalist dream is alive and well. It is fuelled by the media, and many still believe that the story of Horatio Allger will be their story, too. Many still believe that hard work, clever work, and tenacity will open the doors to the sanctum of the status quo. Those who lose faith in this route embrace the "constellation road" to riches through gambling or speculation. For the majority, steeped in the imperative of positive thinking, the status quo must be protected. It is the destination of the eternally, albeit gullible, hopeful.

The second category of responses I expect will come from a smaller group, more accurately groups, likely initially dispersed and disconnected from each other. These pockets of individuals already are doing much good and their efforts contribute to advances in the human condition. Unfortunately, because they are disconnected from each other, their respective impact is a long way from reaching critical mass, an effect which will precipitate the process that will, in five generations, culminate in achieving the goal prescribed in this book. While I very much believe, as the anthropologist Margaret Mead, that much can be accomplished by a small dedicated group, time is a wasting. It may already be too late but, through an exponentially growing coalition, it may just be possible to incrementally turn back the doomsday clock the professional activists are describing. The time for consciousness raising is past. It is now time for reasoned action focussed not on symptoms but on underlying causes. The very future of the human species now depends upon the small disassociated groups who by uniting their efforts, can bring about the solution described in this book.

To mobilize the emergence of existing and new small groups of innovative doers and to mobilize their coalition, admittedly two-thirds of this book is designed to be seductive, to stir as many as possible to action. Action which will include the application of each person's capabilities to this initiative. One-third, Part One, entails a broad sweeping review of the various professional activists' publications categorizing the materials into sections. The next third, Part Two, proffers a particular explanation as to what causes the symptoms. I say 'causes the symptoms', fully aware of the scientific rigour required to establish cause and effect, because I believe it to be a useful belief even if not absolutely true. In Part Two, I offer both meaning and relevance to the action plan that is proposed in Part Three, the last part of this book. The greatest challenge was to write in such a way as to keep you engaged in the very sobering conversation about the "crazy aunt" in the attic whom no one wants to acknowledge let alone do something about. The "crazy aunt" is how we raise our children.

PART ONE
WHAT ARE THEY SAYING?

PART ONE
PREAMBLE

Throughout my life, I have experienced an insidious, gradual disillusionment with how things have been and how they continue to be. Nevertheless, I have remained an eternal optimist about our individual and our collective potential to do better. From my perspective, it is not that there is an absence of goodness; the problem is that it is overshadowed by whatever we call its opposite. This has been and continues to be the case. This kind of thinking, to which I subscribe, is typical of a realist. Being a realist has been an incredibly liberating and energizing experience. Almost a decade ago, I became energized to write my own version of just how bad things have been and continue to be and used as a template Hans Christian Andersen's The Emperor's New Clothes fairy tale. I very much identified with the youth who blurted out that the king on parade, "is in his underwear not magnificent clothing". The spin to my version, thinking myself to be more astute than Mr. Andersen, was going to be that the crowd turned on the dissenting boy, who dared to speak the truth, and reveal how things really were, and stoned him to death. Alas, upon reflection, I quickly faced reality that Mr. Andersen did indeed get it right. The evidence is overwhelming that the speakers of truth, whistle-blowers, social commentators, and activists who dare to break from the politically correct and status quo, are not stoned to death. The very best of these people are politely humoured and marginalised. They realize this and justify their approach by saying that they are keeping an issue alive and, in so doing, gradually instigate change. A good example is Noam Chomsky, who is treated with polite dignity. At the other end of the spectrum, the Michael Moores of the social commentators become marginalised, ridiculed, and exposed for their own shortcomings.

In contrast to the social commentators, most agents of change are assassinated. This was the finale of Jesus. There was a plan to assassinate Mohammed before he heard of it and fled to Mecca. Mahatma Ghandi was assassinated, so were John F. Kennedy, Robert Kennedy, Martin Luther King, and John Lennon. They all spent little time on exposés; their focus was vision and action-driven. They were actually driven to incite people to do things and to do them differently. In my mind, Dr. King's I Have A Dream is singularly beautiful as well as inspirational. So is John Lennon's Imagine. My point is that many "doers" have suffered premature deaths whereas the social commentators go on with their work, albeit marginalised by defenders of the status quo and those who aspire to it.

In Part One, the work and apparent purpose of current and past social commentators is described. I argue that each and every lecture, documentary, and book is necessary but insufficient to precipitate change. The brilliant exposés inform us, raise our individual and collective consciousness, others alarm us and lead to one or more significant changes. This is best illustrated by Rachel Carson's 1962 book Silent Spring. She raised the alarm about the pesticide DDT which eventually led to the substance being banned. Recently, some have argued for its re-introduction to combat malaria-carrying mosquitos in Africa because, in the short term, malaria is far more devastating than the use of the pesticide even though DDT always has broad- and-long term negative consequences.

The dissemination of information by those who make us aware of all that is awry with the human condition is essential. We should be grateful for such watchful individuals even if most are unable to offer meaningful solutions or don't quite understand how one can wholeheartedly agree with something, such as the need to address global warming.

Experience teaches us all significant lessons, which are, difficult for some of us, to recognize and/or accept. The lesson is that most of us know the difference between what is right and what is wrong. If we do not, it does not take much to make us aware of it. Becoming aware, having our unconscious thoughts and motives raised to a conscious level, as is the goal of Freudian analysts, does not necessarily lead to behavioural change. While most of us can learn new knowledge and skills, it is the application of the knowledge and skills in predictably competent ways which really matter.

Application is the "to do" part of our emerging consciousness, our awareness of what is occurring around us. Admittedly, what is occurring around us, now more so than ever before, is both incrementally complex and dangerous. Some are of the belief that the complexity is beyond the capabilities of our prehistoric brains to comprehend. This belief is based on the reality that our physiology has not changed since we were preoccupied with eating, procreating, and surviving the dangers posed by some prehistoric predator or the other tribe just over the hill. Others clearly believe the contrary. The very proliferation of information about how bad things are and have always been is the very proof of this belief. By telling us, by showing it to us in a myriad of clever and intriguing ways, the various social commentators, first and foremost, present themselves as being primarily preoccupied with the task of convincing us of the truthfulness of their message. Some may say, selling us what they are selling. Nevertheless, the very act of presenting us with a message also conveys that we, the masses, have the cognitive intellectual potential to comprehend the message. Unfortunately, we manifest our positive potential intermittently. When we do, however, we do it in ingenious creative ways. Because sometimes we do get it, I have great optimism about the human species. But the world is in trouble and has always been in trouble because of our failure to actualize that of which we are ultimately capable. Understanding our limitations in this respect is the focus of Part Two. Suffice it to say here that, our limitations are not attributable to innate deficiencies or to cognitive intellectual limitations or to deficiencies with respect to learning what is the right and wrong thing to do, even in our complex world.

The myriad of social commentators serve, therefore, a vitally important function. Systematically, skillfully, and many in great scholarly fashion tell us mostly what are the wrong things we are doing. They sensitize us to the nature and severity of the problems facing us. In clinical terms, social commentators provide us with an exceptionally comprehensive statement of the problem which needs to be addressed. Many even do so in operational terms, providing qualitative and quantitative indicators as well as describing the various manifestations of a problem. In most cases, the defined solution to a problem is that the problem no longer exists or is discernibly reduced. The challenge is finding a solution and, of equal importance, the motivation to act. To act requires the actualization of the potential with which we are born. To understand what action is required and how to motivate ourselves and others to action, I review in Part One the literature which tells us of our various problems.

When I first started to plan this book, my expectation was that Part One would be a rather straightforward undertaking. Unfortunately, the troubling adage; "The more I learn, the more I realize how much I don't know", reared its ugly head. In fact, the task of writing Part One became debilitatingly onerous. To overcome this obstacle I had to devise a unique strategy, one which would satisfy a self-imposed standard and would be perceived by the reader as sufficiently informative. Anticipating and appeasing the critics was not a concern in solving the problem. I decided therefore, to organize the social-commentary literature into three categories. I describe, in brief, the major contributions made under the three categories and provide annotated bibliographies. I was very selective in what works I cited for two important reasons. The first has to do with my decision not to write another exposé, one which is void of a comprehensive action plan. The second has to do with making connections among the three parts of this book. This consideration was especially salient with respect to explaining in Part Two the underlying processes revealed by the various symptoms, such as global warming, described in the literature.

Therefore, it is imperative that Part One be recognized as not, in any way, an exhaustive representation of the literature. Moreover, the annotation of the cited materials also must be recognized to be tersely, albeit hopefully sufficient to convince you that there is a problem without having to read every cited publication in its entirety. While, I do not believe it to be absolutely necessary, I do encourage you to read, in its entirety, at least one of the references I provide in each section. If you read more than one, so much the better! You also should examine carefully the bibliography of the work you select to read to see for yourself the vast amount of information there is for consumption. I have made no effort to provide in Part One or in this book an exhaustive list of references. The references I do provide represent most of the major works in print. Although some are obscure, they serve well the task of explaining what meaning can be attributed to the described symptoms and what can be done to fix the root causes.

The first thing I would describe as a mess in the world is the environment and what we are doing to it. Much, if not all, of our destruction of the environment started with the Industrial Revolution, continued with the use of fossil fuels to propel our machines to get us around, all of which is exacerbated by the destruction of our oxygen producing forests, the earth's lungs, for economic reasons. At first the consequences of our assault on the world was called global warming. More accurately the consequences have evolved to be referred to climate change. Regardless of what we call it, the changes are attributed to the increasing concentration of carbon dioxide in the atmosphere. What constitutes an acceptable level of carbon dioxide concentration has been studied and reviewed for several years the current results of which are alarming.

The second thing that is a mess about the world, and always has been is corruption. Corruption is a specific form of people behaving badly, whereby personal gains are extracted at a cost to many. Almost always the concept conveys that those misbehaving are in a position of significant trust, a position which comes with concomitant obligations. It is reasonable that the masses have special, more than the norm, positive expectations of those in position of power, when those in power betray such trust, the consequences stipulated by law, in most countries, are far harsher than the consequences of criminal activities of people who are not in positions of trust. In other words, "buyer beware" when purchasing a used car curbside, whereas the same admonishment applies less when purchasing Enron stocks with your life's savings. Tragically, but also fortunately, we are all far wiser now than before; less willing to assume anything, especially that there are institutionalized provisions in place to protect our individual and collective best interests.

There are levels and degrees of corruption throughout the world. At one end of the spectrum, there is corruption in poor countries of the world, countries which don't give entrepreneurs strong incentives to behave in socially responsible ways. At the other end of the spectrum such blatant and transparent corruption is not evident, and the masses are lulled into a sense of security, a feeling which recent events have taught to be markedly unwarranted. However, fundamentally there are no structural differences in types of corruption. It does not matter where it occurs; it does not matter who is doing it, it is still corruption in its full definition. The only differences are in content, the manner of dress, and how much money is involved. U.S. Assistant Attorney, Jeffrey Cramer, at Sir Conrad Black's trial in Chicago, in the Spring of 2007, compared Black and his co-accused to bank robbers and street thugs. He said, "That's what crime looks like in the corporate world". To the jury, he said, "Every day when you walk in through those doors, you will be in a room with four guys who stole sixty million dollars".

The theme about corruption is how we have been and continue to be swindled daily by people in pretty prestigious business, political, and religious places. People whom we do not expect to lie to us or to cheat us out of our hard earned cash. The operative term is "people" not "corporation", not "government", or "organized/institutionalized religion". It is "people". After all, each entity is comprised of people: It is a person who drafts, disseminates, and implements policies and procedures. The debacle was not perpetrated by Enron, it was perpetrated by its people. The only real difference between the Enron executives and street thugs is opportunity and different skill sets. Moreover, while being swindled can take many forms, whether we are stolen from or lied to for power or monetary reasons, it is all corruption. This formulation applies to all types of organizations, big and small, including multinational or locally operating businesses. This formulation applies equally to overseas organizations as it also applies to the Ontario Lottery and Gaming Corporation (it is being investigated for corruption as I write this chapter).

The third thing that is a mess in the world is people behaving badly. Not surprisingly, as much has been written about people, individuals, and groups behaving badly as has been written about the corruption inherent to corporations, politics, and religion. The difficulty is creating categories which capture the essence of what is being talked about currently and in the past. Also, it is difficult to differentiate among the various symptoms of human problems discussed in Part One since people are the actors in every situation, whether perpetrating an energy crisis or distorting the essence of the messages of the prophets such as Jesus and Mohammed. It is for this very reason that it is imperative to review what is said about individuals and groups misbehaving in preparation to explaining in Part Two, what all this means and in Part Three delineating what can we do about it.

CHAPTER ONE
THE ENVIRONMENT

Global Warming

At the time of this writing global warming, no pun intended, was a hot issue. Subsequently, climate change became the description of what we are doing to our planet. Everywhere climate change is being talked about, written about, and is debated. No serious publication about the state of world affairs excludes the topic. Most everyone has something to say about it. Few discount the process while many argue that it is happening, and will continue to happen unless we immediately do something about it. Some argue that we have even less time to stop the process, let alone reverse it, than previously believed. Some argue that it is already too late. Some argue that, if we act now, we have a hundred years to reverse the process. In the United States, the more famous and persuasive voice about global warming is former Vice President, Al Gore. Just prior to writing this he received an Oscar for his documentary: An Inconvenient Truth. He also has published the same information in a book with the same title. I strongly recommend at least renting the video of his documentary. To say the least, it is thought provoking. In Canada, geneticist, now environmentalist, David Suzuki has been a persistent and long standing voice on this issue. During the winter of 2007 he embarked on a cross Canada speaking tour, seeking as much support as possible, with the intent to take the product of his efforts to the Federal Government in Ottawa. A significant component to his thrust is to get the Canadian Federal Government to abide by the Kyoto Accord. With this intent, he reveals considerable optimism about the benefits that can be derived from an international law. While we should have such a law, while we should abide by such a law, clearly having a law has always been insufficient to have people to do the right thing. Notwithstanding this comment about the law, David Suzuki's position pertaining to global warming should be read. In particular, I recommend reading in its entirety a collection of his ideas: The David Suzuki Reader, published in 2003. It is a fun and informative read.

The reason for recommending the above two commentators is because of their respective abilities to be engaging and to do so in a way with which it is difficult to disagree. I don't believe that you will be bored by what either one of them has to say. Is there more to read, hear, and see about global warming? Absolutely! For example, Thomas Homer-Dixon, in: The Upside of Down, in the chapter having to do with global warming, cites no less than eighty-one references. The referenced works span a broad range of evidence that support the conclusion that global warming is our reality and that to it, there are very dire consequences. The consequences include a variety of measurable occurrences such as lowering the ocean's PH level and increasing the destructiveness of tropical cyclones.

Jared Diamond in his book: Collapse is less expansive in citing references concerning global warming. In the section called: Further Readings to Chapter Sixteen he provides three excellent references, two published after 2000 and one published in 1997. There is much to read, therefore, on the topic, if you are so inclined.

Global warming, or more precisely climate change, essentially has to do with increasing levels of carbon dioxide concentration in the atmosphere. The concentration of atmospheric carbon dioxide, when I wrote this, was said to be 387 parts per million (ppm). According to climatologists, this concentration increases 3 ppm per year. When 425 ppm is reached and maintained for any period of time, according to these scientists, probably all the ice and polar caps will melt. When that happens the sea level will go up 70 to 80 metres (240 to 270 feet). At 3 ppm per year, it will take a short 12 years to reach the 425 ppm concentration. Accepting that there is always a certain margin of error in every such calculation, it would nevertheless be prudent for us to accept an optimal level of carbon dioxide concentration, far lower than the ice melting 425 ppm. Probably, it should be even lower than the current 387 ppm. The bad news is that to reverse the escalating trend in carbon dioxide concentration in the atmosphere we must begin the process immediately and it will take time to first stop it and them more time to reverse it. The good news is that the oceans and the ice sheets react slowly to change but as we are finding out not nearly as slowly as was first believed. Nevertheless, the consensus of climatologists is that conditions which are causing climate change can be stopped and reversed, as long as we act now.

Even a tersely review of the extensive literature on the topic of global warming, therefore, allows for a synopsis of what is contended by the various sources. Before summarizing the essential contents of the various works, it might be useful to define how I came to the position that it is better, adaptive, and ultimately to our collective advantage to take the position that climate change is happening and that we have to take action right now to stop and reverse it. My rationale for arriving at this conclusion, in part, is based on the scientific, logical, and convincing manner in which the various authors argue their case. In part, my rationale for accepting the premise of climate change also is based on a clinical strategy I learned a long time ago. Simply put, potential consequences determine the actions to be taken. For instance, it is markedly prudent to take medication immediately in order to stop one from dying even if the medication's efficacy will not be known until later (especially if there are no lethal side effects to taking the medication). This is exactly the case with respect to what we are told will stop and reverse climate change caused by global warming. The "cure" to global warming has no lethal side effects. Personally, I am not prepared to gamble our collective well-being, perhaps our very existence, on the arguments of the "nay" sayers only to find out, when it is too late, to use the analogy, that my disease indeed is lethal and has advanced beyond the point of no return. Moreover, if the cure has no negative side effects, and if I can benefit from it by more than just staying alive, why would I not take it? As far as I can tell, (and no one has convinced me otherwise) we can only benefit from applying the strategies recommended by the various authors. Strategies, which do not require expensive technology. Strategies, that we, as individuals, can employ on a daily basis for the rest of our lives.

"What is causing global warming" is the logical first question. In a nutshell, global warming is said to be caused by greenhouse gases (mostly atmospheric carbon dioxide). The gases caused by human activities which are in excess of that which occurs naturally, such as forest fires or volcano eruptions. The amount of gases we produce are said to be sufficient to disrupt a very delicate atmospheric balance. The carbon dioxide of our creation, are from combustion and methane caused by fermentation in the intestines of cud-chewing animals. While we have been burning fossil fuels since the discovery of fire, and there have been cud-chewing animals, for a very long time, which humans harvest for food, it is the sheer exponential growth in both which reportedly has caused a shift in the homeostatic balance.

Who could disagree with the blatantly obvious when one simply reflects upon the production and use of the automobile since the first black Model "T" rolled off Mr. Ford's assembly line? Who could ignore the proliferation of fossil fuel-burning, electric generation plants or the increased amount of energy required to generate protein food to an ever growing population?

As will be elaborated upon in Part Two, people, for self serving reasons, do discount information and what they experience. With respect to global warming, discounting it is easy because most of us are unaware of some simple facts. The greatest impact on my level of awareness is that average global temperatures were only five degrees cooler at the height of the last ice age; indeed, small numbers do have huge effects on the delicate homeostatic balance. One degree or five degrees of warming over the next century is a big deal. Certainly, there is no reason to celebrate lower heating bills because, along with this, there are myriad other dire consequences.

In listing the negative consequences of global warming, and concomitant climate change, which are also the proof that it is occurring, the danger is that one's reaction may be: "So what?" Rest assured, there are many unpleasant answers. For example, ice is melting faster than it is accumulating. The world's greatest glaciers and ice fields are retreating. While not all, some are even growing, nevertheless it does not take much to disturb a very delicate homeostatic balance. It would not take a great increase in sea levels to flood much, if not all, of Florida, the eastern United States coast, and Bangladesh to name just a few places. Furthermore, it is reported that almost a billion people, a sixth of the world's population, depend upon fresh water from mountain glaciers.

Melting of the permafrost also is cited as proof of global warming and as a significant negative consequence. It has disrupted much of life where permafrost is needed to simply get around. The melting of the permafrost also has had a significant impact upon insect populations, a species which can and has devastated the earth's very lungs. A beetle infestation, attributed to global warming, destroyed some forty million spruce trees in southern California. This destruction is said to be the largest recorded loss of North American forest caused by insects.

It is hard to say, "So what", to this catastrophe since life depends upon the cleaning of the air and the oxygen production by trees. Admittedly, the diehard "Nay" sayers can argue the beetle infestation had nothing to do with global warming. But what if it did?

Many may also say "So what the ice is melting?" Many may say they have no interest in seeing or climbing on glaciers, "So what if they are shrinking?" Be that as it may, what else are the consequences of ice melting? I already mentioned rising sea levels, a phenomenon which also is not readily accepted by some scientists as a real danger. More difficult to refute are changing weather trends and the severity of events such as heat waves, droughts, floods, many and devastating hurricanes, and tornadoes. Global warming is an increasing strain on our electricity supply for air conditioning during intense and protracted summer heat waves and our financial resources when we need to rebuild our houses after a devastating storm.

Growing food is said to be adversely affected by global warming because many varieties are susceptible to weather extremes. Extremely inclement weather threatens the animals we eat and makes it increasingly costly to raise them. Predictably, the more disadvantaged one is the more negatively one will be affected by climate change. The converse is true with respect to the advantaged, although eventually as Robert Wright so eloquently states: "Wealth can buy no refuge from pollution ... wealth is no shield from chaos, as the surprise on each haughty face that rolled from the guillotine made clear". Sooner than later everyone will suffer the consequence of global warming regardless of bank account, power, prestige, influence or status. Where one lives will not matter either since the hemispheres mix, as revealed by pesticides used on the opposite side of the world to where one lives find their way into the food and the water supply, and the very air that one breathes.

Needless to say, I have barely touched upon the plethora of negative consequences of global climate change. While a full discourse makes for good reading, if you are in any way as I am, after a while, you will tire of the vast amount of information and will focus insistently on what can be done. To optimize the doing, to create a critical mass of "doers" from the individual efforts of some, it is first necessary to know that there are dissenters to climate change being caused by global warming. Some are formidable, authoritative, and even number among the scientific community. It is imperative also to understand their disclaimers but most importantly, their implicit motivation.

It is noteworthy that dissenters of global warming are primarily not mainstream climatologists. It is also important to note that the number of dissenters only appear to be significant because of the disproportionate media time they are receiving. Controversy is always popular, and dissent is judged to be more interesting than boring scientific facts. So, who are the dissenters?

Some will name Dr. Tim Ball as Canada's "poster boy" for those who deny global warming. Dr. Ball claims the earth is actually cooling. He does so despite of the fact that scientific groups such as the Meteorological Services of Canada or the Royal Society's Guide to Facts and Fictions About Climate Change report that the world is indeed warming. Their findings are supported by the National Oceanic And Atmospheric Administration of the United States and the United Kingdom Meteorological Offices. Sceptics such as Dr. Ball also claim that concern for global warming is exaggerated and unnecessarily alarming. Most troubling about the "Nay" sayers is their position that "Kyoto will cost us the earth and solve little". How reducing toxic emissions will cost us the world is never really elaborated. Similarly, there is little evidence offered in support of dissenting formulations about climate change, beyond that it is cyclical and that the cycles are naturally occurring phenomena.

There is also the Danish political scientist and statistician Bjrrn Lomborg. In his 2001 published book: The Sceptical Environmentalist: Measuring the Real State of the World, he asserts that environmentalists most often overstate their claim, abuse statistics, and use data selectively. He marshals evidence that the earth's environment is in an acceptable state, resources are abundant, and that we are not endangering the planet. His difficult-to-dispute point is that our quality of life has improved immensely; however, his claim that our present state of affairs will continue indefinitely, is much more difficult to accept. Nevertheless, he does make some points, points which apply to most sciences, namely that sloppiness exists in data collection, analysis, and reporting. Paradoxically, Lomborg's critics accuse him of the same things. Nevertheless, he is given much voice essentially because of one singularly significant factor. His position is consistent with our basic propensity of not acting, doing as little as possible, and resisting change as long as we can.

Although he is not a scientist, certainly not a climatologist, United States Republican Senator James Inhofe also is given much voice and receives support from business interests, especially those who profit from the burning of fossil fuels. While his argument against global warming lacks scientific rigour, it is, nevertheless, influential since it comes from the chair of the Senate's Environment and Public Works Committee. From his position of bestowed authority and without the need to provide rational elaboration, he has blithely stated, much to the glee of business interests, that he was "becoming more and more convinced ... that global warming is the greatest hoax ever perpetrated on the American people and the world". As will be discussed in Part Two, there are reasons for many people accepting his empirically unsupported bombastic assertion, all having to do with who they are, how they perceive the world, and how they behave as a result.

There are also dissenters among artists, people whose work has considerable popular appeal. The late author, director, and producer, Michael Crichton, is one of the most notable. I have enjoyed immensely almost every one of his books. I have read Jurassic Park at least twice to my children, and I have seen the movie with them an untold number of times. I enjoy, indeed admire, how he weaves science and fiction together to create stories whose entertainment value, to a large degree, lies in the personal conclusion that they are probable. I consider him, therefore, to be a very persuasive individual despite of the fact that he made no other claim than to be a fiction writer, one who writes, albeit about current and globally interesting topics. In his 2004 publication, State of Fear, Michael Crichton tells a story of conspiracy, whereby the information about global warming is manipulated, with great malice, by the very people who are raising the alarm about its reality. Their purpose is described to be a self-serving, monetary one. The plot culminates in discrediting the proponents of global warming and, by implication, in the real, here-and-now world. Stepping out of the fiction novelist role, Crichton draws an analogy between eugenics and global warming. The theory of eugenics postulates a crisis in the gene pool, one which leads to the deterioration in the state of the human race. Eugenics was widely supported in North America and Europe and, to a significant degree, precipitated the Holocaust. Even tangentially, to compare the actions rooted in the theory of eugenics to the actions required to curtail and reverse global warming simply is absurd. Nevertheless, there is a point to being appropriately cautious with respect to jumping on the bandwagon. In Crichton's defence, (not because I like and read his novels but because he makes sense), his ultimate position is that undoubtedly we are harming the environment; this is not a good thing to do, and we should stop it. For Crichton, to what degree and how fast we are doing it continues to be up for debate. As I have already declared, for a good reason, namely because of what is at stake I choose to believe that global warming is real and that we should take decisive action right now. I do not particularly care if this view puts me in good company. What I care about is the perplexing human propensity to behave in self-destructive ways as to cause future generations to ask in the same vein as we now ask about a past calamity: "What were they thinking on Easter Island when they cut down the last tree"?. Therefore, I am less concerned about the views of those who deny global warming than I am about all of us failing to act in our individual and collective best interest, especially when we know what it takes to curtail it.

A chapter about the environment would be incomplete without a brief review of what we are told about our western consumerism, the trend toward emulating consumerism in Third World countries and how this trend is exacerbating the problem of global warming. The theme, which applies to such a discussion, is that what happens in a specific place in some way affects us all, that is to say, the whole world. This reality has been long known and, at one time, was part of most-post-secondary curricula. For the very interested reader, I would recommend reading General System Theory by Ludwig von Bertalanffy. Be warned that it is a difficult read, a fact which perhaps explains the decline in popularity of the topic. More recently, the same principles have been expressed by how a butterfly which flaps its wings in Africa can affect weather patterns in the western hemisphere.

Consumerism

Rabid consumerism and the voracious consumption of fuel in the First World are included in this discussion because these two phenomena exemplify people behaving in maladaptive ways, the negative consequences of which are devastating on our environment. A few years from now, one may ask upon reflection the same question posed regarding the inhabitants of Easter Island who cut down the last tree: "What were they thinking?" The human propensity to engage in the unbridled consumption of food, drink, and stuff is comprehensively delineated by Jared Diamond in his book: Collapse. Whether he is describing the collapse of the pristine Montana countryside or the utterly complete deforestation of Easter Island, the culprits ultimately are human beings. Our voracious appetite for more, invariably leads to trouble and all the more devastating when the source being depleted, such as Iceland, is extremely delicate. By the time Iceland's inhabitants became aware of how delicate the ecology of their land is, it was already too late. To their credit, Icelanders tried to adapt to the environment, one which appeared to be, but was in fact not that which they knew. It took many decades, much devastation, and the loss of many lives before Iceland, the most impoverished of European nations became one of its most prosperous one. Alas, Iceland could not sustain this status mostly because of some of its people behaving badly. Nevertheless, Iceland's success gives cause for much optimism, albeit tempered by the reality that unless carefully maintained, achievements can be and are often lost.

Actually, the dynamics of consumerism are rather simple. Whatever we consume, be it food or the purchase of some material thing, requires resources to produce it. It requires energy, raw materials, nutrients from the soil, water, and so on. With some slight variation, the production of a consumable items is more or less the same anywhere in the world, although the cost of production can vary greatly. It is the cost factor, the wages, which is the reason for offshore manufacturing. It has been decades since a television has been manufactured in North America. Escalating wages have made it infinitely cost-effective for corporations to set up shop in Third World countries. Moreover, wages in Third World countries do not rise rapidly and, when they do increase, the baseline from which they start is so low as to barely affect huge profit margins. Just compare the cost of producing a Nike runner, a shoe which is in the single dollar-digit range, to the price you pay for it at your local mall.

Another significant dynamic of consumerism is the consumers. Proportionately, First World countries are said to consume thirty-two times more resources and generate thirty-two times more waste than do inhabitants of all of the Third World. China's awakening, to say the very least, is alarming. What will happen when they achieve to what they aspire and have as many automobiles, appliances, and as much technology as we? Will the world have the resources to meet the ever growing demands, the resources to dispose of the refuse, and the fuel with which to drive the mechanisation of the advancing Third World. How will their consumer success impact on an already battered climate?

Needless to say, we all assume that growth is a good thing, unless it is a malignant tumour. That growth is a good thing is virtually unchallenged, except by a few. Fortunately, a few dare to speak the unspeakable, namely that a higher income does not make one happier, and a higher gross national product (GNP) does not make for a better country. But we pursue escalating production and consumption with a vengeance and other nations such as China and India are fervently following our example. Why we are seduced by consumerism is the topic of discussion in Part Two. While the worrisome consequences of consumerism are the focus of many, there are detractors. To understand the detractors, I recommend you read about them in the aforementioned David Suzuki's book. You should also become familiar with arguments for and against globalization, and the reliance on rules to regulate its growth. Probably, your best source is a controversial one. You should read George Soros: Open Society: Reforming Global Capitalism and his major critic, Robert Solow, who wrote: The Amateur. You should also probably read Tim

Kasser's book: The High Price of Materialism. These readings are recommended if you need a whole lot of convincing that consumerism and globalization are symptomatic of an underlying problem, a problem which ultimately must be addressed and not just its manifestations (symptoms).

There are as many who praise consumerism as those who raise the alarm about it. Not only is it praised but by many it is aided and abetted. Interestingly, those in favour of constantly increasing consumerism are not all purveyors of stuff for us to buy. The position of purveyors is easy to understand. It makes a whole lot of sense that they want as much demand as possible for the stuff they are selling because it is in their best interest. How economic growth, consumerism, and rising wages are in the best interest of politicians, policy makers, economists, and public commentators, however, is less transparent. Notwithstanding the lack of apparent self-interest in their rationale, many from these groups advocate and take action to create exponential economic growth. A significant justification for their capitalistic vigour is that constant economic growth creates new jobs and industries for those who lost their employment to economic growth in the first place. Greater efficiency, and profitability attributed to increased productivity are believed to create more affordable products. This is said to translate into money left-over to spend on other things. The left-over money, in their way of reasoning amounts to an increase in income. There are significant false assumptions to this position. One of them is illustrated by a story I like to tell about my grandfather in response to the excitement created by discount sale times after the holidays. According to my family folklore, my eastern European grandfather saved money daily by running after, instead of taking, the streetcar to work. He then discovered that he could save ten times more by running after the taxi that drove past his place of employment. The point is that, the thought of saving money makes us do things we would not have done in the first place. Another significant false assumption is that by becoming more efficient, although many workers do themselves out of a job, the profits accrued by corporations lead to new ventures, which then employ the laid-off workers. There is no discernable evidence to this effect. In fact, according to Forbes magazine, there is only evidence of the rich becoming richer as a function of the increased efficiency and cheaper costs of production in Third World countries. In the Forbes article, it is reported that in 2003 there were four hundred and seventy-six billionaires in the world. Some four years later, in 2007, there is said to be nine hundred and forty-six billionaires with a combined worth of 3.5 trillion dollars and an average net worth of 3.6 billion. Comparatively, the 2007 budget of the United States was 2.9 trillion dollars. Therefore, five percent of Americans control nearly half of the country's wealth, and the richest three hundred thousand Americans collectively earn almost as much as all the bottom hundred and fifty million people. These are important statistics. Moreover, the statistics reveal a historically pervasive concentration of wealth with little evidence of benevolent redistribution of it.

The capitalist ideology, that laid off workers will be re-employed by successful corporations, assumes that the masses have an insatiable appetite for material goods. There is no doubt that many people do, regardless of whether they have any disposable income or not. Personal debt load, beyond any reasonable ability to pay out, was a significant contributing factor to the economic crisis that started in the fall of 2008. There is considerable evidence, especially produced by research concerning happiness associated with income, that people sooner than later tire of buying for its own sake and save their extra cash rather than spend it on more stuff. Despite these and other demonstrated fallacies, there are many who continue to believe absolutely that an answer to employment and financial problems is constant economic growth. For many, this includes population growth. If population growth is not created internally, the ideology of growth necessity justifies mass immigration.

Economic and exponential growth of consumerism are supported, encouraged, and fuelled by some very powerful forces. On the one hand, to buy stuff is incredibly easy, on the other, to pay for it, more often than not, is difficult. Consider how easy it was before the 2008 economic crisis to get a credit card and a considerable spending limit. Contrast this to the continued high fees charged by the credit card company not the least of which is the double-digit interest rate if you do not pay the entire balance by the due date. Buying a brand new automobile interest free was and continues to be more the norm than the exception, and you can purchase all sorts of furniture and appliances without paying for a year. We are constantly inundated by the message to do so. Even before built in obsolescence occurs, we are encouraged to buy things because the new models are better: Better picture resolution, better sound, flatter screen, smoother ride, better design, and the list goes on. Most of us, however, lack the fine sense to appreciate the better. Curiously, it is sufficient that we believe it to be there.

There also are economists who are fervent advocates of the growth imperative. Their reasons and supportive argument are based upon the grim lessons of the Great Depression: Less demands lead to price reduction and, in turn, to mass unemployment, a deplorable situation, which creates politically and socially disastrous conditions. From the perspective of these advocates, growth must continue, and any adverse consequences of growth will take care of themselves. Those who made horse buggies and whips are held out as classic examples of human resilience because they found employment in the automobile manufacturing industry.

Not surprisingly, there are those who are concerned about exponentially growing consumerism, and there are those who absolutely are in favour of it. I cannot see how anything can continue indefinitely, especially unlimited exponential economic growth but I can see it imploding on itself. I believe that constant growth in consumerism is not adaptive human behaviour. However, it is certainly consistent with who we have been so far and continue to be to this day.

Last but by no means the least, let us not forget that most of what we are manipulated and persuaded to buy are designed and manufactured to deliberate inferior and obsolescence specifications. The gas tank exploding Pinto is a well known blatant example, but there are many more subtle ones such as the toaster that cannot be fixed or the coffee maker for which you cannot purchase a replacement carafe. Ralph Nader has been the quintessential consumer advocate, drawing attention to the manufacturing maleficence of corporations which actually resulted in companies designing and manufacturing better products.

Without his relentless efforts, the improvements probably would have been much longer in the coming, if at all. In spite of his successes, Ralph Nader, more recently is largely marginalised and essentially thought of as the throw back, frugal eccentric, in the rumpled suit and army boots, who splits the Democratic vote when he runs for the U.S. Presidency. Unfortunately, he is seldom referenced in recent sweeping books on the state of consumer affairs, since focus has shifted from how well made are the things we buy to why do we need so much stuff in the first place. Notwithstanding his diminishing stature, Nader was a significant iconic pioneer just as Rachel Carson was with respect to alerting us about DDT's negative impact on the environment. As will be revealed subsequently, individuals such as Ralph Nader and Rachel Corson represent very specific types of people whose very presence is good cause for the optimism conveyed in this book.

Nader also has authored many books, commenting on more issues than manufacturing. I would recommend his most recent work: The Seventeen Traditions. In this work, Nader describes how he, like all of us, is very much a product of his environment, specifically the parents who raised him. Nader chronicles how he developed his world view and personal values, which he has applied to broader global issues and to how he lives his life. What he says about dissent being the genesis of change, and the need to challenge paradigms, are particularly relevant to the changes which are advocated in Part Three of this book.

Energy Crisis

Two aspects of another symptom of a most worrisome human propensity and the impact this has on our environment, is our consumption of fossil fuels and our blind faith in what we are told about their availability. Jeremy Rifkin in his 2002 book: The Hydrogen Economy, talks about oil production, with emphasis on when its production peaks and, most importantly, what will take place when, not if, it happens. Needless to say, there is considerable disagreement as to when oil production will peak, but there is no disagreement that it will. When it does, the remaining reserves, Rifkin reports, will be found in the Muslim countries of the Middle East. As a result, the current power balance in the world will be altered, and we will turn to burning dirtier, fossil fuels. Notwithstanding the power issue, the far greater concern is that global warming will be accelerated by the burning of dirtier fuels. Assuming we survive the burning of dirtier fuels, and when we run out of such, the next logical question is: "What do we do when we run out of such energy sources?"

To slow down energy consumption there are many who advocate the free market system. If consumption is allowed to escalate, they say let the supply and demand principle flourish (we charge you whatever we want because we can), people will exercise restraint. Slowing down consumption will then afford us time to bring technology to the rescue. Such thinking, however, is completely oblivious to history and personal experiences we all have had. Let me illustrate my point, by recounting briefly, a personal story. In the mid 1960s I commuted in a four cylinder, six volt PV444 Volvo some eighty kilometres to university. As long as I had five dollars in a crisp note or a pocket full of equivalent change, I was safe to instruct the attendant to "fill her up" and be assured that I had enough money to purchase the gasoline. Now, I usually do not carry enough cash to be able to say, "fill her up", because the cost of a full tank of gas hovers around sixty to seventy dollars. Incidentally, I still drive a Volvo, one which sadly is bigger, more powerful, and uses premium gas. From a five to seventy dollar fill-up, each price increase was noted with much disdain. Fortunately, my earnings also have increased but my point is that eventually I habituated to each increase in the price. Seventy-dollar fill-ups for me have become the norm as eventually will eighty, ninety and so on. Judging by the absence of mass revolt and the wholesale turning away from gas-guzzling, automobiles, most people have had the same habituation experience.

Perhaps, there is no energy crisis. Perhaps, the crisis is what we are obliged to pay for our insatiable appetite for fuel, however, my review of the literature leads me to think that yes, prices are exorbitant but we are in real trouble with respect to fuel availability, the pollution created by the use of fossil fuels, and we are doing very little about it.

Furthermore, we are doing very little about our addiction to fuels and improving fossil fuel consumption technologically. A few hybrids do not a solution make, although their introduction is a step in the right direction. Electric cars have always been heralded as the mode of transportation for the future since they were first introduced in the early 1900s. Witness, however, the early and ongoing replacement of electric streetcars by gasoline burning or diesel-spewing buses. I can still remember when trolley buses were used in my home town. While they consumed electric energy, they at least did not contribute directly to pollution at the street level. Elsewhere, as for example in Los Angeles, the network of electric streetcars collapsed into bankruptcies in the 1920s and '30s. The right-of-ways allotted to the electric streetcars was bought up by automobile manufacturers and subdivided to make it impossible to rebuild the network which could then compete with the gas burning modes of transportation.

According to Jeremy Rifkin and others, there are some very viable technical solutions to the energy crisis. In his book, he discusses two broad strategies of producing hydrogen energy. The premise is that hydrogen is a viable replacement of fossil fuels and can propel our various ways of getting around, especially our personal automobiles. Hydrogen energy also is considered, by many, as a viable replacement fuel for generating electric power. And the combustion of hydrogen does not pollute the environment. Rifkin explains admirably how this can take place. The benefit of hydrogen-generated energy is said to be considerable. For example, fuel cells which operate on this principle, are said to be up to two and one-half times more efficient than internal combustion engines: To better grasp this idea, apply it to how far you can go on a litre of gasoline; then compare it to going two and a half times as far on hydrogen and your utility bills will be two and a half times less than it is now. Not only does all this sound good but also it is eminently believable. Once again, technology potentially comes to the rescue! I certainly believe in it, and I suspect that so will you if you review, even briefly, the book by Rifkin. However, technology cannot solve all of our energy problems, especially our exponentially growing demand for it.

Rifkin is not alone with respect to heralding a technological solution to our energy problem. For example, in the Washington D.C. based: World Watch Paper, Seth Dunn in his articles: Hydrogen Futures: Toward a Sustainable Energy System and Micropower: The Next Electrical Era, convey the same message as Rifkin about hydrogen as a viable alternative. The problem is the rate at which technology is progressing and whether it can rescue us from ourselves. So what is holding up its progress? There is no shortage of innovators or entrepreneurs who believe in the vision of hydrogen as the clean energy source of the future. Ballard Power Systems of Burnaby, British Columbia and Plug Power of Latham, New York are two capable corporations committed to making hydrogen a cost-effective clean power source. They have been at it for some time. Progress is slow, however, turning automobiles into small self generating power plants because, as Rifkin puts it, "automobile companies are reluctant to manufacture direct hydrogen fuel-cell cars for fear that the energy companies will not invest sufficient funds to create thousands of hydrogen refuelling stations". By the same token, the energy companies are said to be reluctant to commit to hydrogen production in case automobile companies do not manufacture enough hydrogen fuel-cell vehicles. This stalemate is predictable because for both interests its all about money, and neither will really do anything significant unless absolutely forced to do so. I add to this that in various ways both groups' self interest is tied to fossil fuel consumption. From their perspective, there is much fossil fuel still to be consumed before there is a profound need to produce vehicles which will run on alternate forms of clean energy or produce hydrogen refuelling stations.

The same can be said about generating electrical energy. This idea was best expressed by a stand-up comedian (whose name I cannot recall). He said that his strategy is to drive the most fuel-guzzling vehicle in order to accelerate the depletion of our fossil fuel reserves because no one will really do anything until they are all gone. His humour is diminished by the concern that by the time all fossil fuels are "gone", it will be too late (not to mention the devastating consequences the fossil fuel burning has on global warming).

Our failure to act on the information that fossil fuel energy resources are rapidly depleting and their use is a significant contributing factor to global warming is underscored by a report prepared by an illustrious panel of faculty at the Massachusetts Institute of Technology who spent three years studying the role of fossil fuels in the twenty-first century. The panel was chaired by John Deutch, a chemical engineer, and Ernst Moniz, a theoretical physicist. The panel's published report states unequivocally that fossil fuels will remain the most important source of primary energy for decades to come. According to this report, fossil fuels supply 80% of the world's energy. Oil supplies 35%, coal 25%, and natural gas, 20%. Some may be surprised to know that nuclear power supplies only 6.5% of the energy consumed globally, harnessed water 2.1%, biomass 11%, and solar wind and geothermal sources only 0.4%.

Most worrisome in the MIT report is the reality that not only is coal the most abundant but also the cheapest source of energy. Coal delivers the same amount of energy for one to two dollars (U.S.) as oil or natural gas does at a cost of six to twelve dollars (U.S.) . Moreover, coal is available in vast quantities all over the world. Not surprisingly, the panel predicts that "coal use will increase under any foreseeable scenario because it is cheap and abundant". The fact that coal can be one of the dirtiest sources of energy is treated as irrelevant when the issue is real or perceived need. China is case in point.

The MIT report is quite definitive in its claim that China's alternative energy source to oil and natural gas is coal. Currently, China increases its coal-fired electricity production every year by an amount equal to the entire production of Great Britain. The MIT report goes on to say that for the next twenty-five years China and India will account for seventy percent of the incremental demand for coal in the entire world. The MIT scholars also predict that India probably will surpass China in both coal consumption and in population growth. Needless to say, there are profound global warming consequences to this prediction.

The MIT group's proposed solution is nuclear power, an energy source which will have to be heavily subsidized by governments willing to develop it. The report qualifies and cautions, however, that governments should avoid "picking a technological winner".

Unfortunately, the MIT panel reports the objective realities without broaching why we place emphasis on the satisfaction of our immediate needs, for energy, and why we do not forsake fossil fuels. At best, their report implies that our attraction is based upon affordability and availability, especially of coal for the next quarter century, at least.

Despite the reality that energy is our master resource and any significant disruption to its availability will create catastrophic consequences, there are those who genuinely are not worried about its supply. These also are the same people who deny global warming. The fundamental premise of energy-crisis deniers does not discount the fact that all fossil fuels are non-renewable resources. They regard those who believe that resources are imminently finite as alarmists whose opinions are to be discounted. Simply put, these deniers believe that there is so much available that no shortage will occur even in the remote future. Consider, for example, the various reports concerning oil reserves, specifically light oil, the kind that gushes out of the ground. There is little disagreement about how much has been removed from the ground in the past hundred and forty years. Most geologists agree that it is more than eight hundred and seventy five billion barrels. Geologists disagree, but not significantly, on how much conventional oil is still left to be harvested. Some of the disagreement is attributable to semantics, the definitions of what constitute reserves and resources. There is also the problem of defining concepts such as "inactive","probable", "inferred", and "undiscovered", to list just a few. The consequence is that it is possible to "fudge the figures" if one is so inclined for political and/or economic reasons.

Rifkin points out that to accurately calculate the total amount of oil left to be harvested, it is necessary to factor in an estimate of oil reserves - a projection of recoverable oil yet to be discovered - and how much conventional oil already has been harvested globally. Using sophisticated geochemical, computer-generated modelling, the U.S. reportedly has fourteen percent of its oil unharvested; Russia has thirty-nine percent; and Saudi Arabia has seventy percent of its oil still in the ground. To complicate calculations further, it is noteworthy that the U.S. Securities and

Exchange Commission qualifies reserves as proven only if the oil lies near a producing well and there is a "reasonable certainty" that it can be recovered profitably at current oil prices and by using existing technology. Some countries and experts argue that the criteria is too narrow and thereby does not produce optimally accurate calculations of reserves or resources.

In the final analysis, the question is rather simple. When will oil production peak and reach half the estimated recovery of what is ultimately available? The difference in the range of the data is not monumental. One calculation predicts a peak in global oil production between 2030 and 2040, while another predicts a peak between 2020 and 2030. Regardless of when the peak occurs, let us say for the sake of discussion 2030, oil prices will begin a steady, uninterrupted rise based upon real shortages and not on politically or economically motivated claims of unavailability. The question therefore, is not if oil production peak will occur, but when it will occur. There is little solace if oil production peak occurs ten years later and to argue the point amounts to nothing more than an academic exercise. Unfortunately, it is an academic exercise which serves a very narrow and short-term agenda, and is one which I am certain has a huge financial windfall associated with it for a very small select group. In Part Two, reasons why we become unwitting participants in this ridiculous, potentially species extinction process, is explored.

CHAPTER TWO
CORRUPTION

Corporate Corruption

Since the financial collapse of Enron, World Con, and the international consulting firm Arthur Andersen, much has been written about the corporate ideology which precipitated the events. Previously, there were movies about corporate corruption in full bloom, such as Wall Street and, more recently, the documentary based on the book by Joel Bakan, The Corporation. Of all that is available, I recommend Bakan's book as the best example of what you should know first hand. The movies, however, teach us the best lesson on corporate corruption at any level. The lesson is that corporations, indeed all organizations, are not abstract, conceptual entities. The collective, represented by the concept, is really made up of individuals. The actors portray the individuals, and draw our attention to the fact that it is someone doing something, and not some ill-defined, abstract entity. Without individuals who are in sync with the corporate ideology or individuals who are readily co-opted to the ideology, corporate corruption could not exist.

I disagree vehemently with the notion that otherwise decent, valorous people can chameleonize themselves to villainous, corporate doers, who fit into the work place culture and then return to their virtuous selves in the suburbs. Anyone who has longevity and some form of corporate success represents a pretty good fit, with the culture of their corporation, such as that for which human resource personnel are purportedly looking, when hiring a person to perform a specific role and associated functions. Undoubtedly there are exceptions, although it is difficult to imagine how anyone could lead a life of profound disharmony for any length of time.

So what is it about corporations whose ethos lead to debacles such as that experienced at Enron? It is really very simple. By law, corporations are required to be profit driven. By law, corporations also have been granted the legal status and rights of a person. This development in the nineteenth century has contributed greatly to the fabricated and corporate-encouraged view of themselves as entities in their own right as opposed to a collective of individuals who will do whatever it takes to make a profit. Invariably, to make a profit a corporation must exert great, unquestioning influence. The same can be said of politics and religion. Suffice it to say that corporations have become one of the world's most powerful economic forces, sharing this status only with religious and political organizations. Corporations have evolved to influencing virtually everything in our lives: What we eat, what entertainment we watch, what we drive, what we wear, what we buy, where we live, where we go, what we value, indeed what we believe, in short, how we live our lives. The character, the makeup or what is emphasized by such a powerful force over our lives, therefore, ought to be well-known and understood.

The following is as terrifying an examination as any description of Islamic terrorists devoted to the annihilation of Judeo-Christian people. In his analysis of corporations, Joel Bakan applies a globally recognized, mental state diagnostic label, to describe a particularly chronic and pervasive psychopathology known as psychopathy. Infamous psychopaths such as serial killer Ted Bundy are without conscience, remorse or empathy. They are driven by self interest and absolutely are without the ability to relate to community standards, let alone, live by any of them. Applying this characterization to corporations, the people who work in them and who manage them, is made only worse by the reality that not only are their amoral actions sanctioned by law but are also required by it. Failing to maximize corporate profits can expose an executive to potentially negative consequences from the corporation's board of directors and its shareholders.

It is noteworthy that, the now defunct, Enron's horrific characterization is not something new. In fact, corporations from the time the first emerged in the late sixteenth century were almost immediately in disrepute, and for very good reasons. Whereas partnerships entail a group which owns and operates a company, the setup of a corporation is markedly different. Specifically, corporations separate ownership from management. Directors and managers run the company, while shareholders own it. From the very beginning, this arrangement was believed to be ripe for the picking by corrupt, dishonest, and psychopathic individuals.

As early as 1776, Adam Smith warned that managers cannot be trusted to steward other people's money. He should also have warned that given the mandate to be profitable, managers cannot be trusted to accomplish this by being socially responsible.

It is noteworthy that in 1720 the British Parliament banned corporations, following the unravelling of the South Sea Company which bilked investors of huge amounts of money with promises of fabulous profits. Fortunes were lost, lives were ruined, and one of the company's directors, John Blunt, was shot by an angry shareholder. Much of this, with the exception of the shooting, sounds very familiar. The question becomes, therefore, how did this business arrangement not only survive but come to flourish, and continues to do so, despite the Enron, World Com, Hollinger Inc., Adelphia Communications Corp., Tyco International, and Health South Corp debacles just to name a current few? The answer is really very simple.

There are many, indeed the majority, who believe the misbehaviour of people can be curtailed, subdued or altogether stopped by rules and laws. And there are many rules and laws crafted to control the potentially corruptible or the corrupted, who are in charge of other people's money. Why such measures invariably fail, and why the people, or at least our so called elected representatives, continue to do the same things, make laws, and expect something different will be discussed in Part Two. Suffice it to say here that the greed of shareholders and management combined are far too powerful a force to be curtailed by any law. To illustrate the point that laws do not solve the problem of corporate corruption, the Fair Labour Standards Act of President Franklin Roosevelt's administration serves extremely well. Despite its intent to curb the garment industries callous disregard for its employees, still sweat shops and dangerous work conditions prevail in North America. Sixty-five percent of all apparel operations in New York City are said to be sweat shops. Out of fifty thousand workers in forty-five hundred factories, only seven thousand earn a dollar or two an hour. Conditions in Los Angeles are said to be no better.

The CEOs of corporations and some of their henchmen are the benefactors of misdeeds, not some nebulous entity. It is a real person who pockets the money, and these people, once caught, become fair game for the media to expose. It seems like everyone is writing about the bad behaviour of corrupt executives but not about how they came to be who they are, and how they came to be in a position to commit their misdeeds.

To reiterate, it is a markedly perplexing phenomena, whereby we engage in mass insanity when we treat a corporation as something other than a concept, one which represents a collective of individuals. At least in part, our collective insanity can be blamed on the law which granted corporations the legal status and rights of a person. A very special person whose antisocial behaviour we tolerate, condone, and indeed prescribe by law. The same behaviour of real people we would condemn. This needs to be explored further by first examining the legally sanctioned expectations of a corporation.

By law, the executives of a corporation are required to set the interests of their companies and shareholders above all other interests. The same law forbids them from being socially responsible. Henry Ford learned about this edict the hard way when he treated his company not just as a profit machine. When

Ford cancelled company dividends in order to make the Model T cheaper and more affordable, his partners, the brothers Dodge, took him to court. To this day, the precedence set by Dodge v. Ford still stands for the legal principle that managers and directors have a legal obligation to put the shareholder's interest above all others and that managers and directors have no legal authority to serve any other interests. Since then "the best interest of the corporation" principle has perpetrated all sorts of harm in the name of legally mandated self-interest, void of any social responsibility, which, if carried out by a real person, would be completely abhorrent to most of us.

There are many examples of corporate psychopathy. A few will suffice to illustrate the point. Bopahl is one of the most salient examples of corporate corruption which resulted in the loss of life because toxins were released callously, without concern for who would be adversely affected. The release of toxins was a simple matter of economics. The environmental disaster created by the Exxon Valdez falls into the same category of the corporate mandate to externalize costs without regard for the harm such actions may cause to people, communities, and the environment. Closer to home are the atrocities committed by General Electric, which include environmental contamination with PCB, discrimination practices, defrauding government in defence contracts, pollution, and the list goes on. Bakan chronicles no fewer than forty-two significant infractions by this iconic corporation starting from 1990 to 2001.

Curiously and paradoxically, while laws which govern and mandate corporations prevail, those who excel at being the best at what corporations do, when caught obscenely benefiting themselves are severely sanctioned. As near as I can tell, the excessive lining of their own pockets, as opposed to the pockets of shareholders, is unacceptable. It would seem that when they cross some undefined threshold of greed, their own kind turn on them. This is reminiscent of an old sociological study of Communist Russia's pervasive, black marketeering. It was tolerated as long as greed and conspicuous ill-gotten wealth was not flagrantly flaunted. When it was, someone informed the authorities who were then compelled to take action in order to conserve the status quo. It seems that this old lesson was lost on the likes of Sir Conrad Black of Hollinger International Inc., John Rigos of Adelphia Communications, and others.

The magnitude of the greed to which corporate leaders rise and the misbehaviour in which they engage is in itself an informative study. When reduced to its common denominator, it still amounts to the individuals being common criminals except that they wear suits and ties and have access to enormous amounts of money to steal. The most accomplished of this nefarious group probably is Bernard Ebbers. Some reports have him overseeing an eleven-billion dollar fraud at World Com. John Rigas was found guilty of stealing hundred-million-dollars from Adelphia Communications and hiding a 2.3 billion-dollar debt from investors and regulators. Dennis Kozlowski of Tyco was found guilty of looting six-hundred-million-dollars from the corporation by concealing the bonuses and loans with the aid of his Chief Financial Officer Mark Swartz. Richard Scrusky of Health South Corp allegedly orchestrated a 2.7 billion-dollar fraud to inflate the earnings of his corporation. Jeffrey Skilling and Kenneth Lay of Enron infamy were charged and convicted of conspiracy and securities fraud, the total amount of which probably never will be known.

The consequences the caught, errant stewards of corporations, must face when convicted, are significant and convey a disdain, I think, for the magnitude of their greed but not so much for their crime. For example, John Rigas of Adelphia Communications Corp, at the age of eighty was sentenced to fifteen years in prison. The sentencing judge added that "were it not for your age and health, I would impose a sentence far greater than I do today". The son of Rigas, Timothy, the corporation's former Chief Financial Officer was sentenced to twenty years of incarceration.

Not surprisingly, there are apologists for both the legal mandate of corporations and for the executives as well as the managers who run them. The most blatant apologists are the legal defenders of the fallen/caught executives. As a prelude, it will be useful to reflect on what executives earn on the open market and thereby from where they start when seeking more through the corporations they direct. The salaries of corporate executives become particularly poignant when juxtapositioned to that of the worker. As so aptly reported by the Canadian Centre For Policy Alternatives, by the time the average worker arrives at work in the morning, the highest paid CEOs will have already earned the worker's annual salary. According to this 2007 study, minimum-wage workers will have barely rolled out of bed on New Years Day by the time the country's top earners pocketed fifteen thousand, nine hundred and thirty-one dollars that will likely take low-paid workers all of the year to make. Canada's one hundred, highest-paid, private-sector executives earn an average salary of thirty-eight thousand and ten dollars by nine forty five a.m. of each working day. By the six p.m. news the average CEO pockets a staggering seventy thousand dollars.

These are not only staggeringly impressive figures but according to Edward Greenspan, Lord Conrad Black's Canadian lawyer representing him in Chicago, they are nothing of which to be ashamed. In fact, Mr. Greenspan is reported to have told his lawyer friends at their Canadian Corporate Counsel Association conference in 2004 that there is nothing wrong with being greedy. According to Mr. Greenspan society has mistakenly equated greed with crime and has made these out to be dangerous times for rich executives. He went on to say that society's views of rich corporate executives is as ridiculous as the view that most poor people commit property crimes. Such beliefs, he said, are dangerous. Mr. Greenspan then went on to compare the investigation, trial, conviction, and imprisonment of Martha Stewart to the fear and burning of witches in Salem. By characterizing the burning of witches as not the proudest part of American history, he more than implied that the way Martha Stewart was treated also is nothing of which to be proud. He said, in fact, that Martha Stewart was not sent to jail for her "so called" crime but rather for her lifestyle and the envy that she instilled in others. "In other times Martha Stewart wouldn't have been investigated, let alone charged". This is an interesting spin on the part of Edward Greenspan, counsel and advocate for the rich and famous. Arguably there is very transparent self interest at work in what he says. There are others, who have less transparent self interests, who say very similar things.

Trevor Cole in the University of Toronto magazine (2005)

writes that while we are being told through the stories of Enron and the rest that there is something terribly wrong, no one is telling us why corruption of such magnitude is happening. Cole begins his treatise by quoting an expert who states; "The problem isn't the lack of understanding of what one ought to do, it is just the failure to do it". In stating that "people are morally imperfect" and that "well-designed institutions" are required to govern us all, he argues the flaw is explicitly not with corporations and the people who govern them but rather with the lack of laws or rules with which to do it. Cole underscores this view by quoting the philosopher Immanual Kant who said that: "A well-ordered, constitutional society could govern even a nation of evil".

The theme which supports the mandate of corporations continues in Cole's article wherein he blames corruption on environmental factors. Specifically he quotes Professor Murka of management studies: "If the media concentrate on acts of wrongdoing, they will create the belief that wrongdoing is common, which will increase the amount of wrongdoing". Further, quoting yet another academic, Professor Callahan, author of the: Cheating Culture, Cole excuses the inherent flaw in corporations and the people who are drawn to them by saying: "As the race for money and status has intensified it has become more acceptable for individuals to act opportunistically and dishonestly to get ahead". The getting ahead is in reference to the corporation not the individual executives who are dissatisfied with the above described exorbitant salaries they are being paid.

Cole concludes his analysis with further efforts to absolve the individual executives and their corporations by referring to the people as having lost their sense of a higher authority and a connection to the common good. The operative term is "lost", which explicitly conveys that they had it at one time. Cole cites brain research to argue the same point. He refers to the work of Donald Stuss, a professor of psychology and medicine at the University of Toronto and director of the Rotman Research Institute at the Baycrest Centre for geriatric care. According to Stuss and the work of others, the more we do something, such as cheat or lie, the less we think about it and, the more the pattern is established, the less work the brain has to do. In other words, this is consistent with the mind's relentless desire to find the path of least resistance. Cole concludes his article by saying that we are mistaken if we dismiss the cheating executive as merely a bad apple. I could not disagree more but for very different reasons. Barbara Ley Tofflen, who is from the defunct accounting firm Arthur Anderson, became co-opted by the firms illegal practices believes that "anyone has the potential to be a bad apple" Cole contends that there is no evil intent only a best decision being made at a given time.

The purpose in citing this article is to illustrate that a rather comprehensive treatment as to why corporate executives behave badly, inadvertently conveys support for corporations and their managers. More precisely, executives and managers, the people of corporations, are portrayed as victims of their environment and circumstance as opposed to manifestations of a much broader human species malaise, one which has been with us since the beginning of recorded history. At best, Coles' article describes a symptom but not the underlying cause of it. At worst, Cole implies that we would all be susceptible to being co-opted by corporate culture, the culture of the people already there, when we arrive. This begs the question, where did the existing corporate members come from, those before them, and the ones before them who first conceived of the idea as a means of tapping into the greed of people to give as little as possible to get as much as possible by offering them shares?

Roger Martin, Dean of the University of Toronto Joseph L. Rotman School of Management justifies the actions of corporate executives on the grounds that it is required by Canadian law. He states as Bakan, that chief executive officers are required to put their company's interests first. This can create a conflict, according to Martin, for well intentioned, socially responsible executives. A conflict, which, he believes, can be resolved in innovative ways and can preserve corporate profits while simultaneously being socially responsible. To this end, the school of management, of which Martin is Dean, has created the Institute for Corporate Citizenship. Martin proclaims: "We plan to become a global centre for thinking about good corporate citizenship and how to put that into action". As is the norm, Martin also places much emphasis on law, one which demands from executives corporate interest first, and one that demands socially responsible behaviour, such as not releasing toxins into the environment just to save the corporation money. Martin concludes by invoking the notion of business ethics as being a significant part of their institute's curriculum. Assumedly, since he does not define it, business ethics refer to rules which require from executives socially responsible behaviours.

Richard C. Powers, also from the Joseph L. Rotman School of Management, believes that the corrupt behaviour of individuals, such as Martha Stewart and Lord Conrad Black, can be controlled by regulatory measures and corporate governance. It just has to be done better, a view which reveals an all too familiar response to misbehaviour - we will just make more rules, enforce them better, and impose harsher consequences to transgressions. Powers also conveys, without explicitly stating so, that there is merit to corporations and the profit edict by which they operate.

Peter Drucker, thought by many to be the world's leading management thinker, in 1946 was one of the first to analyse the corporation in his book: Concept of the Corporation. In response to current trends, recently he stated that corporate social responsibility is a dangerous distortion of business principles. "If you find an executive who wants to take on social responsibilities", Drucker said, "fire him fast". Milton Friedman, Nobel Laureate and one of the world's most eminent economists, also believes the new moralism in business, is in fact immoral. Noam Chomsky, Friedman's intellectual ideological nemesis, on this point shares his view that corporations must "be concerned only with their stockholders not the community or the workforce or whatever".

As many as those in opposition to corporations and the corruption they breed, there are those who see them simply as entities. Neither good nor bad, neither moral or immoral. Corporations just simply are. Corporations have no interest in political systems beyond whether a political system serves or impedes its self interested purposes. This is a very clear and transparent support of corporations which, to a large extent, despite all which has happened over the decades, explains why the institutions continue to exist, indeed flourish, albeit with almost predictable episodic down turns out of which they get bailed out, by monies from tax payers.

You will have noted that the lines are considerably blurred between corrupt corporate practices sanctioned by law and corrupt, executive practices prohibited by law. For corporations to enrich themselves with little regard for the social and community impact of what they do is not only acceptable but is prescribed by law. It is unacceptable that an executive, who is mandated to enrich the corporation, should generalize the behaviour to enrich him or herself beyond the agreed upon compensation package. Some form of double standard seems to be in play or at least naiveté and unwarranted shock and surprise when the fox invited into the hen house starts to eat the chickens. The board of directors at Hollinger, to whom Lord Conrad Black reported, only became outraged when they discovered that he was more interested in enriching himself than the board and shareholders. What does this say about the board of directors, the shareholders, and Lord Conrad Black? I think pretty much the same things.

Political Corruption

There are many who would argue that using the words "political" and "corruption" together constitutes a redundancy. According to this group both concepts represent self-serving interests through a power or influence base. While there are certain ideological parameters which indicate how a political group pursues self-interests, the name of the game for any political group is to get into power and to stay in power, doing whatever it takes, as long as the strategies stay roughly within the ideological parameters of the group. Those who tell us about political corruption come from all the ideologies; from the left, right, centre, and now from the green. Their message, almost always, is that the other political ideologies are corrupt and implicitly that the political group to which they belong is not. The attacks are personified and sometimes even ideological in nature.

My favourite commentary on politics is George Orwell's Animal Farm. If you have not read this brief but poignant work, I strongly recommend that you do. My understanding of this work is that it was written as a general commentary on politics and not simply as a scathing commentary on the feared Communism which was coming into prominence when the book was published. A very brief summary of Animal Farm is that all the animals unite and as a collective rise up against their human rulers. Shortly after the animals' successful revolution the group starts to notice that the pigs are increasingly less of a presence in working towards the collective good. Finally, the taller of the animals who can see into the farmhouse through the windows, much to their shock and dismay, report to the others that the pigs are walking on their hind legs, conducting themselves exactly like the humans who were deposed by the group in their uprising. The lesson, from my perspective, is that eventually the pigs will end up walking on their hind legs regardless of how noble or well-intentioned their striving for power initially was conceived. Said differently; "Absolute power corrupts absolutely". This is why we need a system of checks and balances, a system which is said to be best accomplished in a democracy. Even in democratic systems, however, checks and balances can be circumvented and as Michael Moore put it in, Stupid White Man, "a man no one elected (sic 7 November 2000) sits in the White House".

Currently Noam Chomsky, Michael Moore, and Al Franken are some of the loudest and most often cited revealers of political corruption. They are critical mostly of the established right, the most fervent protectors of the establishment. Also there are critics of the central liberals and some find it necessary at this time in history to attack the outdated far left. The point being, there is no shortage of individuals or for that fact, organizations raising the alarm about political corruption.

The most scholarly, best informed, and greatest of elderly statesmen among corruption tale bearers, especially of a political nature, is Professor Noam Chomsky of the Massachusetts Institute of Technology. You should read at least one of his books, perhaps 9/11. He points out the magnitude and sophistication of the U.S. government's and corporations' capability of disseminating propaganda against which the efforts of the old Russian or Communist regime pale by comparison. Also, Chomsky is a tireless exposer of forces intent on maintaining the status quo. Among these forces he includes the Pentagon, which he claims justified itself initially as an organization created to defend us from the Russians. Long after the Cold War slipped into historical oblivion, the Pentagon not only continues but is expanding exponentially. Chomsky rhetorically asks, "How stupid can you be and how indoctrinated can you be? Don't you ever ask a question about what happened? What happened is, it is there for the same reasons it always was. How else are Newt Gingrich's rich constituents going to stay rich? You obviously can't subject them to market discipline". These few words in the book: Class Warfare, should suffice to convey that Professor Chomsky does not mince his words or shy away from saying that which he believes. To reiterate an earlier comment, as far as I can tell he has only been marginalised by the status quo there have been no attempts on his life because he has no real plans to change things. His apparent expectation is that raising consciousness will serve to mobilize individuals to eventually create a critical mass, one which will precipitate a tremendous, social upheaval. My concern is that this has not happened so far, and I cannot imagine what it will take to create the critical mass necessary to precipitate sustainable change which is required in response to Professor Chomsky's revelations..

The other, more popular but less scholarly quixotic bearer of tales is the scruffy, bespectacled, cap-wearing, overweight, duel hot tub owner, who does not readily give interviews himself, and who actually met with Roger but excluded the interview from his documentary, Michael Moore. Not only does he expose corruption but he does so in a very "in your face" manner. I am especially intrigued by Moore who is also marginalised by the status quo and there are no apparent attempts to assassinate him. But then, beyond admonishing us to "get involved", Moore also does not have a real plan for change. Nevertheless, he has become a very popular voice who dares not be politically correct. He speaks often in painfully revealing ways about political and corporate corruption. My personal favourite of Moore's work is Stupid White Man. Reading or viewing on DVD any one of his other works would serve just as well to familiarize yourself with his brazen approach. As brazen, if not more so, is Al Franken. His book, Lies and the Liars Who Tell Them, is number one at the time of writing this on the New York Times best seller list and classically illustrates what you can get away with if you expose but have little, if any, solutions to offer.

Political corruption is not a new phenomena. The history of the Roman Empire or more precisely, its eventual demise in the fourth century, is an illustration of incompetence, corruption, and decay, hundreds of years in the making. While the content of the history is quite different from modern times the underlying structure of periods of growth, decline, prosperity, scarceness, internal strife, and external threats virtually is the same as today. In reality, perhaps corruption is more sanitized now, but perhaps not even. The only reason for thinking of political corruption as now more sanitized is that most of us don't experience the concomitant mayhem firsthand. We mostly experience it through the media. We can sit in the comfort of our living rooms as opposed to the seats of the Colosseum with the Roman sun scorching us and the winds blowing our way the stench of death only a few metres below our feet.

If you have not realized it so far, corruption, especially political, always comes with lethal consequences to very real people but never people from the privileged classes. Consider for example, Haiti, where a relentless, economic crisis has eroded all their public institutions and has created and perpetuated a climate of pervasive, political corruption, a climate which fuels vicious, lethal fighting among political factions. In the Philippines, chronic poverty is exploited by a tenacious Communist insurgency, and in Rwanda corrupt regimes precipitated bitter hatreds and violence which led to the unspeakable horrors of the 1994 genocide. In the Darfur region of the Sudan political corruption, attributable to a myriad of factors, have allowed the massacre of hundreds of thousands of farmers and precipitated the movement of a million refugees, which may yet equal the horror in Rwanda.

These instances represent political corruption in poor countries and implicitly convey that it is a far greater problem there than in rich, industrialized, technologically advanced, and well educated, western cultures. This, however, is not the case. Don't think for a minute that there were ever the "good old days" when a handshake was enough and when a man's word was as good as gold. There were never any "good old days". There has always been political corruption of one sort or another perpetrated on the public by every ideological perspective imaginable. There is of course the Nixon, "I am not a crook" debacle, and the infamous buying of votes in Chicago and New York at the turn of the century. Then there is the more current U. S. Presidential election in 2000 when Governor Jeb Bush gave his brother George W. Bush, as Moore puts it, an early Christmas present, the State of Florida. Notwithstanding the satirical humour of Moore, his point and that of others is that political corruption has been and continues to be the bane of all organized societies. To date, no one advocates the abolition of politics, nor the abolition of the management of cities, regions, and states by elected individuals who are, for the most part, untrained for the onerous responsibilities bestowed upon them by the electorate. Some advocate for larger government stewardship while others for lesser interference in the lives of people. Some want all of it run by government and attribute to those who aspire to the role unbridled benevolence, altruism, and good will. While no one advocates for the abolition of politics, opposing factions invariably advocate for their brand of political power, seemingly oblivious to Orwell's allegorical warning that the pigs always end up walking on their hind legs.

From my perspective, it is not surprising that in spite of the widespread corruption in politics which has always existed and continues to do so, and in spite of the proliferation of those who criticize political ideologies and their leaders, the only real choice available is a change in the name of the party or individual we elect. The jury is still out on President Obama and the people who he assembles around him. Democracy continues to be propagandized as the best form of governance, despite Winston Churchill's admonishment of it based upon a very real evaluation of the masses who do the voting. Democracy, from time to time, is subverted even by democratic nations who wish to put into place other forms of governments to suit a particular self serving purpose. The point being that it seems to be an axiom of the human condition that leaders eventually emerge and others follow. We are glad for the aspiration of those who want to govern, until they get there, at which time the leader is immediately criticized and/or ousted. On this point, and somewhat tongue in cheek, it is lost on most people that Italy is a persistently pervasive example of how a nation can function without a real, stable, central government presence.

No discussion of political systems, however brief, would be complete without, at least, a passing commentary on the bureaucracy which actually runs things despite the attempted interference of politicians who, from the perspective of the civil servants, are just a nuisance to be tolerated. The British television series of the 1980s: Yes Minister, is not far off the mark. It portrays an interesting arrangement, whereby those who actually have a permanence, history, and a direction, right or wrong, have to incorporate into the process elected officials. The worst part of this arrangement is that every bureaucrat knows the elected official will not be long at his post, but just long enough to make some sort of a stir. The challenge for the bureaucrats always is to allow, indeed to participate in creating the stir, while keeping it under sufficient control as not to disturb very much what the bureaucracy actually is doing. Curiously, little mention is made of this arrangement by the pundits cited above. It is as if this enormous cohort of people does not exist and plays no part in the political process. Arguably, they do at least by enabling political corruption and by feigning subservience to their political masters, whoever they may be at any given time.

Curiously, political commentators just do not focus on bureaucracy or on the enormous influence and power they have over what is accomplished and in what direction various services, such as education and health care are set upon. We should be mindful of the fact that the military also is a civil service bureaucracy, the only difference being, the equipment and the uniforms they are provided. All police forces fall into the same category. In reality, elections are applications for the job of managing, not the country, state or province but the specific jurisdiction's bureaucracy. In most instances, the applicants offer an ideology, seldom if ever, management knowledge, and the skills required to truly take control of the civil service. It is no wonder therefore, that politicians barely are tolerated by civil servants but are viewed as necessary, unavoidable nuisances not unlike those depicted by the aforementioned British television series. Similarly, it is no wonder that elected officials are content to impose mostly meaningless initiatives; their focus lasts no longer than the duration of their term. Their significant concern is that some bureaucrat will not commit some serious transgression on his watch.

It is markedly worrisome that government bureaucracies are afforded such behavioural latitudes, almost as if there has been some conspiratorial agreement to treat them as non existent, indeed, invisible entities. They are not. Both corporations and bureaucracies are made up of people whose decisions and actions are not nearly as directed by their political overseers as we believe or as we would like it to be. Moreover, what bureaucrats do is derived more from who they are than from anything else. As such, they, too, are self-serving actors in pursuit of the satisfaction of their own needs, little influenced, if at all, by the political ideology of the time.

Over three decades ago, Lawrence Kohlberg and Peter Scharf, in a brief and somewhat obscure article, exposed just how powerful and dangerous bureaucracies can be. They accomplished this by analysing the Mylai Massacre in Vietnam. The same analysis could easily be applied to the Abu Dabue Prison debacle in Iraq and the torture of prisoners in Guantánamo Bay, or for that fact, anywhere else the torture of prisoners is committed with the knowledge and complacency of countries who are officially opposed to such human degradation. According to the article of Kohlberg and Scharf, their formulations are just as relevant today as they were then, bureaucratic violence essentially is a function of blind obedience to power, the power an officer has over an enlisted soldier, and the power high-ranking officers have over the officer at the scene, even though physically far removed from the action. Analysing transcripts, it was obvious that all those involved in Mylai had only the barest understanding that killing babies is not acceptable conduct. From the perspective of all those involved it was quite irrelevant that there is a Geneva Convention which requires officers and soldiers to test the legality (in terms of international law) of orders given to them. It is even more irrelevant what might be the ideology of the elected political party at the time. Because of these realities, on reflection, I suppose that, ultimately, it is better to have fewer politicians and a smaller civil service to minimize the misbehaviour and harm of which clearly they are capable. For certain, at least at this time, politicians are, for the most part, unable to protect us from the civil servants of the bureaucracy, and the bureaucrats, for strategic purposes, also for the most part, are unwilling or unable to protect us from the corrupt shenanigans of the elected representatives of the people.

Religious Corruption

This section is not concerned with the transgressions of various religious people from all denominations. The transgressions of Catholic priests, television evangelists, and Islamic Imams or Mullahs, to name just a few groups, are simply just that: people misbehaving. Similarly, religious organizational coverups of malfeasances are simply just more of people misbehaving. The focus of this section rather is on systemic corruption which obstructs that which has great potential to elevate the human condition from the base, rabid territorialism, tribalism, and unmitigated pleasure seeking which has characterized it since the beginning of recorded history.

So far, I have not been able to find one significant readily-identifiable voice, although satirist Bill Maher may fit the bill, about religious corruption. Dan Brown, author of Da Vinci Code claims to have written a fictional book, yet he has popularized the reality that all sorts of corruption has occurred and continues to occur in all religions, especially the well-established and long standing institutionalized ones. The inspiration to Dan Brown's fictional work appears to be The Holy Blood and the Holy Grail by Messrs Baigent, Leigh and Lincoln. It is an extremely dense book, chock full of detail; the relevance of much of it is difficult, if not impossible, to discern. Their point and the fictional theme of Dan Brown's book is that the deification of a man called Jesus was the corrupt chicanery of Constantine in the third century C.E. The motivation, as for all corrupt actions, was power and wealth, specifically assigning to Rome king-making rights in the rest of the world. The Vatican, Westminster Abbey, and other opulent Christian edifices bear witness to how successful Constantine's creativity has been. The total combined wealth of all organized Christian-based religions is unimaginably staggering to the point that I have never seen an estimate of it. Adding to this Christian-based, religious wealth and the wealth of other religions makes the very idea of a number-value even more staggering. Such colossal wealth and power over people requires more than the simple, powerfully positive message of men such as Jesus, Mohammed, Buddha, and Confucius. It requires a well thought-out, tenacious corruption perpetuated and embellished over centuries.

For the purposes of this book, I am not at all concerned with the question of whether Jesus ever existed as an historical person. I am satisfied with the idea of a Jesus and the message he purportedly had. It is the distortion of the person and of the message which is of concern. Similarly, I am not at all concerned with whether Jesus rose from the grave, married or had descendants. My concern is with how Christianity evolved in its early years to become what it is today because of the powerful, political figure Constantine, who believed that embracing and escalating the Christian movement was a better thing to do than to fight it.

The message of Islam has been similarly distorted, to achieve markedly self-serving interests. Instead of elevating the human condition and serving as a catalyst to promote the optimal development of human potential, the two major and opposing religions Christianity and Islam have obstructed our innate propensity to think for ourselves in principled ways and act accordingly. They have subjugated their followers and have enticed them with the promise of an afterlife to compensate for the misery created by humanity. While mainstream religions are very much committed to subjugation, fundamentalists are especially good at it. Regardless of which denomination they subscribe to, fundamentalists represent extreme positions, and their numbers are growing seemingly exponentially. Their sheer numbers are as alarming as what they represent.

Of all places, there is a brief but revealing exposé of the fundamentalist agenda for America in the Rolling Stone Magazine by Bob Moser. In this article, he mentions a conference of fundamentalists representing all fifty states held in Fort Lauderdale, Florida, just after the so-called first election of George W.

Bush. The name of the conference was "Reclaiming America for Christ". The delegates were celebrating their success as the nation's most effective, political machine. Despite their success, they reportedly profess to consider themselves as a persecuted minority Moser writes, "Waging a holy war against the godless forces of secularism". Justified as the mediaeval crusaders, the biblical literalists are in pursuit of world domination by imposing their views, values, and beliefs upon the American people first and then upon the rest of the world - all in the name of service to God. This end then justifies the means. These fundamentalist Christians terrorize the heathen with threats of eternal damnation for not joining up, whereas Muslims terrorize the infidels with threats of death for not being one of them. Neither gang of zealots is being true to the message of their respective prophets: both have distorted the "truth" to serve their own ends apart from what the prophets intended. As such, this, too, is a form of corruption no more or less than that which is evident in corporations and politics.

Before going further, it is important to note here that most historical philosophers say that religion was created to explain natural phenomena. For example, before Christianity's presence in Norway, the Vikings attributed thunder to Thor and since thunder and lightning is followed by rain, something important to Viking farmers, Thor was worshipped as the God of Fertility. In fact, Indo-Europeans before and after the birth of Jesus believed in the existence of many gods, who were ascribed certain human or animal personas. As well, both of the two great Oriental religions, Hinduism and Buddhism, are Indo-European in origin. It also is noteworthy that the idea that deity is present in all things has been around for a very long time. This notion continued after the birth of Christianity and, as Christianity grew, it became the basis for a culture which unified many who believed in the prescribed doctrine. While empiricism started a gradual separation from the theology of the church, the more important events for our discussion occurred in the early years of Christianity. These are the events which mark and exemplify the corruption of religion at the hands of men, and I do mean men, in a very gender specific way.

One of the first events which occurred in the early years of Christianity was the gradual exclusion of women, with the exception of the mother of Jesus. Another significant event was the birth of the state and church acting in unison, essentially out of Constantine's self interests. This co-operation was aided and abetted by the self interest of the Bishop of Rome.

The book: The Holy Blood and the Holy Grail is presented by the authors not as a criticism of Christianity but as a thorough, extensively researched, historical study of the man known as Jesus of Nazareth. According to the authors, Christianity, contrary to popular conception, is not a single specific homogeneous entity. There are numerous forms of Christianity, from the very beginning, evolving to this very day. A new version of it may be in the making at the very moment that I am writing or you are reading this. There is, however, a single factor which arguably unites an otherwise diverse, Christian entity. It is the New Testament and in it the unique status ascribed to the crucifixion and resurrection of Jesus. What the authors say about these writings, especially the four gospels is much. It is overwhelmingly much, requiring much effort to read, let alone absorb. If you are tenacious and truly curious, about all that is said and interpreted about the gospels, struggle with the entire Holy Blood and the Holy Grail book. For our purposes, I will draw selectively on what illustrates the existence of corruption in Christianity.

The premise of The Holy Blood and the Holy Grail is that Jesus was, as described by his first followers, a holy human teacher and profit. As prescribed by the custom of his time, he married Mary Magdalene, procreated, escaped crucifixion, and created a bloodline lineage. This is a markedly shameful simplification of a five hundred page treatise. The simplification is justifiable on the premise that whether or not Jesus existed, let alone was/is God, is not relevant to the corruption to which the idea of his existence and, more importantly, his message was subjugated. First, it is noteworthy that around the year AD 304, the pagan emperor Diocletian ordered the destruction of all Christian writings which could be found. As such, Christian documents, especially in Rome, all but vanished. This is said to be an important event insofar as it casts aspersions on just what materials the New Testament and the four gospels are based.

Shortly after Constantine came to power in Rome his influence on Christianity is ascribed much importance but not in the way described in the official Roman Catholic document known as the "Donation of Constantine". The intent of this document is said to have been to confuse, misrepresent, and mislead subsequent Christian writers. This eighth-century document is said to have been an effort to cover up the corruption to which the ideas of Jesus and his teachings were subjugated by Constantine. To illustrate, according to the "Donation of Constantine", Constantine converted to Christianity, and gave to the Bishop of Rome his imperial symbols and regalia. These items became the Church's property. Then, according to the document, Constantine was the first to declare the Bishop of Rome as the "Vicar of Christ" and offered him the status of Emperor. In his capacity as "Vicar of Christ", the Bishop then allegedly returned the imperial regalia to Constantine, who wore them subsequently with ecclesiastical sanction and permission.

This is the Roman Catholic version of how the Bishop of Rome came to exercise supreme secular and spiritual authority over Christendom. With the support of Constantine, the Bishop of Rome came to possess the unchallengeable right to create or depose kings. From the conversion of Constantine, therefore, came the subsequent power of the Vatican in secular affairs. In other words, coronations became the creation of a king through the authority of the church. Constantine, however, was not nearly as magnanimous as the "Donation of Constantine" would lead us to believe, according to The Holy Blood and the Holy Grail discourse. He was, in fact, quite to the contrary and self-servingly corrupt as well. According to the authors of The Holy Blood and the Holy Grail their research reveals that Constantine was a pagan, who subscribed to pagan beliefs and practices all his life until he was baptized on his death bed in CE 337 when he was too weak to protest. This, then, begs the question as to how he came to be associated with the emergence of the papacy and the strengthening of Christianity's foothold on which it has thrived for millennia.

Reportedly, in the interest of unity, Constantine deliberately chose to blur the distinction between Christianity, Mithraism, and Sol Invictus, (the latter two religions emphasize the status of the sun). He deliberately chose not to see any contradictions between Christianity and the other two pagan beliefs. Out of his self-serving need to rule and to do so with expedience, Constantine tolerated the deified Jesus and probably rationalized him to be the earthly manifestation of Sol Invictus. From Constantine's perspective, therefore, there were no contradictions in building Christian churches and pagan temples. While Constantine was not the good Christian which later tradition depicts, he was an expedient ruler who consolidated the religion in the interest of unity, Christian Orthodoxy did not necessarily attribute to him corruption of the message of Jesus. The Council of Nicea which he convened in AD 325, however, very much enshrined him in this role.

Constantine set the agenda, and it was carried out accordingly. For example, it was at this Council that the dating of Easter was established, rules were framed which defined the authority of Bishops, and by vote it was decided that Jesus was a God, not a mortal prophet. Moreover, as a God Jesus then could be associated conveniently with the pagan Sol Invictus. Insofar as virgin birth was a prerequisite for deities it then became necessary for the mother of Jesus to have conceived him without intercourse. This voted upon decision of Jesus being a deity also required that he be distanced from women in his life and, subsequently, from any notion that he married and had children with a mortal such as Mary Magdalene.

A year after the Council of Nicea, Constantine sanctioned the confiscation and destruction of all works which challenged the Christian Orthodox teachings which he commissioned and orchestrated. Christianity thus started to serve self interests not unlike the corporations discussed earlier. By Constantine's design and for his self-serving purposes, he allowed the council to define the authority of Bishops, and in so doing, he initiated a concentration of power in ecclesiastical hands. This initiative was elaborated upon a year after the Council by Constantine who arranged for a fixed income to be allocated to the church. Simultaneously, he installed the Bishop of Rome in the Lateran Palace. Interestingly, it was not until C.E. 384 (some 58 years later) that the Bishop of Rome called himself Pope for the first time.

In C.E. 331, six years after the Council of Nicea took place, Constantine commissioned and financed new copies of the Bible. This allowed the custodians of the created Christian Orthodoxy to revise, edit, and rewrite the content of surviving documents and information as they saw fit, in accordance with their tenets. It was at this point in time that most of the crucial alterations to the New Testament probably were made and Jesus assumed the unique status he has enjoyed ever since.

It is the contention therefore of some, who consider themselves as historians rather than critics, that the New Testament represents an act of corruption since it is essentially the product of Constantine's appointed editors and writers. The fourth-century authors were appointed custodians of Orthodoxy with vested interests to protect. It is noteworthy that many books with different versions of events were deliberately excluded from the Bible. For example, the Apocrypha casts a markedly different light on accepted accounts. So also the Nag Hammadi Scrolls, which depict Jesus escaping his death on the cross through an ingenious substitution.

The salient point of the critics or as most prefer to be known, historians, is that the person and teachings of a man known as

Jesus was subverted to serve specific, immediate state needs. That which was created by Constantine perpetrated, albeit in new innovative ways, the relationship between the secular state and the tenets of religion. While this clearly defined relationship no longer exists in its original and very transparent form, it nevertheless continues to thrive to this day. Some would say every bit as blatantly as it did, for example, during the Inquisition.

The most alarming manifestation of the close relationship between the state and religion, according to Bob Moser's article in the magazine Rolling Stone, is the American Christian Fundamentalist Proliferation and its pervasive influence over the far right political ideology. In the year 2004, nine hundred of America's staunchest Christian Fundamentalists gathered in Fort Lauderdale, Florida. The name of the conference, proudly displayed, was "Reclaiming America for Christ". This group of evangelical activists who are considered to be America's most effective political machine, brought more than four-million, new Christian voters to the polls to re-elect George W. Bush back to the White House and thirty-two, new, pro lifers to Congress. In spite of their unprecedented power, the group proclaimed itself to be a persecuted minority, one which was waging a holy war against the godless forces of secularism. Within this group are the Dominionists or biblical literalists, who believe God has called them to take over the U.S. Government. This group wants to re-write school books to reflect a Christian version of American history, to fill the nation's courts with judges who follow Old Testament laws, post the Ten Commandments in every Court House, and make it a felony for gay men to have sex and women to have abortions.

The founder of the Dominionists is D. James Kennedy, a former Arthur Murray dance instructor. He launched his Florida ministry in 1959 and built it into a thirty seven million dollar a year empire. He also helped to create the moral majority in 1979 and established his vast influence to the extent that George W. Bush sought his blessing before running for President and, throughout his two terms, consulted top Dominionists on matters of federal policy. In their view, the founding fathers of America never intended to erect a barrier between politics and religion. The First Amendment, they say, was not intended to separate the church and state. In fact, according to a virtual army of Dominionist-trained lawyers, the Constitution was actually designed to "shield" the church from federal interference and to pave the way for Christians to take their rightful place at the head of the government. At the beginning of the conference, we are told, by Moser, the Dominionists recited an oath they want to be recited in every classroom: "I pledge allegiance to the Christian flag, and to the Saviour for whose kingdom it stands, one Saviour, crucified, risen, and coming again, with life and liberty for all who believe".

Indeed, Constantine would be pleased with the longevity and fervour of his commissioned Christian Orthodoxy. Probably, he would be quite bemused by the exercise of literacy license in re-writing and interpreting the Bible he had ordered and would take solace in the fact that the primary tenets of Jesus, which declared him to be a deity who was crucified and then rose from the dead, have been unequivocally retained.

The relationship between state and religion is alive and well. It is alive and well most everywhere. In fact, it is thriving as much as it ever did. Religious ideals are being corrupted to serve the power and influence motives of both the state and church and obscure the very idea of each prophet as well as his respective messages.

Before discussing in Part Two how all religions, due to being corrupted, have failed to realize their respective powerful potential to elevate the human condition to that of which it is capable, it will be useful to first explore how religion, as it has come to exist, obstructs human development. To illustrate this criticism of institutionalized religion, I have chosen James Hollis. He is a trained Jungian analyst, lecturer, and a person who has had first hand experience with religion. There are many others but for me, his insights about this travesty are the most concise of any.

To begin, religion is from the Latin religare, essentially meaning to "reconnect with". Regardless of what we agree to be the object of our desire to reconnect with, the point made by the Jungians is that this motivation is natural and pervasive. So far, so good. Since we cannot go backward, however, it is said that a human life-long quest is to satisfy this need symbolically through relationships with individuals, institutions, ideologies or the sky-parent God. What the Jungians don't say is that the motivation represents a developmental phase from which, under the right conditions, we can transcend to subsequent stages. Instead of facilitating the development of the human potential, institutionalized religion relies on fear, insecurity, and the need for prescribed direction to obstruct human development. In fact, this obstruction of development has been the bane of the human condition since the beginning of recorded history.

Hollis says it best: "Fundamentalism is a flight from adulthood and appeals to many because life is so scary. If I can turn my fears over to the rigidity of a dogma, turn my choices over to my pastor, subscribe to an ideology which rationalizes the suffering of life for me, then I will have happiness." While, as Hollis says, it is no crime to be fearful, it is a crime to relinquish control of our life-journey to someone or something else. For the Jungians, the coercive hysteria of the fundamentalists, regardless of denomination, is based on the fact that their dogmas not only decrease or alleviate anxiety but they also perpetuate cultural infantilization. Moreover, to be bewitched by literalism, to fall in love with our own constructs, Hollis contends, is a form of insanity, or as will be discussed in Part Two, a profound manifestation of a pervasive, cultural developmental deficit. It is the child-like creation of pleasing fantasies, which in the hands of physically mature adults, has and continues to create much harm.

In contrast to many who raise the alarm and unabashedly stick our collective faces into the profound harm and human degradation which has been committed in the name of one religion or another, there are those who contend that the messages of the prophets were not distorted, and if applied as intended, they can be instrumental in optimally developing the human potential. It requires some effort, however, to ferret out such individuals, and in some cases overlook their respective penchant towards some Orthodoxy, one which pertains mostly to deification and resurrection. One such person is the Anglican Bishop, John Shelby Spong. To his utmost credit, the Bishop acknowledges that, indeed, security has been and continues to be the primary goal of every religious system. Security, he says, not truth is well-served by controlling thought, disciplining deviation, and purging critics. An ultimately vast, impersonal, and frightening universe encourages religious zealots to surrender their freedom for the security of being told what to think. Bishop Spong asks; "When will we recognize that religion is always in the mind control business?". At least in part, the answer to this question is that as long as there is systemic cultural infantilization, the masses will remain susceptible to being controlled. Therefore, we cannot look to any religion, new or old, regardless of denomination, for change. Nevertheless, the prophets and their respective messages can give much direction of which the good Bishop speaks extensively.

For example, according to Bishop Spong, Jesus did not say, "I have come that you might be religious". Instead Jesus said, "I have come that you might have life and have it abundantly". This is a good message. It speaks of the human potential which was not then or now realized. The message also acknowledges that life's journey is not an easy one, that it requires courage, and that we all need, from time to time, to various degrees, guidance. But guidance to achieve what? Spong quotes Dietrich Bonhoeffer, a German martyr in World War II who said; "To be a Christian does not mean to be a religious man (or woman). It simply means to be a man (or woman)". I believe the very same has been said about being a Muslim, a Shiite, a Jew, or Buddhist and has been said by those who have not been corrupted by self-serving distortions of the messages. Hamlet's soliloquy captures the idea best: "To be or not to be is the question". Not barely being, not adequately being, but being everything of which we are capable. Sadly, the potential benefits of the prophets' messages have been corrupted to the point that, instead of promoting optimal development, the messages have served, along with most other social institutions, to curtail it. Fortunately, there are people out there, even among the clergy, who see this clearly and are sufficiently courageous to speak of it openly.

Spong contends that old mythologies and literal interpretations may have worked in an ancient world but are no longer relevant in post-Darwinian times and in light of our current knowledge. He advocates for reformation and not the abolition of the Christian message. He predicts that without the reformation, Christianity is unlikely to remain a viable system. Spong, as I, believes in the prophet's message and certainly is unwilling to throw out the baby with the bathwater.

While Hollis, as described above, is critical of religion, particularly fundamentalism, he has, as Spong, much that is positive to say about the idea of a Jesus as well as the message he disseminated during his brief life. Interestingly, neither Spong nor Hollis (among many others who see the great potential) bother themselves with the historical facts as to how the New Testament was shaped by secular self serving interests. Perhaps as I do, they don't particularly care to whom the surviving message of the prophets can be attributed. It is sufficient that the message exists. Hollis writes: "To make this Jewish prophet more than human is to render him irrelevant to our common condition of living in a perilous place, struggling with our own fears and uncertainties. In The Last Temptation of Christ, the gravest temptation of Jesus, the carpenter, is to have an ordinary life, untroubled, comfortable, married with kids, living in the suburbs, commuting to work. Jesus, however, did not choose this." The struggle of his life, according to Hollis, is precisely what makes Christ relevant today. Deified and resurrected without real blood, real fear, real suffering, Hollis says, "demeans the carpenter and renders his passion (message) irrelevant to our daily lives. It is only in his choice and suffering that we see a model for our own journey. When we model Christ, leaving some familiar stance in life and move into the unknown, we open ourselves to developing the maturity of which we are capable, including thinking for ourselves, a state that is completely antithetical to fundamentalism."

Of the human potential embodied in the message of Jesus, Hollis cites the Gnostic Gospel of Thomas, wherein Jesus said: "The kingdom of God is spread all over the world and we do not see it". Instead of accepting suffering in hopes of a heavenly afterlife, the message is that we have the potential to create it here. As the artist Paul Elbard also suggested: "There is another world and it is this one."

Albert Nolan in his book: Jesus Before Christianity, writes about a man who lived in first century Palestine. Nolan's intent is to depict this man and his message as seen through the eyes of his contemporaries. Nolan also speaks at length about the man's message and not his divinity. Most important is the message of our potential to be different and to live differently. For example, Nolan writes that many Christians have been mislead for centuries about the nature of God's "kingdom" by the well-known mistranslation of Luke 17:21: "The kingdom of God is within you". Today, all serious scholars and translators agree that the text should read: "The kingdom of God is among you or in your midst". Through a discussion pertaining not to the meaning of words but the manner in which they were used at the time of Jesus and shortly after, Nolan asserts that when Jesus spoke of a "kingdom" what he had in mind was a politically structured society of people here on earth. Insofar as it was said by Jesus that the "kingdom" is not of this world, Nolan says the accurate meaning is that the values of the "kingdom" are different from, and opposed to, the values of this world. Nolan concludes: "There is no reason for thinking that it means the "kingdom" will float in the air somewhere above the earth or that it will be an abstract entity without any tangible social and political structure". Incidentally, Nolan also does not acknowledge the aforementioned Council of Nicea and what effect this had on the scriptures he cites. Instead, he references the discovery of the Dead Sea Scrolls. This implies that his interpretations are based on information not destroyed or corrupted by the edicts of a Roman emperor.

It would be wrong to conclude this chapter without reiterating that for enlightened developmentally mature religious scholars there were other prophets besides Jesus. All harboured a message of hope, based on the human potential to rise above the secular corruptions of the time. It is heartening that, without exception, the various prophets' motivation was to improve on the human condition and that their respective plans now can be interpreted as relying on the populous achieving a "mature" level of reasoning. As a point of reference, you need only to consult the Islamic Creed for some of the names of the prophets; Abraham, Ishmael, Isaac, Jacob and the tribes, Moses, and Jesus. The greater challenge is to sift through the distortions about the persons and their messages. Hopefully, now that we are a little better informed this will be a less onerous task, if you are so inclined to learn more. Whatever you do to become more informed, keep in mind the focus of this book. Specifically, develop an explanation as to what has been going wrong and based on the Part Two definition of the problem, apply strategies with which to rise above the cultural infantilization which has and continues to rob all of human kind the potential of which we are capable.

CHAPTER THREE
MISBEHAVIOUR

The Misbehaviour of Criminals

Arguably criminality is an extremely broad topic, one which has been pondered and explained in various ways since the beginning of recorded history. Even the classification of criminal behaviour is onerous and subject to debate. For the purposes of clarity, I have chosen three groups of criminal behaviour for discussion. Those who commit property crimes, those who perpetrate violence, and those who use illegal substances. Prior to reviewing what is reported in the literature about such transgressions it is noteworthy that in some circles, especially in academia, there is considerable debate about how illegality is determined and what strategies ought to be used to curtail it. The first person I recommend for your review is a former teacher and mentor, John Eisenberg. In his very scholarly work: The Limits of Reason, he describes very easily discernable, universal propensities to curtail criminality through the creation and enforcement of laws. While his book is dense and difficult to digest, it is an important work you should know about.

Views about criminality over the centuries range from very simplistic notions to sophisticated, socio-cultural, political debates. Responses to criminality include the hardliners with a punishment perspective which, even today, barely disguises the now ridiculous belief that so called bad people are possessed by the devil. Tragically, this belief justifies "beating the devil out of" the so-called bad person. The beatings are coupled with longer periods of incarceration; a call for harsher environmental conditions during incarceration, and the loss of all societal rights for the remainder of the offender's life. Alternatively, there is a trend to medicalize deviance and to turn misbehaviour into a sickness. Hence, the medical concepts of rehabilitation and re-integration are used in the treatment of offenders. If you are interested in what is being said about efforts to address deviance and why it is failing, I recommend reading: Deviance and Medicalization: From Badness to Sickness, by Conrad and Schneider. I also recommend Bruce Alexander's book: Peaceful Measures, if you are interested in reading a sound, reasonable, and informed critique concerning how substance abuse and the legal response to it is viewed. While published more than a decade ago most, if not all, of what Alexander says is poignantly relative to this very day. More recently, Gabor Maté has written In the Realm of Hungry Ghosts which is about the exponential growth in substance use and abuse and about the futility of the so called war on drugs.

In addition to the conceptualizations of the causes of crime and how best to respond to it, there also are two other broad areas of discussion. The first concerns our collective perception regarding the magnitude of the problem. In the context of objectively determining magnitude, as well, there is considerable debate as to what constitutes an illegal act. There is a goodly number who argue that much of criminality is manufactured as a function of various political agendas mostly as a response to an alarmed populace which is reacting to media representations of what is going on in our immediate communities and broader afield. Also included in this debate are various views as to how terrorists and/or anarchists should be categorized. Notwithstanding these debates, the most important issue to be aware of is the propensity, as described by John Eisenberg, to make more laws. According to Eisenberg, the common perception is that the purpose of various efforts to create social order, especially laws, is to improve things and to enable citizens to lead ordered lives and to avoid chaos. This perception is reinforced by instances in which laws do seem to make a difference as, for example, when seat belt laws are correlated with a decrease in traffic deaths and injuries. Eisenberg cautions, however, that law is not needed to solve the problems we have or is law the most effective way we have of controlling our collective destiny. The only real reason law is important, especially in troubled times, is because we believe it to be so. A belief that politicians and the legal profession are quick to reinforce, each for their respective self-serving purposes. The legal profession for very obvious reasons, it is good for business. Politicians see the law as a necessity for more convoluted reasons, ones which ultimately translate into pandering to the grossly misinformed populace for the purpose of securing the majority vote at the time of the, always imminent, next election. Everyone seems to forget, however, that from prohibition to the war on drugs, there has never been a successful global ban on any behaviour. Yet we continue to indulge ourselves in a mass fantasy that what we do not like can be legislated out of existence.

At the time of this writing, the Mayors of Toronto, Buffalo, Detroit, and Windsor are forming a coalition to stop street violence, shooting, and killings with hand guns by stopping the smuggling of these weapons across the border. Clearly, the coalition and the rhetoric is a reaction to weekly and occasionally daily shootings and killings among young and primarily disenfranchised men. As elected leaders, circumstances are forcing them to do something, anything, to stop the cycle of violence. To offer a long-term solution simply would be unpalatable at a perceived time of crisis. Moreover, there is no reason to believe that any of the Mayors in the coalition fully understand the nature of the problem and what would bring about a sustainable solution. Similarly, in lieu of knowing what else to do, joint police forces round up street-gang members, create a correctional resource to house the large numbers, and additional Court services to process the charges. Few argue with such a tactic. At least these delinquents are off the streets, goes the rhetoric. Seldom is it mentioned that the void created by their absence will soon be filled by opportunistic wannabes. I also believe that, if through some magic, all firearms could be removed from everywhere, these testosterone laden, disenfranchised, and violent young men would be shooting each other with bows and arrows or hacking each other to death with machetes or stabbing each other to death with sharpened sticks.

The other side of the discussion about crime comes from social scientists such as Professor Tony Doob, from the Centre of Criminology at the University of Toronto. Doob and others argue that the real, statistically supported, incidents of crime is on the decline. They acknowledge the media created perception that the sky is falling but maintain the hard numbers support a different conclusion. Admittedly, statistics can be manipulated to serve a purpose. However, the data on which criminologists rely are not obtained through complicated, statistical procedures. Statisticians simply count incident rates and report them relative to population size. If the relative number of crimes to population size is not factored in, the numbers would be meaningless; it would be like comparing oranges to apples. This per capita notion also reveals much about the influence of police on crime. There is a rather old, but salient study, conducted by Daniel Koeing, from the University of Victoria, in which he found that increased levels of per capita police strength precede increased crime rates, rather than being a response to increased crime rates. Moreover, the increased police strength does not correlate with a decrease in criminal rates. There is, however, an exception to his findings when it comes to violence. Specifically, lower levels of per capita police strength are associated with higher rates of violent crime. Therefore, increased levels of violence are used to provide the rationale for increased levels of per capita police strength. However, the increased levels of police strength merely generate increased police activity, activity which is not necessarily targeted or is capable of containing, let alone eradicating, violent crime.

I have included the preceding to alert you to the existence

of rather complex academic, statistical, and ideological debates in which it is all too easy to become embroiled. In so doing, we become distracted from the real issues. Enforcement, containment, laws, more police, and harsher penalties at best are reactionary. Such tactics produce little, if any, long term sustainable results. Also, I believe the preceding serves to illustrate two extremely important points, both of which are encouraging. The problem of crime is not so great as is depicted by the media, and the corollary is that there are far more, especially among the youth, who are developing into mainstream productive adults than there are those who belong to violent, criminal gangs. Even if the magnitude of the crime problem is not as great as it is generally perceived, the" ninety-and ten-percent" axiom of life prevails. Simply put, ten percent of the youth cause ninety percent of our crime problems. The same axiom applies to adults who commit criminal acts when compared to the general population. For this reason, I believe it is important to examine what is being said and written about crime and then address what it means, in Part Two.

The most important point about crime is the aforementioned, well-defined dual perspective. To reiterate, the first is a medicalization of deviance, and the second is a demonization of it. These two views, at quite opposite ends of a continuum of beliefs, seem to coexist simultaneously. No wonder traditional interventions, notwithstanding that they are primarily reactionary (i.e. they fix a problem rather than prevent it) have been mostly ineffective. Moreover, three major forms of crimes; property, violence, and substance abuse are treated the same way.

The medical view of crime is that all three types of offenses represent a form of illness over which people have little, if any, control. From this perspective, the breaking of rules by individuals is not attributed to an absence of knowing what is and what is not acceptable. According to Conrad and Schneider, the medicalization of deviance has a long history, beginning at least as early as Ancient Greece. The idea is that disease can cause deviant behaviour, and that deviant behaviour, as an illness, has existed in various forms for thousands of years. They go on to say that, concomitant with the emergence of the medical profession in the nineteenth and twentieth centuries, the medical designations of deviance became the dominant definition of people behaving badly. They also make the point that the physician driven medicalization of deviance did not just happen; it was championed, and the conceptual framework while challenged was successfully defended. I believe it continues to characterize much of the rationale underlying how we respond to crime and how we contain it. Academically, as always, various debates flourish but it is what is practised which really matters.

First World nations have cultivated an extraordinary faith in science as a way of making sense of experience and as a source of solving all of our problems. Concomitantly, the medicalization of a non-medical problem was and continues to be a welcomed approach because of our collective ideological delusion about who we are. Specifically, First World nations such as America, Canada, the United Kingdom, and others see themselves as lands of opportunity. Anyone can aspire to greatness and achieve it. One's success is measured by material wealth, influence, power, and fame. The opportunities are there for the taking if a person is hard working and tenacious. Communities think of themselves in the same way. So also do nuclear and extended families think about the opportunities they provide their children. It is convenient, therefore, to explain deviance as an illness as opposed to something precipitated and activated by environmental conditions.

The resilient and pervasive use of the two concepts of rehabilitation and re-integration in the field of corrections also illustrates the point of medicalization. For almost three decades, I have challenged the use of these concepts to no avail. My challenges invariably are dismissed as splitting the proverbial, semantics hair or as superfluous since everyone really knows what we are talking about. Even that statement is incomprehensible because I only see the wrong tools being used and, therefore, a mess being created and perpetuated. No wonder interventions do not produce sustainable and desired outcomes. In a medical context, however, the concepts of rehabilitation and reintegration not only make sense but also give clear direction as to what strategies produce the best results to accomplish the two objectives. A case example will serve to clarify this vitally important point.

A young man who demonstrates considerable athletic prowess, especially at kicking a football, in a moment of lapsed judgement, jumps on a moving freight train, falls off, and has both his legs, below the knees, cut off by the wheels. After a lengthy stay in an acute trauma ward, during which time he became addicted to morphine, administered to ease his pain, he is transferred to a rehabilitation facility. By definition, the singular goal of the place is to return him, as close as possible, to the state in which he was prior to losing both his legs below the knees. To achieve this goal, several objectives are identified along with empirically proven methods with which to accomplish them. For example, he had to learn how to use prostheses, he had to be weaned off the morphine, and he had to regain the physical conditioning which he lost as a result of being bedridden for several weeks. Of course, this is not an exhaustive list but should suffice to demonstrate what is entailed in the activity of rehabilitation. At the same time, as all these rehabilitative interventions are taking place, the young man's world gradually became that of the facility and the attending staff. Progressively, circumstances forced on him a disengagement from the community whence he came and whither he was destined to return. Therefore, an integral part of his rehabilitation involved reintegrating him to the community from which he became 'unintegrated'. At the end, the young man was able to function almost as well as he did prior to having his legs cut off below the knees and after the invocation of specific strategies, once again felt himself to be a part of the community to which he belonged prior to sustaining the injuries.

No great intellect or wisdom is required to recognize immediately that the above process absolutely does not apply to most, if not all, correctional clients. Anyone would be extremely hard pressed to argue even from some abstract perspective that offenders need to be returned to some former state or that they were integrated members of mainstream communities. The majority of offenders, if not all, never really fit in. For the most part they report always feeling alienated from the mainstream. Consequently, they gravitate to others with similar interests and identify with them. Surely, no one would want to reintegrate them to the sub-culture group with which they identified prior to being convicted of a felony. A significant part of identifying with their peers, for almost all offenders, is that members of the group are similarly maladaptive, dysfunctional or otherwise are obstructed from fulfilling their potential. How they are obstructed is the focus of Part Two of this book. Suffice it to say here that no one in his right mind would want to return (rehabilitate) as close as possible an offender to the level of maladaptive dysfunctionality, which characterized his life prior to being convicted of a felony. Hopefully, this is as self evident to you as it is to me. Nevertheless, the two medical concepts of rehabilitation and re-integration, for the most part, continue to be used and continue to influence what is done in correctional institutions.

What is done in response to illegal transgressions also bears some elaboration. Before so doing, I want to acknowledge that there are many excellent, correctionally-based interventions which produce desired sustainable results. In fact, I rely on this fact heavily, in Part Two, to justify what is advocated in Part Three of this book. For the most part, however, consequences to illegal behaviour entail punitive and deterrent components. The Canadian judiciary are compelled by the Superior Court of the land to include in their disposition of a convicted felon these two principles. They are compelled to do so despite the fact that, at best, punishment simply grabs the person's attention for a brief period of time. Moreover, we know empirically that people accommodate to anything, including negative consequences, so the severity of the punishment gradually becomes irrelevant. We also know that a hundred years of studies have not produced any compelling evidence which indicates that specific or general deterrence curtails, let alone eradicates, criminal behaviour.

As Eisenberg cautioned, people wearing their seat belts or not driving after drinking alcohol, cannot readily be attributed to a fear of punishment. Many continue to break the law, and the majority who do not, do so not out of fear but because of a heightened sense of awareness and a value system they did not have before. More will be said of this in Part Two.

The medicalization of deviance continues for the most part to coexist with the demonization of offenders. This marriage is based on a markedly archaic perspective, whereby an illness and misbehaviour were interpreted to be caused by the possession of the individual by demon spirits. In lieu of knowing what else to do, the strategy was to use the colloquialism beat the devil, out of the individual. This belief system served to justify the various abhorrent ways in which both the mentally ill and criminals were treated. The point of the beatings is to make the body possessed by the demon so unpleasant a sanctuary as to cause it to leave. Every time we respond with or demand some form of retribution/punishment, we are invoking this belief system and forsaking the very fundamentals of how we learn to behave appropriately. To illustrate this point in workshops, I ask how many participants toilet trained their child or taught their child to cross a street safely by slapping them about the head when they behaved in non desirable ways. Invariably, the participants of the workshops respond with incredulity that I would even ask such a question, and then exclaim that, indeed, they use principles of positive reinforcement to shape their child's behaviours. I then ask them at what age or stage of development do they/we decide that those principles no longer work and that we can only garner acceptable behaviour by reacting to misbehaviour with punitive measures. No one really has ever offered any rationalization other than that some behaviours accrue a negative consequence, such as being burned when one touches a hot stove. The debate usually fizzles when I ask: Would it not be better if we taught the child not to touch the stove in the first place?

The three major types of transgressions, property crimes, violence, and drug use are attributed sometimes simultaneously and at other times interchangeably, to a form of illness or to a manifestation of willful badness or to a disregard for doing the socially acceptable thing. The medicalization of substance abuse is particularly intriguing. Alcoholism has been defined as a disease since 1940. Not only does the medical profession define alcoholism as a chronic disease but the profession considers it to be a major health problem. Not only because of the negative affect alcohol has on the body but also because of the very fact that the person is addicted to alcohol. The goal of medical treatment is first detoxification, which can include anti convulsant and sedative drugs to reduce withdrawal stress, vitamin supplements, rest, and supportive care. Subsequent medical intervention includes individual or group psychotherapy, relapse prevention, discussion groups, various behavioural techniques, and sometimes the drug Disulfiram commonly known as Antabuse.

The debate about whether alcoholism is a disease or not is most evident in the way it is viewed in Alcoholics Anonymous. The twelve steps, self-help program was begun in 1935 by two men, a physician and a stockbroker. Previously Bill W. (the stockbroker) was greatly influenced by the Oxford Group, a religious movement which flourished briefly during the 1930s and was characterized by small discussion groups, confessions, honesty, talking out of emotional problems, unselfishness, and praying to God as personally conceived. Additionally, doctor W. D. Silkworth, a physician, treated and advised Bill W. He had great influence on Bill W. It is not surprising, therefore, that the official view of the program is that alcoholism is a disease.

The notion of an obsessive craving for alcohol, linked to a physical allergy to alcohol, became the fundamental proposition on which the Alcoholics Anonymous program developed. The themes that alcoholism is a disease and alcoholics are sick people run through all AA publications and speeches. The physical allergy view of alcoholism is said to have offered an advantage over competing definitions of excessive drinking behaviour as a type of mental illness or a psychiatric condition. Although the Alcoholics Anonymous ideology holds that a compulsion to drink drives the alcoholic, it rejects the notion that the abuse of alcohol is a manifestation of an underlying mental problem. Therefore, Alcoholics Anonymous members do not consider psychotherapy to be a relevant intervention to alcoholism. Since alcoholics are considered to suffer from a form of an allergy, the medical definition of excessive drinkers as "sick" people is legitimized. People with allergies are seen as victims who are not to be held responsible for their conditions. Some have postulated that the disease model served to remove any stigmatization or negative labels applied to alcoholics and replaced these labels with more socially acceptable labels such as sick, repentant, recovering, and even controlled.

The paradox is that while the medicalization of alcoholism remains firmly in place, despite much criticism, Alcoholics Anonymous takes a very dim view of any medical treatment of alcohol abuse. Despite its ideology, which serves to abdicate environmental etiological responsibility, Alcoholics Anonymous, in essence, treats what is defined by them as a medical problem non-medically. A very curious paradox which works for the twelve-step based, self help program but inadvertently obstructs sound environmentally based, preventative measures. These measures are discussed in Parts Two and Three of this book.

Not surprisingly, other twelve-step based, self-help programs such as Narcotics, Gamblers, Sexaholics, and other anonymous groups also subscribe to the same paradoxical view. They medicalize the problem, thereby, they abdicate familial and environmental responsibility, only to treat the problem as non medical in nature by invoking environmental strategies. The success and the trouble with the medicalization of non-medical problems are that the medicalization is accomplished through decontextualization. Simply put, the ideology is embraced because medicalization absolves all of us of responsibility for the environmental conditions in which the adult alcoholic was programmed as a child. Unfortunately, the ideology serves to perpetuate an otherwise preventable condition if we only could accept that alcoholism is a later-life, negative consequences of adverse, environmental conditions to which the person was exposed as a child. That holds true for all addictions. Moreover, medicalization is embraced because mistakenly we believe science has readily available solutions. We don't even care if the solutions only entail a violent, physical reaction to alcohol if the person is taking the medically prescribed drug, Antabuse.

ALEXANDER T. POLGAR, PH.D.

The Misbehaviour of Groups

At the top of the list is the much maligned legal profession. Virtually from Shakespeare to former Vice President Al Gore, everyone has had something negative to say about this discipline. For instance, when a group, eager to pounce on anything from which it could profit, discovered how to profit from the misery of others, the legal profession was born. People malign the profession's fee structure and the contingency arrangement in some jurisdictions which encourage frivolous legal actions. Some are critical of the self-serving way in which the profession exacerbates acrimony for its own profit. Others complain of over representation of the profession in politics through which legislations are crafted and from which the legal profession profits the most. Literally, there is probably an infinite list of accusations and criticisms of the profession. Suffice it to say, the profession arguably warrants first billing under this subheading.

Curiously, there is no one person who readily can be identified as being a critic of the legal profession. Perhaps, because everyone has and continues to malign the profession so pervasively, no one person has risen to the top. At best, I would recommend that you peruse the book: Coercing Virtue, in which Robert H. Bork writes at length about the judiciary usurping the legal process by making laws, which, in a democratic system of government, is the job of the duly elected representatives of the people. Curiously, Bork does not comment on the profession of law from which the judiciary he criticizes all come. His apparent oversight perhaps may be explained by the fact that he is a partner at a major law firm and taught Constitutional

Law at Yale Law School. He also served as Solicitor General and Acting Attorney General of the United States and was a U.S. Court of Appeal Judge. His omission, in itself, is quite telling. In contrast, there are many whose criticism of the legal profession is all inclusive and not restricted to the judiciary. Such criticisms date back virtually to the beginning of recorded history. We are reminded of Shakespeare's suggestion to do away with lawyers when the revolution comes. Of course, I have seen this sentiment interpreted quite differently, not surprisingly, by the judiciary. The point is that the legal profession has suffered from a negative public relations image since it came to be recognized as an entity. Despite this negative image, there always has been and will always be bright-eyed, idealistic youth who enter and stay in the profession.

To better understand the negative public image of the legal profession, I recommend reading a history of how our current adversarial system developed. A dated but relevant article by Neef and Nagel should suffice. They contend that the adversarial system of today still use techniques that have their roots in the ritualistic practices of primitive tribes, ancient societies, and the "Dark Ages". The practises are described as having evolved from efforts to mediate disputes in small communities to adversarial and permanently divisive strategies or communities grew and individuals became disassociated from each other. The practice of "trial by combat" while long abandoned in content continues to prevail in structure. As such, in today's court proceedings, according to critics of the adversarial system, bloody battles destroy lives, ruin litigants financially, and cause irreparable psychological damage. It also is noteworthy that the adversary system with which we are so familiar, especially through the popular media, is unique to First World countries. In other jurisdictions, there are worse examples and in some far better ways of resolving competing claims.

A more contemporary, critical perspective of the so-called justice system, and by extension, the legal profession, is by Professor Alan Young. In his book: Justice Defiled, Professor Young takes on the system for creating criminals out of law abiding citizens who simply do not conform. His position parallels that of psychiatrist Thomas Szasz who decades ago argued and continues to do so to this day that a label of insanity represents nothing more than a punitive social response to nonconformity. I recommend to you, Justice Defiled, because the work blatantly illustrates our collective responsibility for the debacle our legal system has become, largely due to having abdicated to lawyers our responsibility to resolve conflict. In the hope of avoiding the dirty business of justice, Professor Young contends, we have created far worse conditions and we had plenty of eager help to do so from the legal profession. While not specifically explicating it, Professor Young describes a business run amuck because we, the people, allowed to happen only to hate (lawyers) what we have created.

Another contemporary, academic writer has a more focussed, critical perspective in her book wherein she deals with judicial decision making. Unlike Bork, who chastises the judiciary for making laws, a task which is completely outside of their scope or mandate, Professor Margaret Wright exposes judicial decisions which are made based on self-delusional expertise instead of relying on the law. According to Wright, by definition, the law is nothing more than a system of rules, crafted by well-intentioned representatives of the people with the aid of many from the legal profession and simply are intended to promote order and harmony in our social existence.

There is no lack of authors who exalt the profession of lawyering. They base their premise on the idealized notion of how competing claims best can be resolved but they completely ignore the realities of how the activity actually is practised. While complex, tedious, and at times difficult to follow, there are philosophers and contemporary scholars who address admirably the complexities of creating and administering the law. Most notable are Ronald Dworkin and John Rawls. In Taking Rights Seriously, Dworkin addresses what is law, who must obey it, and when. In A Theory of Justice, Rawls exhaustively argues justice to be fairness and a cornerstone of constitutional democracy. Such scholarly deliberations justify the comments of Ontario's Chief Justice Patrick LeSage given at an annual breakfast meeting of lawyers. He referred to the attendees as "members of a proud and noble profession", a sentiment not in accordance with how the profession is practised and more importantly perceived. In fact, within the profession, at all levels, there is a pervasive, collective delusion which is precisely captured by the Chief Justice's characterization of lawyering. To illustrate this just a little further in his book: Understanding Judicial Reasoning, Roland Case, another professor of law, claims such idealized views generate shock and awe about Canadian lawyers who ascend to the bench.

To understand better the ill repute of the legal profession, a historical perspective informative. The fundamental essence of all that is negatively said of the legal profession is based on the fact that it is founded on an adversarial system. Its successful practitioners by aptitude are ideally suited for it. Even the most idealistic, because of their aptitude, are quickly co-opted to the profession's various tenets as they prepare for their Bar exams in a field where most of what matters is the billable hours the aspiring lawyer can generate on a daily basis. Idealistic articling lawyers, without the compatible aptitude for the profession, quickly fall away from the pack and often leave the profession in much dismay. They do anything but lawyering despite the effort and sacrifice which went into their education and training. The problem with the profession, its major critics contend, is that the adversarial system is no longer relevant. Their point is that there are better, more constructive ways of learning the truth when two parties have diametrically opposed positions. The critics point out that the adversarial system prevails only in the United States, England, and its former colonies. In the adversarial system, each side is permitted to withhold (subject to certain guidelines) facts which might compromise their respective position and to present those which support it. The method originated in criminal proceedings, where the dispute was between a prosecutor and an accused. Subsequently, it became the method used in civil proceedings, where the dispute is between a plaintive and a defendant.

In contrast, the European, continental procedure is an inquisitorial system. In this system, the judge is less neutral and more active in the cross-examination of a witness than the judge in the adversarial system. It is noteworthy that the continental system has its roots in the Catholic church's fear of the anti-Catholic movements. This fear extended to the Spanish Inquisition, which resorted to such tactics as the rack, thumb screws, and flogging to extract confessions from accused heretics. The powers of judges grew to such an extent that limits were imposed on their authority. Suffice it to say, the current inquisitorial system is said by many to be no better than the adversarial system. It is simply different. The only noted advantage to the inquisitorial process is that all witnesses (expert and non expert) are given great latitude to present their testimony rather than being restricted by the rules of evidence of the adversarial system.

In both systems, especially the adversarial one, critics say the problems lie with the lawyering profession. It also is noteworthy that the role and associated function of juries also evolved over the years to the point that a significant problem has emerged concerning the abilities of jurors to understand complex arguments. The major criticism is that often juries are not comprised of peers, rather they are comprised of people who could not find good reasons to be excused from jury duty. Active, professional, gainfully employed, and involved citizens more often than not do not end up on juries, so the argument goes in many sectors. Originally, judges were representatives of the King. Offenses were considered to be transgressions against the State and not individual parties. As such, judges were like civil servants appointed by the King. The practice gradually evolved into selecting judges from among lawyers who were perceived as worthy individuals and could be trusted in such a position of authority. This practice prevails in Canada, the United Kingdom, and other former colonies but in the United States judges, at all levels, are elected. The crux of the criticism about what the legal profession has created, in part, is based upon the fact that prior to being appointed to the bench, judges were practising lawyers who were steeped and socialized into the profession. Therefore, so the argument goes, judges are complacent perpetrators of a fundamentally flawed system.

Initially, a lawyer's mandate as an Officer of the Court, was to seek and to speak the truth. When the profession adopted the attorney-client privilege principle, lawyers acquired a special status of immunity from certain obligations. The argument is that this first gave sanction to lies of omission and then to lies of commission. Critics of the profession argue that lawyers are trained in law schools and in practice to be liars. Concomitantly, the mandate for lawyers to be voracious advocates for their clients took precedence over being Officers of the Court. This is the present state of affairs. Therefore, the argument is that the system basically encourages lies of omission. It encourages withholding information which could compromise a client's position. Critics say, regardless of how you rationalize it, omission is lying. Moreover, critics say that teaching law students to utilize the tactic of omission is a "deceitful and despicable practice". The argument that the other side is very likely to bring out what is withheld is not a valid one because often the other side may not be aware of the fact that such information exists in the first place. The argument concludes by characterizing the fundamental flaw of the adversarial system: "When one embraces a system that is intrinsically deceitful, one cannot expect those who implement it to use it in an honest manner". Insofar as all behaviours tend to generalize, especially when successful (having the client acquitted), it should be of no surprise that the lies of omission are accompanied by lies of commission, and truth, as in all wars, becomes the immediate and inevitable fatality.

The legal profession first and foremost, like all other professions, is in the business of making money. An adversarial system, like all wars, is ideally suited to accomplishing this objective. This is the very reason why, in family matters, the highly emotionally-laden concepts of custody and access are retained, despite the fact that in most jurisdictions, a "no-fault" system to grant divorce was legislated decades ago. By retaining the emotionally-laden concepts of custody and access, the abolition of the adversarial separation and divorce process is circumvented insofar as children become objects which are "won" or "lost". When children are treated as chattel, concerns about the emotional impact litigation has on them become hollow. In the name of business, adversaries are created to fuel an adversarial process. Admittedly, however, when estranged parents are intent on destroying each other, thinking that legal proceedings is the way to do it, it probably does not matter very much, what words are used when it comes to a ruling as to who plays what role in their children's lives. Notwithstanding this reality, my point is; why throw gasoline on an already raging fire? Why not tell dysfunctional, warring parents, up front, that legal proceedings do not produce winners or losers? At best, legal proceedings deal with provable facts and also, at best, can define the details of parental responsibility for the children.

Most law professors and judges invited to speak at lawyers' breakfast meetings or conferences are the primary supporters of the adversarial system. It is probably reasonable to assume that in all law schools students are taught that the adversarial system is not perfect. It is also probably reasonable to assume that they are taught that it is, however, the best we have. They are taught that the best way of finding out who is telling the truth in situations of conflicting claims is for both sides to present to an impartial body (a judge and/or jury) their respective arguments, in accordance with well-defined procedures. Essential to the doctrine into which lawyers are socialized is that the impartial body expertly uses general or specific rules of law to resolve the dispute. Professors of Law and guest speaking judges also claim that criticisms, especially concerning the withholding of information, do not give proper credit to or are respectful of the higher principles taught at law schools. Many claim that law students are imbued with the highest ethical and moral values known to humankind. The very manner in which this claim is stated is nonsensical and constitutes a perfect illustration of the imprecision with which concepts (ethical and moral) are used and accepted as conveying something important. In fact, such statements mean nothing. More of this in Part Two.

Without belabouring the point as to who justifies the workings of the adversarial system and how practitioners conduct themselves in it, the process of socialization bears some examination. The concept refers to gradual but extremely well-defined procedures which teach ideas, values, and behaviours of the group to which the novice must subscribe in order to belong. Since belonging represents a myriad of desirable consequences most, if not all, neophytes become willing participants and emerge at the end of the socialization process looking and sounding more like the group than not. Everett Hughes in his book: Boys in White, eloquently describes the socialization of physicians. The process he describes applies also to how every profession indoctrinates its newcomers.

Before proceeding to a discussion of the medical profession, I am compelled to warn you about deceptive rhetoric in attempts to compare the legal to the medical profession. The medical profession is portrayed as the better group, almost always by a medically trained individual. For example, the argument is that the medical profession is a helping one which embraces the principle that all pertinent information must be brought to the forefront to inform decisions about the treatment of a patient. While the principle is correct and probably all physicians believe in it, the discipline is as much a business as lawyering, albeit perpetrating harm differently. Since their actions are well intentioned as opposed to adversarial, the medical profession contends that if an error is made it does not warrant invoking an adversarial process. Assuredly, medical errors are made, the nature of which is a significant point for discussion when the misbehaviour of groups is a topic of discussion.

The challenge in discussing the helping professions, especially physicians, is to capture the negative and the positive criticisms levied against them and to differentiate between the physically and mentally-focussed disciplines. Both groups are broadly represented. Those which focus on the physical include physicians, naturopaths, holistic practitioners, chiropractors, and practitioners of Chinese medicine, to name the most prominent ones. In the area of mental health there are psychiatrists, psychologists, clinical social workers, and a host of others who assess and treat the mental and emotional angst of the populace. Despite the vast subject matter, the task of addressing the essence of what is being said about these two groups misbehaviours is not insurmountable. To reiterate, it cannot be overstated that helping professionals also are primarily business people. They all expect to be paid for their services, and their pay should be commensurate with their education and expertise. Of course, there are always commendable exceptions such as Doctors Without Borders. It is also crucially important to understand that health promotion and the prevention of illness, despite an aging population, is still not a significant focus. As such, the training and practice of physicians and others focus on reacting to problems. In their zeal to fix problems, there is an exponentially growing reliance on pharmaceuticals and, to a lesser degree, very sophisticated surgeries. The greatest, dissenting voices, interestingly come from within the medical profession. So-called alternative, medical practitioners publish newsletters and booklets; some even sell their manufactured or endorsed vitamins, minerals, and compounds, and exalt their virtues as opposed to the use of pharmaceuticals. Most notable of this group are two alternative, medicine physicians, Julian Whitaker and David Williams. Whitaker publishes: Health and Healing, and Williams: Alternatives for the Health Conscious Individual. There are a host of others. The gist of their collective explicit and implicit message is captured by Whitaker who reports that in a year, three hundred and fifty thousand people die as a result of mistakes made by physicians. Whitaker says there are never protests or marches about this, whereas there was much protest over the fifty thousand who died in the seven-year Vietnam War. Implicitly and explicitly, alternative medicine practitioners convey the message that their approach is both less dangerous and more effective.

A fervent, albeit marginalised critic of physical medicine, is G. Edward Griffin. In his book: A World Without Cancer, he describes, at painstaking length, conspiracy, collusion, and malfeasance perpetuated by a very few on the very many. His treatise about the pharmaceutical industry, in concert with the medical profession and the suppression of a naturally derived cure for cancer, was first published in the 1970s. It has been reprinted numerous times. The book makes more sense than not and reveals our susceptibility to consume readily misinformation because it fits with our biases and values. The book also provides insight into what extraordinary lengths the status quo will go to perpetuate harm from which it benefits. Unfortunately, the effort of Griffin as that of most other activists, fizzled. As is the case of most others, he, too, engages in rather magical thinking namely, that exposing something for what it is somehow will make a difference. It has never done so in the past and will never in the future. Nevertheless, Griffin does serve a necessary purpose, he makes us aware of essentially hidden information. I recommend you at least familiarize yourself with the content of Griffin's exposés.

The effects of paid for biases by the pharmaceutical industry become really alarming when you consider the well-intentioned help but erroneous actions of physicians. Because of physician errors, it is reported, as discussed earlier, that approximately three hundred and fifty thousand people die annually. This number can be further broken down to reveal one of the greatest causes of this tragedy: prescription drugs. The actual numbers fluctuate, depending upon whom you read and when. The aforementioned Julian Whitaker cites a rather credible article published in the Archives of Internal Medicine. This article reports on adverse and deadly reactions to prescription drugs. Moreover, he states that the two hundred and fifty thousand deaths do not account for unreported deaths caused by prescription drugs or deaths incorrectly blamed on a disease. Therefore, he states the total number attributed to the misuse of medications could be as high as two hundred and fifty thousand per year. Whitaker concludes: "Over a period of five years, prescription drugs likely kill more people than were lost in World War I, World War II, the Korean War, and the Vietnam War combined!"

The pharmaceutical industry reportedly earns a hundred billion dollars per year (more than one million per hour). While pharmaceutical companies are quick to point out the high cost of bringing a new drug to market, they neglect to mention that to every dollar allocated to research and development, half of it goes toward drug advertising and promotion. The greatest, financial ally the pharmaceutical industry has is the practising physician. While the figures are never consistent, the number is always in the ballpark of more than nine thousand dollars spent each year on U.S. physicians in one way or another to promote the use of medications. Even more disturbing to the critics is the exponentially growing practice of direct-to-consumer advertising. Whitaker cites the Hippocratic Oath, which all physicians take upon graduating from medical school. Physicians pledge "...

to work for the good of the patient, to do him or her no harm, to prescribe no deadly drugs ...". He then says that instead of being open-minded about using a myriad of interventions such as vitamin and mineral supplementation, interventions which could be of value to a patient, the current system of medical education and patient care focuses primarily on drugs and surgery. This, he says, makes the system "unbelievably corrupt".

Whitaker has a litany of examples of bad medications. For example, at the top of his list is Prozac, the drug with which the Columbia High School massacre perpetrators were being treated. Into this group, he includes other selective Serotonin reuptake inhibitors. Cholesterol - lowering drugs, of the "statin" group also are vehemently maligned as responsible for devastating side effects. There are many more on his list, with some notable exceptions, such as the use of antibiotics when clearly indicated. Whitaker also is highly critical of conventional treatment for conditions such as cardiovascular disease. His position is that there is no scientific justification for the use of angiography, balloon angioplasty, and bypass surgery to treat most cardiovascular disease. These aggressive approaches, according to longitudinal studies, do more harm than good. Nevertheless, the heart-surgery industry, according to Whitaker; "has been steam-rolling patients for 25 years". At least, in part, this is attributed to the obvious financial incentives for performing the invasive interventions and, in part, to patients and family members who expect and insist on aggressive management.

Lest you think Whitaker is the lone voice in the wilderness who speaks out against the noble profession of medicine, rest assured he is not. There are many others some of whom are on the fringes but more are from the physical sciences. The most convincing of the critics come from within the profession. There are, however, also noteworthy critics from the fringes. For example, from what I think to be from the fringe group, there is the Montreal Canada-based physician Roman Rozencwaig. He was, perhaps still is, the melatonin hormone advocate. Among other benefits, he claims that hormones, especially melatonin, can stave off old age. Some adherents take it a step further and embrace other hormones such as DHEA. They do this all in the name of making aging bodies look and behave as young ones. To reiterate, conventional medicine primarily is concerned with fixing only a problem with medication and/or surgery. In what appears not to be in the fringe group, there also are medically trained critics of conventionality, of the same ilk as Whitaker. There is David G. Williams, who publishes the periodical: Alternatives, John A. McDougall, who publishes another periodical: To Your Health and a roster of various experts who publish: What Doctors Don't Tell You.

While critical of conventional medical practice, it is noteworthy that each of the above authors is all too willing to cash in on the legitimacy of the medical profession, in which he was trained and to which he belongs. Those who have the prefix doctor use it, and Whitaker is mostly pictured in his white frock, the proverbial stethoscope draped over his shoulder. The descriptive concept alternative is particularly telling, since each is selling a product, namely, monthly or quarterly newsletters and booklets which cover a wide range of conditions which benefit from alternative approaches, and, of course, their own brand of supplements, vitamins, and minerals. The advocated use of preventative, daily doses, which include a number of substances, can cost many tens of dollars a month. Whitaker and Williams also claim curative benefits from their alternative approaches. Suffice it to say, therefore that, for all intents and purposes, the most fervent, especially insider critics are simply selling something else. They justify their actions by claiming that what they sell is not as dangerous or potentially as lethal as what is currently done by conventional medical practitioners. Moreover, as said earlier, their interventions are purported to produce better results, even a cure.

The counter argument against alternative medical approaches and the critics of modern medical practices also comes from within the profession. The most salient point is that while pursuing untried and unproven alternative approaches, patients are losing time, health, and the benefits traditional interventions could produce for them. This debate is well illustrated by the differences of opinion between alternative practitioners and mainstream medicine as represented by the University of California, Berkley Wellness Letter. The Berkley publication bashed chromium picolinate, a supplement used to improve health and encourage weight loss, asserting that it is not only ineffective but also dangerous. According to the alternative practitioners, the warning issued in Berkley Illness Letter was based on two, insignificant, test-tube studies. In contrast, the alternative practitioners assert that the chromium benefits have been studied for well over forty years and demonstrate its positive effect on metabolizing sugars and other carbohydrates. Also it improves the activity of insulin and facilitates the uptake of glucose into cells.

Interestingly, mainstream medicine mostly takes the high road by not engaging in a smear campaign against its critics. Instead, it chooses to acknowledge the existence and some benefits which could be derived from alternative approaches. Therefore, it would be extremely informative to review, briefly, the content of newsletters published by the so called establishment. Recognizing the reality of an aging population and not to be undone by the various, alternative strategies to battle the inevitable, the most renown among the mainstream, Johns Hopkins Medical Institutions, publishes a monthly newsletter called: Health After Fifty: Taking Control of Your Own Health and Medical Care. To their credit, the publication covers such topics as keeping cancer at bay by dieting; the benefits of garlic, which drugs are dangerous, how to take control of Chron's Disease, how to evaluate dietary, supplement labels, and how to respond to various scare tactics. Interspersed within these non-traditional approaches is a disproportionally longer list of conventional approaches. The most frightening, advocated, traditional approach in one of its publications from some two decades ago, is the continued, selective use of Electro Convulsive Therapy (ECT) as an effective alternative to treating depression. The target group is said to be patients with severe depression who do not initially respond to standard antidepressant drug therapies: These patients are at risk for suicide and starvation, and they exhibit an intolerance to antidepressant drugs. In this article, it is acknowledged that delivering an electric shock to an individual's brain has garnered a bad reputation as a brutal procedure, one which breaks the spirit of a nonconformist such as the character played by Jack Nicholson in One Flew Over the Cuckoo's Nest. While acknowledging this unsavoury reputation, other difficulties such as those discussed previously; and which pertain to diagnoses and antidepressant medications, are not mentioned at all.

Other topics in the Johns Hopkins publication are aimed at those who are over fifty and include: improvements in radiation therapy, reasons for hope with lymphoma (cancer of the lymph system), the use of estrogen to prevent osteoporosis, glaucoma:

arresting this thief of sight, managing cardiovascular disease and diabetes, and a genetic screen for cancer. The list of topics goes on. Significantly, the publication does not limit the topics to traditional medical interventions. There are articles about alternative approaches, albeit, every one is sanctioned by the medical profession. The aforementioned, Berkley publication also combines conventional, medical interventions with topics which fall into the alternative range. Topics tend, however, to be critical of alternative strategies, often with the implicit message that while you are messing around with herbs, minerals, and vitamins you could be benefiting from our lifesaving mainstream procedures.

One last topic, probably of greater relevance to the position which will be elaborated upon in Part Two, concerns the nature, genetic or innate propensity disposition, advanced by the medical profession and widely embraced by the populace. This theme bears repetition because if unexamined, opportunities for change are lost or put off while we all wait for the medical profession to rescue us. The best example comes from the field of mental health. The director of the Schizophrenic Society, after a tragic preventable homicide of a child, wrote to our local newspaper that "Schizophrenia and other mental illnesses are biological and must be treated as medical illnesses. They are not personality flaws or weaknesses; they are not caused by family dysfunction". This sentiment is shared by many and serves as an impetus to advocate for better and more timely access to medical and allied mental health care professionals. While this is a welcomed position by many about mental illness because it absolves us all of environmental responsibility, the position does not satisfactorily explain how the mentally ill caught the biologically-based disorder in the first place or does the position explain the absence of any physical markers of the condition. Sometimes, implicitly but with equal frequency explicitly, the genetic argument also is made. Therefore, the primary hope is to find the genetic structures and then find ways of manipulating them, as with other diseases in order to eradicate the occurrences of mental and behavioural dysfunctionalities. Instead of invoking environmental interventions, as will be discussed subsequently, we wait until the genetic, silver bullet remedy is found and used.

Treating mental health problems, therefore, is big business, especially for physician-specialists in psychiatry and their business allies, the pharmaceutical industry. The most readable resources are Duncan and Miller and the pamphlets distributed by the Church of Scientology. I do not know much about the Church of Scientology, and, most certainly, I do not endorse their religious beliefs or their proselytization of it. Their treatise concerning psychiatry, however, represents most of what is said about the misbehaviour of this professional group. The first and most important point to know is that there is no physiological or scientific basis for diagnosing a mental disorder. In other words, there are no physiological markers for the majority, if not all, of the diagnostic categories in the DSM-IV. Blood work does not reveal the presence of a mental disorder nor does the use of any of the sophisticated imaging technologies available. Even when symptoms are attributed to a biochemical disorder, there is no physiological evidence to support such a claim. To many, this may sound incredulous, especially since the use of certain medications, for some people, does produce much sought-after relief, albeit from symptoms, symptoms which invariably are troublesome behaviours to those who are in the life of that individual. Duncan and Miller in their book: the Heroic Client, make this point in no uncertain terms. To reiterate, to arrive at a label or a categorization of a symptom or a cluster of symptoms, is accomplished absolutely differently than it is to arrive at a diagnosis of a physical disorder such as diabetes. Moreover, while diabetes will always be diabetes, mental disorders, to say the least, are incredibly flexible insofar as categories are created or destroyed based upon a committee consensus or the political climate, prevailing fashions, and a myriad of other factors, none of which conform to the methods of physical science such as independent reliable observation and quantification. There is no doubt in the mind of the critics that the diagnosis of mental disorders lacks both the scientific requirement for reliability and validity. Their fervent belief is based on elaborate, longitudinal studies as opposed to the committee, consensus process which determines what is included and what is excluded from the DSM-IV.

So what is the purpose of labelling dysfunctionalities and how is this representative of another group misbehaving? To understand this, you have to realize that specialists in psychiatry were first trained as physicians. As such, they are all steeped and socialized into the medical model. They have sacrificed and suffered much to become physicians, and they are not eager or willing to abandon the fundamental way in which their discipline functions. It is not surprising, therefore, that mental-health diagnoses have been developed and promoted primarily by psychiatrists who are interested in prescribing medical treatments. The developers of diagnostic categories primarily are interested in pharmacotherapy; ie., prescribing drugs for specific disorders. For specific disorders or groups of disorders there are specific drugs, the effect of which at best is some relief from symptoms. Given the lucrative nature of how all this works, it is perfectly predictable that others are eager to play in this game. In the United States, there is a concerted effort in motion, initiated by some psychologists, also to be allowed to prescribe drugs. Fortunately for all of us, there are strong status quo forces keeping them out. We certainly do not need yet another profession prescribing drugs.

It is noteworthy that the most vocal and fervent critics of psychiatry have been psychiatrists. Most notable is the late Scottish psychiatrist, R. Laing, whose critical voice was loud and clear in the nineteen sixties and seventies. His views about psychiatry are captured by Robert Boyers and Robert Orrill in: R. D. Laing and Anti-Psychiatry. To say at the least, Laing's views are unconventional and not pharmacologically-driven. Around the same time, Thomas Szasz also spoke out against psychiatry. His seminal book: The Myth of Mental Illness, published in 1961 continues to be relevant and referenced by current writers in this area. If you are going to read anything further on this topic, it is this book which I recommend highly. The position of Szasz is that society and the discipline of psychiatry create mental illness in response to nonconformity. Paula Caplan, a psychologist, is an even more scathing critic of psychiatry who exposes the discipline as committee-based rather than science-determined in the classification of so called mental disorders. To reiterate, psychologists, Duncan and Miller in: The Heroic Client, point out that despite the virtual exclusive reliance on medications by psychiatry, there are no true markers for any of the diagnostic classifications used by mental health professionals. In a more recent publication, Models of Madness, Read, Mosher and Bentall reiterate this position. Additionally, the Church of Scientology, under the guise of the Citizen's Commission on Human Rights, has published and disseminated widely anti-psychiatry literature, which has to do specifically with "betraying and drugging children".

The critics demonstrate by using sound, research methods, that there is no magic pill or silver bullet with which to cure any mental illness. They demonstrate that far less is known about how medications work than we are led to believe. The point is illustrated by the fact that antidepressant medications also are used to alleviate the symptoms of bulimia, panic disorder, obsessive-compulsive disorder, attention-deficit disorder, migraine, and irritable bowel syndrome. Most troubling is that children also are being treated increasingly more with the same drugs as adults. This fact is emphasized by the pamphlets distributed by the Church of Scientology. Between 1985 and 1999, the number of children who were on Ritalin and other anti-depressants reportedly rose from 1.1 to 3.7 million. These numbers now must be astronomical. According to a host of carefully conducted studies, there simply is no discernable evidence that the use of medication with troublesome children does anything more than suppress symptoms and, at best, only temporarily. Studies which report otherwise are demonstrated time and time again to be flawed methodologically. So how is that parents allow their children to be medicated, and that the use of medication to address mental disorders continues to thrive despite such massive evidence to the contrary? The critics say, "just follow the money". To follow the money will reveal much about the growth of the pharmaceutical industry. For example, 96% of research studies of a particular drug, funded by the manufacturer of the drug, find in favour of that drug. Fancy that. Given this reality, it is even more troubling that most pro-drug articles are published without disclosing the investigator's ties to the manufacturer of the drug being studied. While there are well-defined rules about this, it happens any way, all too often. The imperative to "follow the money" becomes even more revealing when the amounts spent by the drug industry are analysed. In 1992, Consumer Reports estimated that of the sixty-three billion dollars spent by the industry that year, five billion dollars were spent on promotion and publicity of its products. Since then, these numbers have only grown. Others have estimated that drug companies pay an average of ten thousand dollars per physician, per year, toward their continuing "education". This includes underwriting the budgets of associations and conferences.

Notwithstanding the obvious differences among the three major mental health disciplines-psychiatry, psychology, and clinical social work - there is much which is overlapping in what they say and do. Despite their collective edict to do no harm, each of the three, probably mostly inadvertently, perpetrate much harm. Another good example of departure from the ethos of the three is their involvement in the legal process. Instead of being expert, independent, and objective friends to the Court, almost always the disciplines align themselves with one or the other side. In so doing, they extend their business into the adversarial realm, the very essence of which is to harm the other side. Most familiar and troublesome are mental health professionals who continue to conduct Custody and Access Assessments in contentious and highly acrimonious divorce cases. The very use of such highly emotional concepts as "custody" (winner) and "access" (loser) is antithetical to being a helping professional, especially when there are alternative approaches available. It is all business, however, and most everyone is doing it, so the inadvertent perpetuation of harm goes on.

While each discipline in mental health does considerable self promotion, there are no distinguishable individuals in any of the major three who currently speak with convincing authority about their respective group. Interestingly, there is no end to authors who claim to have developed a theory, a method or intervention, one which is said to be powerful and effective in the treatment of all or specific types of physical or mental disorders. Most but not all innovators promote themselves do not critique others. Nevertheless, there is no mistaking the fact that every aspect of all the helping professions is, first and foremost, a business.

Obviously there is much good and much not so good about alternative and conventional approaches to what troubles us physically and mentally. The preceding discussion barely scratches the surface of this topic. Hopefully, however, our discussion did to reveal that both sides of the coin represent business ventures. From my perspective, it is not about good versus bad. It is simply about differences in how one makes money. No sooner does the alternative group advocate something such as L'Argenine as a remedy for male erectile dysfunction, then its price soars in the health food stores. This is no different from the exorbitant prices charged for prescription remedies for erectile dysfunction. Viagra is probably the most familiar, a discovered-by-chance medication which does not bear the often touted development cost used to justify its cost.

In conclusion, the point I hope to have conveyed is that approaches to physical and mental ailments overlap in some places and are diametrically opposed to each other in other places. At the end of the day these approaches represent different ways of conducting business. I have no issues with anyone earning a good living. My issue is what price to us is this business of medicine and mental health treatment conducted?

The last but by no means the least group which misbehaves is the news media. They are as corrupt as the previous groups discussed simply because they too are a business, primarily profit-driven and, as such, are prone to misrepresent themselves as acting in the public interest. They do not and have never done so. Some will argue this point or nostalagize it. For example Michael Crichton, in his novel: Airframe, characterizes the news media of the past as focussed only on information, seeking an accurate picture of a situation, and willing to see things from the other's perspective to understand what is really going on. Even if the reporter disagrees, according to Crichton's romanticized version of the past, a reporter sees it as a matter of professional pride to accurately state a person's view before rejecting it. In the past, so the characterization continues, an interview with a reporter was not very personal because the focus was on the event the reporter was trying to understand.

Few serious analysts of the news media would agree with the fanciful description of the past in Crichton's novel but they would certainly agree with a progressive deterioration in the profession as he contends is representative of what it has become. In his novel, Crichton describes modern journalism as intensely subjective, indeed interpretative, as opposed to fact finding. He says reporters start with a bias and proceed to prove what they already think they know. They don't want the information so much as they want information of villainy. Journalism, he says, has become a personal assault on credibility with a singular effort to trip you up, to catch you in a small error and then amplify the mistake to prove the journalist's preconceived notions. Not only does Noam Chomsky agree with this characterization of the modern tactics of journalists, he says much more that is not at all complimentary. His premise is that capital tends to concentrate and that, institutionally, the propensity has always been to centralization. In the news media industry this is manifested by a well-defined, consistent approach to criticism. Chomsky says that what the news media do not like being said about them they simply ignore. Since the business more often than not is on the side of the powerful, this tactic is very successful. In journalism, more so than in most other professions, it is very easy to simply ignore or deflect critical analysis. In journalism, says Chomsky, a position is commonly considered objective if it reflects the views of those in power. An integral component of journalistic propaganda is to create and perpetuate the myth that it is objective and balanced. If the media were honest, Chomsky says, "they would say, look, here are the interests we represent and this is the framework within which we look at things". They cannot admit to such a thing because the pretext of balance and objectivity is a crucial part of propaganda. The propaganda function is further enhanced by the news media's misdirection of the public by presenting themselves as adversarial to power, as subversive, ones who dig away at powerful institutions and undermine them. In reality, however, the media are supportive of powerful interests. They distort and often lie in order to maintain those interests. If those interests are not served, according to Chomsky, you do not survive long. Therefore, in the media, there is a distorting and propaganda effect.

Chomsky, more so than any other critic of the news media, characterizes them as a sophisticated propaganda apparatus from which the old Communist Soviet system could have learned much. Not only is the news media a powerful propaganda apparatus for the status quo but because their executives are financially driven, they also cater and pander to the well researched appetites of the masses for sensational gore, sexual deviance of all types, and especially the voyeuristic propensities of the masses, which include a need to escape the miserable realities of their harsh existence. Even the most distinguished journalists conduct interviews under the guise of seeking understanding as debates. Instead of seeking clarification to foster understanding, they listen for weaknesses to discount and devalue who is being interviewed. I listened with disgust and much discomfort, wanting to turn the station, to a Canadian Broadcasting Corporation female interviewer who relentlessly prodded someone not about his position or idea but to make the person denigrate another who has a different position. To the credit of the person being interviewed and to the very evident frustration of the interviewer, he did not take the bait. This strikes me as being curious behaviour on the part of the interviewer, since the station is publicly funded and thereby not driven by advertising dollars. Perhaps, she was trying to be current or was simply co-opted by the norm to which the news/information media invariably regress.

On the positive side, no one takes issue with the fundamental principle of free speech, although there is much debate about what, if any, restrictions should ever be imposed on this right. On the positive side, the crux of the argument is always that the financially-driven, information media have simply done their homework and, on the basis of what they found, give the people what they want. The argument goes on to say that as the people change their "attitudes" the media will be responsive. Unfortunately, so called "attitudes", or more precisely, how people reason about what is acceptable and what they emphasize, have not changed significantly in structure since the beginning of recorded history. It has only changed in content. To appease the masses, people get what they want just as they did in the Roman Coliseum.

At this juncture, a brief digression is warranted. The concept of propaganda needs to be examined since its creation and dissemination is a central critical theme directed at the media. To reiterate, people such as Chomsky are of the belief that the western, capitalist media are far better at spreading propaganda than the Communist regime ever was. Both by definition were, and the capitalist media continues to be, intent on disseminating information to influence people in favour of or against a particular doctrine or idea. Simply put, whatever is said is biassed and thereby not subject to being informed by a full range of information. The agenda "don't confuse me with facts, my mind is made up" applies exceptionally to the media. They behave badly and are as corrupt as any other self-serving corporation because their livelihood is achieved at a tremendous cost to the majority. Moreover, it is achieved through a well-orchestrated deception of doing exactly the opposite.

Should you think the only person who speaks badly of the media is Noam Chomsky, rest assured, there are many others. Criticisms are more similar than dissimilar among critics, Chomsky is the best at conveying these views. He does it with scholarly acumen, whereas someone such as Al Franken, does it with sarcastic humour. In his exposé, Franken identifies two broad media camps. One is biassed toward the right; the other toward the left. He identifies himself with a liberal ideology, and revels in exposing conservative biases. From my perspective, this is yet another illustration of differences as opposed to one being better than the other.

Even if only for a brief minute, we cast a personal critical eye on the media, it is not difficult to discern that in all their various manifestations, they are truly nothing more than an industry which has always tried to sell us something. At times, the sale is blatant and at other times it is very subtle. By most of us the sale of products is easily detected. Whereas the sale of ideas or the value of an ideology as opposed to another is less easily perceived. Assuredly, the focus is not on presenting all the information, although information is used to influence us to embrace a particular value, idea or belief system. The corporate media impetus is seldom, if ever: "We give you all the information we could collect, you do with it what you will, independent of efforts to influence you in any direction." Judging from what critics say, the presentation of comprehensive information on which to base independent decisions is seldom, if ever, the practice of any media source regardless of its political ideology.

While critical of the media industry, to his credit, it is Noam Chomsky who points out that there are exceptions to his generalizations of what the media are. He speaks of the media's potential as imbued in the individuals who work in the industry. Many are believed to have within them something which drives them towards integrity, honesty, and an accurate depiction of the world. Chomsky refers to this as "personal integrity" which exists independent of the industry in which these individuals work. This is said to be best illustrated in the business press, which Chomsky observes to be doing a better job of reporting accurately all the pertinent information available. He attributes the accuracy in reporting to the people in power who need to know the facts in order to make financial decisions in their own best interest. As such, it is also in the business media's best interest to provide their consumers with information they want. Therefore, perhaps Professor Chomsky is overly magnanimous, when he gives credit where none is due. None is due because the business media knows to serve the interest of big business. To illustrate his point, Chomsky states that the Boston Globe was one of the first newspapers in the United States to lead the crusade against U.S. intervention in Vietnam. The Globe much agonized over editorial, however, was not printed until a year after Wall Street had turned against the war. A year and some time after the business community determined the government should withdraw from Vietnam because it was harmful for the U.S. economy, the news media timidly began to say that perhaps the business community was right. Nevertheless, the mainstream media never really conceded that the Vietnam

War was a war of U.S. aggression, first against South Vietnam, then all of Indo China. Chomsky concludes, "Some elementary truths are too outrageous to be allowed in the printed page". From the hallowed halls of academia where autonomy, critical, and analytic thinking are valued, indeed are a requirement for success, the media as they exist are curiously justified. In fact, academia gives credence to the subterfuge perpetrated by the media that they are adversarial to power. While academia finds fault with how subversive to the establishment the media can be, in so doing, it inadvertently legitimizes the strategies with which propaganda is so effectively disseminated.

To conclude this discussion, it is appropriate to acknowledge the principle for which much has been given, freedom of speech, which applies especially to the press. In a constitutional democracy there are well-defined protections of certain liberties, particularly, the right to be informed, a right which invokes another constitutionally enshrined liberty to choose our sources of information. While deception, under any circumstance is unacceptable, greater weight is given to the freedom to say whatever you want as long as all sides have equal opportunity to express disagreements, alternative perspectives, and how and what and when information is presented. The operative term is "equal opportunity", which no one would deny is afforded to the gamut of ideologies which are advanced implicitly or explicitly by the media. The liberal left has just as much of a chance to advance its particular agenda as the conservative right. Similarly, each has the right to do it in its own way. The challenge of course is for consumers to be fully aware of the cost at which freedom of speech is guaranteed and that they receive all types of information with an optimally focussed critical eye. Caveat emptor should be at least a mandatory suffix to every news media title. Consumers should be cautioned to beware of what it is they are being told (sold) and to admonish everyone to critically evaluate both the content and the intent of what is being said. The same principle should be applied to all forms of communication, including the rhetoric of corporations.

Finally, let us all be very clear that there are limitations on all constitutionally guaranteed liberties. For example, to openly publish and disseminate hate literature is unacceptable as is the practice of deliberately, with malice, maligning another. When it does occur and when the perpetrators get away with it as with the news media, which perpetrate propaganda, it is simply because we allow it. We allow it for a variety of reasons not the least of which is our collective inability to understand how such deceptions obstruct our human developmental potential. This is the focus in Part Two of this book.

The Misbehaviour of Individuals

This topic overlaps the previous discussion about the misbehaviour of criminals. In many respects, it overlaps all the previous discussions, insofar as all misbehaviour is perpetrated by individuals and not by corporations, not by religion, not by the media, not by government, not by the civil service but by individuals. All entities or collectives, after all, are made up of individual people. This cannot be overstated. To firmly drive home this crucially important point is the rationale for allocating a separate discussion about what is generally being said about individuals behaving badly. There is no limit to what is reported and written about this topic. All you have to do is look at the front page of your local newspaper or tune into your local, national or international news broadcast. There is always someone stabbing or shooting someone else, mostly testosterone laden young men assaulting each other. There are domestic murder-suicide incidents and, thankfully, fewer reports of mass or serial killings. Most recently, there are daily reports of some corporate executive or fund manager being arrested for malfeasance of one kind or another. To make the topic more manageable and in the interest of keeping within the limits I set for myself to present three parts of equal length, I will focus on the worst kind of misbehaviour of individuals, starting with murderers. Much has been theorized, studied, and written about the behavioural abominations of these thankfully few, human aberrations.

There are many specific examples of mass murderers, serial killers, historical figures such as Adolph Hitler, and local sexual predators or child molesters we read about in our daily newspapers. One of the most repugnant individuals in my jurisdiction is Paul Bernardo. He is a serial rapist who murdered his sister-in-law and two teenage girls. He was aided and abetted by his wife Carla Homolka. While a familiar name in south-central Ontario, he is virtually unknown in other provinces of Canada and the USA Unknown perhaps because each jurisdiction has its own notorious figure and because of proximity the media report and repeat information which is of local interest. Most are known to the local police, court personnel, child-protection workers, and correctional institution staff. All those who deal with such individuals are busy, the jails are full, their children are taken into care because they are deemed to be at risk, and there is never enough staff or hours available for anyone to adequately do his job. In response to public outrage, especially against violence, public officials respond with get tough rhetoric and strategies. This seems to please the masses if one judges by their parroting of the ill-conceived reactions.

Of great curiosity is the public interest in what nefarious individuals have done, how they did it, when they did it, how many times they did it, and so on. This great interest is revealed by the proliferation of television documentaries, ones which range from the emotionally serious to the ridiculous Dog the Bounty Hunter. Moreover, there are a number of publications, about the likes of Paul Bernardo, Clifford Olson, Jeffrey Dahmer, and other human aberrations who for some part of their respective lives, existed amongst us undetected. I do not recommend or do I want to fuel your morbid curiosity about what these individuals have done. Also, I beseech you to stop watching the television shows which chronicle sensational crimes. Perhaps a declining viewership may become a populace created impetus for a change in programming. Personally, I would prefer another cooking or decorating show to a crime-based reality exposé.

There are two readings I recommend as information about individual misbehaviour. The first is written by a social worker, mediator, and lawyer, Bill Eddy. In his seminal book: High Conflict People in Legal Disputes, he describes the phenomena known as "personality disorder". People who are so afflicted cause a great deal of damage not only in the context of what Eddy writes but to most everyone who come into contact with them.

Most disturbing is that there are many such people around. It is estimated that twenty-five million North Americans meet the criteria for borderline, narcissistic, antisocial, or histrionic personality types. Another thirty million exhibit elements of these disorders. Notwithstanding the previously mentioned problems and criticisms of diagnostic labelling, these are truly substantial numbers and, as such, we should be better informed.

The second reading I recommend is by psychologist Professor Robert Hare. In his book: Without Conscience, Professor Hare describes at length psychopathy, another form of personality disorder. He delves into the onerous responsibility of arriving at a diagnosis and the various extremely troubling manifestations of the disorder. Named as probable psychopaths or more correctly, meeting the criteria of having the disorder are: John Gacy, the Illinois contractor and volunteer clown who murdered thirty-two young men in the 1970s; Kenneth Bianchi, one of the "Hillside Stranglers" who raped, tortured, and murdered a dozen women in the Los Angeles area; Richard Ramires, convicted of thirteen murders; Ted Bundy, responsible for the murder of several dozen young women, and the list goes on. Professor Hare makes the point that not all psychopaths are serial killers but that they all cause havoc and much distress for anyone who comes into contact with them. Interestingly, Professor Hare only offers a vague estimate of how big the problem is but he certainly implies that it is significant. Since psychopathy is a form of personality disorder, it would not be unreasonable to conclude that the numbers are embedded in what is reported by Bill Eddy.

It is most curious that what is reported in the broad media about people who behave so badly is that there is little said as to where they come from and how they came to be so bad. Professor Hare, on the one hand, comments that it is unthinkable and a "monstrous" idea that children simply are "born bad". On the other hand, his main theme is that people who meet the criteria of psychopathy since infancy were difficult, willful, and hard to get close to. He says that all children begin their development unrestrained by social boundaries but certain children remain stubbornly immune to socializing pressures. They are said to be inexplicably "different" from normal children - more difficult, willful, aggressive and deceitful. Professor Hare underscores his emphasis on nature and not nurture when he says: "The parents of psychopaths can do little but stand by helplessly and watch their children tread a crooked path of self-absorbed gratification accompanied by a sense of omnipotence and entitlement".

Instead of throwing up one's hands and exclaiming as Professor Hare, "I don't know where and how people become so badly behaved" one should review the many studies which offer plausible solutions. At least, so argues physician and past, medical school dean, Frasier Mustard. In 1999 he co-authored the: Early Years Study with a followup publication in 2007. In these two volumes, there is unequivocal evidence concerning the incredible influence environmental conditions pre and post-natally have on the development of a child. The influence is pervasive. The influence of environment reportedly affects all aspects of physiological, personality, and emotional development. These sentiments are echoed by family physician Gabor Maté who attributes increases in the mental-health problems of children, escalating violence, and drug use among youth to what he calls the "breakdown of the family". As will be elaborated in Part Two, Maté does not blame parents, but he certainly takes the mystery out of children and adults behaving badly. In so doing, along with Mustard, Maté offers hope.

In contrast to the position or nurturing advanced in the Early Years Study publications, there is an interesting publication by Professor James McBride-Dabbs, in collaboration with his wife, entitled, Heroes, Rogues and Lovers: Testosterone and Behaviour. As revealed by the title, the work correlates male and female testosterone levels to behaviour. In so doing, the emphasis starts out to be on physiology, on innate propensities. This emphasis is reflected in Immanual Kant's statement that "the normal state of man in nature is not peace but war". The subjects of McBride-Dabbs' study were violent offenders most readily found and accessed in prisons. Professor McBride-Dabbs empirically demonstrates Kant's premise by measuring testosterone levels in the saliva of violent male and female incarcerates. His methodology seems to have been reasonably sound, and his findings not terribly surprising. Both groups compared to non-violent offenders were found to have significantly higher testosterone levels. We do not know, however, how this finding can be generalized to the population. For example, we do not know how many high testosterone-level individuals there are in the general population or the extent to which such individuals learn to control their innate physiological propensities and behave in socially acceptable ways. What we do know from this publication is that those incarcerated and having high testosterone levels certainly did not learn ways in which to override or otherwise control the innate propensity with which they were born. Nevertheless, the publication is significant because of its findings and, more importantly, because its focus is not entirely on physiology. It is noteworthy that while much emphasis is placed on nature, the importance of environmental factors on development and behaviour is not at all discounted. The importance of this cannot be overstated since it thwarts the efforts of those who are inclined to abdicate personal and social responsibility for violent aberrations in behaviour. Immanuel Kant should have qualified his statement by saying that "the normal state of some men in nature is not peace but war".

In the Heros, Rogues and Lovers publication, it is acknowledged also that people who are high in testosterone "come together to join the same clubs, enter the same occupations, listen to the same radio talk shows, and support the same political candidates. They influence each other, their special interests affect the overall tone of society. They begin to shape foreign and domestic policy".

McBride-Dabbs continues by stating that "many cultures channel the effects of testosterone towards specific goals. Biology provides the hormone and its potential effects on our actions. But whether we act, and exactly how we act depends on other factors, including culture". What is being described here will be discussed in Part Two as a reference-group, developmental perspective and the bane it has been to the human species since the ape-like ancestors of human beings began to stand and walk upright some four million years ago, and who evolved a hundred thousand years ago what we have become biologically. Socially, however, various institutions, including the family, are said to play a crucial role by teaching us what to do and how to control our impulses, especially those which come from testosterone.

When social institutions fail, biology dominates behaviour and it is mostly men who misbehave; who find themselves in trouble with the law, and who use and abuse all sorts of mood-altering substances. Not surprisingly, high testosterone men, who the various social institutions failed to socialize, also are low in socio-economic status and manifest disproportionate degrees of delinquency. In contrast, testosterone is reported to have fewer bad effects among men who are solidly embedded in positive, social networks; who grow up with strong parental support and have high levels of formal education, stable marriages, steady jobs, and numerous friends and social contacts. The determining factor, even for high testosterone men, therefore, is not the biology with which they were born but the adequacy of their environment to tame the innate propensity of the hormone. We control ourselves with skills we learn from our families, our communities, and social institutions.

Professor Hare describes a slightly different but nevertheless very discomforting pattern when it comes to the behaviour of a psychopath. He contends that although psychopaths have a "hair trigger", and they readily initiate aggressive displays, their misbehaviour is not out of control. When they act violently, he says, they know exactly what they are doing. As one inmate told him "No, I keep myself in control ... I decide how much I want to hurt a guy". The difference between high testosterone and psychopathy related misbehaviours is that children who become adults, who meet the criteria of having a psychopathic personality, were strange and unusual from the beginning. They are said to be so before puberty, before their testosterone kicks in: They leave home early, engage in repetitive, casual, and seemingly thoughtless lying and they are unable to understand the feelings, expectations or pain of others. They are said to be defiant of parents, teachers and rules, to be persistently aggressive; they bully and fight, and manifest a pattern of hurting or killing animals. The list goes on but by now you can see the overlap with the misbehaviour of high testosterone males.

It is noteworthy that among the so called psychopathic group there are also females, although only a small number. Similarly, among the high testosterone subjects it is noteworthy that there are some females, although again few in numbers. What is markedly disturbing about the phenomena of psychopathy is that most researchers, notably Professor Hare, say that its development and its adult manifestations cannot be brought under control. No amount of parental or other social institutional interventions can change the course identified early in a child's pattern of behaviour. Professor Hare says that "the forces that produce a psychopath are still obscure to researchers". Nevertheless, crucial to the central theme of this book, Professor Hare does say that there are several rudimentary theories about the causes of psychopathy. At one end of the continuum, psychopathy is said to be the product of genetic or biological factors and, at the other end, the product of faulty, early, social environmental conditions. Professor Hare concludes, but seemingly not consistently, that "psychopathic attitudes and behaviours very likely are the result of a combination of biological factors and environmental forces". This conclusion, albeit less definitive, is the same as that offered with respect to the misbehaviour of high testosterone individuals. Undoubtedly, both groups pose a huge challenge, especially to parents and institutions. Both are for most of the time under some sort of siege and are fighting for survival as financial constraints increasingly strangle their innovative efforts to respond with creative effectiveness to the troublesome child.

An exacerbating factor to both high testosterone and psychopathic related misbehaviours is the natural process of procreation, whereby there is an exponential growth of intergenerational perpetuation of both biological and environmental factors. Delinquent adults pass on their biological factors and because of their ineptness as parents they are virtually incapable of curtailing any of the emerging misbehaviours of their own children. Unfortunately while Hare includes among his list of psychopathic serial killers such as Ted Bundy and Clifford Olson, he has no information about the environment which spawned them. Assumedly, it was not idyllic but then again Hare also contends that people who meet the criteria of psychopathy can and do come from "the best of homes". With all due respect to this academic scholar and researcher, I see no evidence of his skill or expertise to apply a psychosocial perspective to the analysis of this group of misbehaving individuals. Therefore, as I will argue in Part Two, while psychopathy may well be, in part, an innate propensity as is high testosterone, environmental factors are determinants of their respective actualization.

In the popular literature, produced for mass consumption, appealing to the surveyed interest of the people, there is much written about the actual atrocities of serial killers. Some movies are similarly oriented, for example the Silence of the Lambs. The masses are interested in the gore and mayhem, and those monetarily driven are all too willing to satisfy this perverse appetite. Fortunately, some social scientists have a broader interest, namely, where do the human behavioural aberrations come from, how are they created? Always, the answer entails an interaction between innate disposition and environmental conditions, environmental factors which fail to instill in an innately predisposed individual internal control mechanisms as discussed previously about men who have high testosterone levels. There are other environmental factors which create propensities, the dynamics of which are complex and subject to much debate. The manifestation of the dynamics, however, establishes a relatively well-defined pattern. For example, Elliot Leyton describes modern, multiple murderers as class-conscious and socially conservative men who are obsessed with status, class, and power. In a culture which glorifies status, class, and power these serial killers live desperate lives of unfulfilled aspirations for success. Layton contends that the serial killers focus on successful individuals they envy. They continue to kill enviable successful people until they achieve some level of satisfaction, satisfaction derived from considering themselves as having achieved that to which they aspired or until some external force stops them. Layton may not be alone in his characterization of serial killers but his views are not shared by everyone. Notwithstanding the quibblings and the citations of exceptions to the characterization of serial killers, there is a persistent theme of environmental factors interacting with physiology.

Scientific analyses of men who kill for sexual reasons reveal various biological, physiological, and sociological factors in complex interaction with each other. A study conducted by Stone found that 86.5% of the serial killers meet the Hare criteria for psychopathy. Moreover, sadistic personality disorder was also a significant variable in this group of men. A disorder, which is said to be the result of severe aggression in childhood. Sadism, from a developmental perspective, is said to be an "antidote" against having been abused. Those who were victimised, so the adage goes, become victimizers as adults.

I want to conclude this discussion of individuals misbehaving by examining further the phenomenon of personality disorder. I am compelled to do so because of its vast prevalence in North America and throughout the world. To reiterate, among adult Americans, thirty-eight million present at least one type of personality disorder. This corresponds to 14.79% of the population. Worldwide, the incidents of personality disorders in the general population, range from ten to fifteen percent. These numbers are disturbing when the defining features of this classification are taken into consideration. Notwithstanding the aforementioned problems with the DSM-IV system of labelling, the pattern of behaviours is markedly informative when considering the disharmony we experience with some others in our personal lives, in our communities, and intra and internationally. To the credit of the majority of mental health researchers and practitioners, few consider the phenomenon to be attributable solely to some organic process, disease or genes. The majority consider the etiology to be attributable to a combination or interplay between innate propensities and well-defined environmental factors. In Part Two, I elaborate at length on the Early Years Studies and the correlation between failed attachment and later-life negative consequences which include personality disorders.

In general, the category of personality disorders, while

difficult to "diagnose", does represent an unmistakable pattern of effectivity, excitability, impaired integration of impulses, attitudes and conduct, all of which manifest themselves in the interpersonal relations of the individual. Such individuals always are problematic and with whom it is difficult to form a relationship. People with personality disorders are unproductive when assessed from a contextualized psychosocial perspective and over the long term almost always are unable to achieve autonomous independence. Their behaviour is usually chaotic, their ideas incoherent, and their actions are ruled by a need for immediate gratification.

Bill Eddy, in his previously referenced seminal work, characterizes people with personality disorders as high conflict individuals whose emotions are often exaggerated. He says their behaviour is repeatedly inappropriate and their minor problems become major disputes. They engage in adversarial processes long after others let go. There is an urgency and drama to their daily lives. Most importantly they always have someone to blame. The pattern of always blaming, never accepting any responsibility for the circumstances of their lives is particularly worrisome about this group of people. This is often made worse by the fact that people with a personality disorder often find, what Eddy calls, negative enablers. Negative enablers agree and support the personality-disorder view that the difficulties people with personality-disorders encounter in dealing with other people or tasks are external to them, and generally independent of their behaviour or input. With the support of negative enablers, these individuals sustain a fixed belief in being victimized by others or by the system. Independent of what happens externally, people with personality disorders escalate their maladaptive problem-solving methods as far as they can, until someone or something stops them. In western society, what stops them is often the court system.

I agree with Eddy that it is not necessary to diagnose a personality disorder. It is sufficient to see an enduring and unconscious pattern of dysfunctional behaviour. In other words, their behaviour is not situational and is not open to ordinary feedback. The behaviour of the person is resilient and impervious to treatment, interventions, notwithstanding the claims of some clinicians who combine mood stabilizing medications with cognitive behavioural interventions. If, indeed, the condition is difficult or as some contend, impossible to treat, what then is the relevance of raising the topic in a book such as this? The answer is twofold. First, a description of the disorder serves well to explain much of the disharmony, acrimony, and interpersonal as well as mass violence which have and continue to exist within the human species. Second, and most salient, is that the disorder is primarily environmentally induced or activated. It is a formative stage task failure having to do with attachment. While such dysfunctionalities are almost always intergenerationally perpetuated, we can do something about it, by gradually making improvements in a child's formative stage environment. Much more will be said of this in Part Two.

Counter arguments to the etiology of antisocial personality disorders, psychopathy, and borderline personality essentially are technical hairsplitting in nature. No self-respecting academic can avoid finding fault with a position, regardless of how rigorous the research, survey or analysis. Fault can be found with polarized positions as well as with compromised views such as interaction between innate propensities and environmental factors. Even Professor Hare waffles on his position concerning the etiology of psychopathy. While acknowledging a probable environmental factor, his more persistent position is that the cause is unknown. Psychopathic personality types, he says, come from the best of families, although he professes no expertise in assessing family dynamics or dysfunctionalities within the family. My personal experience has been that opposition to the influence of environment emanates primarily from the afflicted general public. When confronted by the realities of a progressively troublesome child who develops into dysfunctional adolescence and early adulthood, parents either blame external factors or, in extreme cases, invoke the demon-seed, genetic explanation: An inherited, evil propensity from a distant relative in the old country who committed vile but unspecified acts. The parents of a particularly deviant individual actually told this to me.

At least, implicitly, opposition to the nature/nurture position concerning the development of a well defined propensity to misbehave is embodied in the medicalization of the problem. As discussed previously, if deviance is caused by illness than no one is to blame. If the so-called illness responds to some form of medication, even if the response is simply to diminish the magnitude of symptoms, this serves to reinforce the medical explanation and serves as good reason to look to the medical profession for a cure. The fact that some psychologists also are vying to join the group of professionals who prescribe pharmacological interventions is viewed by many as confirming their abdication of personal responsibility for how their child came to be a maladaptive, misbehaving adult. Most curious is that the same individuals who abdicate responsibility for the misbehaviour of one child take great pride in the success of another. Whenever they do it, it is clearly self-serving in the immediate here and now and is void of any appreciation for the broader and long term implications of their beliefs.

In conclusion to this discussion and to Part One, suffice it to say that I am fully aware I have not by any stretch of the imagination given exhaustive regard to all which is said about what is wrong with our world. I admit that I have not given due regard to the materials I summarized. I can hear the criticisms already. But frankly, my dears, I don't give a damn.

I did not want to find myself mired in the vast amount of materials and repeat most of their content. I would be so exhausted by the task that I would be unable to explain, let alone offer, solutions to the problems here under consideration.

My intent was not to cast aspersions on the literature beyond reporting to you that very little time, effort, and space is devoted to explanation and offering solutions to problems. While I have made an effort to provide a short list of references and an even shorter list of what I recommend for you to read in their entirety, honestly, I hope you will not waste your time. For the foreseeable future, you will continue to be bombarded by bad news whether you purposely look for it or not. Instead, I hope you will seek out and familiarize yourself with certain references, in their entirety, which will be provided in Parts Two and Three because they are full of optimism about the human potential to evolve out of the quagmire we have been in since the beginning of recorded history. The optimistic references are worth your effort. My intent from here on, in Parts Two and Three, is to convince you of the potential good of which we are all capable. At this juncture, it is time to ask: "So where are we?" and to answer: "Where we have always been!" To paraphrase Joseph Campbell, philosopher and anthropologist: The world is a mess ... it has always been a mess. Since the beginning of recorded history someone, somewhere has been saying this. For saying as much and then trying to do something about it, the Greek philosopher, Aristotle, some three hundred years before the birth of Jesus, was himself assassinated. The Roman orator, politician, commentator, and philosopher, Cicero, a hundred years before the birth of Jesus, said behind every great wealth you will find a great crime. Such insights and the courage to say them have always been a part of our social fabric. The fact that little has changed in the human condition in no way denigrates the efforts of past or current social commentators. What they have done and continue to do are absolutely necessary, albeit their efforts are clearly insufficient to take us beyond the quagmire in which we are stuck. Moreover, I would hate to think where we would be if not for the social critics' efforts to raise our consciousness about world conditions at any given time. Therefore, my sincere hope is that there always will be those who watch all of us, watch what we do with a critical eye and have the courage to speak their views and accept the marginalization which comes with it.

In Part One, I only briefly touched upon those who were catalysts of change in history: I shall elaborate on the importance of their efforts and existence later. The point I hope to have conveyed is that great forces corrupted what were herculean efforts to bring about sustainable change. If not for the corruption by man of their message, our human developmental potential would long have been actualized. On the grand scale of things, from a very broad prospective, I believe we are being obstructed from "break[ing] out through to the other side", to quote Jim Morrison of the Doors, by very little. As little as a thin sheet of rice paper. In other words, as an elephant is conditioned from birth to be tethered by a flimsy chain, we too, remain where we have been by the efforts of very few and largely ineffectual social institutions, ones which have been quite effective at protecting the status quo. In one respect this is good news because it means there is less of a need for force than there is for creative, informed effort. We really need to work smart not hard. This approach is always easier, especially if we know how to work smart and what our goal is. I certainly do not advocate force no matter how smartly conceived. I certainly also do not advocate the Judeo-Christian figurative or literal beating the devil out of obstructionists forces. What I do advocate, promoting the optimal development of all children, I cannot take credit for nor claim it to be some brilliantly conceived intervention. This focus is familiar to all of us, and in some, perhaps many places, already is being implemented. My intent is to spur this focus on the development of our children on, to marshal more to the initiative by elaborating on why it will produce the goal of actualizing our full developmental potential. My authority, indeed the authority of all those already engaged in the school system based process, rests like all effective authority on the capability to provide reasoned elaboration for what is required or requested. What is required is a grass roots activation of the often said but poorly understood axiom that our future lies in our children.

Simply saying something does not make it so. Agreeing with the axiom also does not make it so. It is like agreeing with, and signing on to the Kyoto Accord. Real, concerted, and sustained action is required and for this to occur we must overcome great inertia. But once we start to move, we are likely to stay in motion simply because success begets success. Hence my belief that what obstructs the human condition from realizing to its potential is nothing more than a thin sheet of rice paper, we must overcome the eons of conditioning so that we are no longer like the proverbial pachyderm tethered by a flimsy chain.

PART TWO
WHAT IT ALL MEANS!

PART TWO
PREAMBLE

My optimism, is not based on some idealistic notion of human beings. We have been, we are, and we will always be pleasure seeking organisms. There is nothing wrong with this. The problem concerns what we seek, how we seek it, and how fast we need to be gratified. So far our pleasure seeking innate propensity has worked against realizing our fullest potential. My plan is to subvert this conditioning of the pachyderm paradigm and to use our innate propensity to work for us by invoking the simple principle involved in modifying behaviour. The principle is to do it generationally (five generations), to progress in small, achievable, incremental steps in order to ensure that each effort is successful and rewarding. After all we always, or at least should, repeat that which is rewarding and abandon that which produces unpleasant results. Even when we keep doing the same thing, expecting a different (desired) result but failing, the pleasure seeking principle is at work, albeit not well. In such cases the process/method not the principle is at fault.

Before I venture into explicating an action plan, I want to address the question: "Why something should be done at all?" Fortunately, there are many who not only understand but also contribute significantly to the development of children. My intent in Part Two is to entice many more to similar actions and to encourage greater links cross culturally. All this, I hope will culminate in a blanket of emphasis on the cognitive and emotional development of our children; through optimal parenting, especially of infants. In my view, focussing on the cognitive and emotional development of a child is as important as a child's scholastic achievements. For far too long we have placed far too great and largely unwarranted value on cognitive intelligence (IQ) and scholastic achievement. I would prefer a person capable of principled reasoning and above average emotional intelligence to one of above average, cognitive intellect. A world populated mostly by people with such attributes and abilities would be a world unlike any we have ever known, a world which for now, only exists in our imaginations and is created by our fanciful images of what it is like in heaven.

To excite you to action, I shall provide you with a framework for analysing why we are in such a mess, and how is it that from time to time, in some places, some individuals have been able to rise above it all. Clearly, rules and laws, including the Kyoto Accord, have limited utility. People can agree but fail to act fully on that to which they agree. The question, therefore, is unavoidable: "What prevents most of us from doing in sustainable ways that which we must?"

Part Two is a synthesis of three, empirically supported theoretical frameworks, to explain, in a way that leads to well defined actions, why the world has always been and continues to be a mess. The culprits are people, not entities, not abstractions like corporations, not groups, not nations nor religions. The culprits are attachment failed, cognitive developmentally delayed, emotionally unintelligent, destructive to life people. All such people are the products of discernable sequence of environmental events. The sequence of life determining events have a short duration, starting from gestation to the end of the first two years of life. This is fortunate because the focus of required intervention to make things better is so well defined and short in duration. Because the time span is so short and the focus is so well defined this reality also is unfortunate. Much harm has been and continues to be perpetrated on children in a very short time. And we all pay the consequences as these children fail to realize their developmental potential. In Part Two the intent is to make abundantly clear that children of competent parenting, during the most crucial formative stage of life, grow up to be physically and mentally high functioning life enhancing adults. In contrast, children of incompetent parenting grow up to be the adults whose negative impact has been exponentially growing to this critical state that now defines the first decade in the new millennium.

In Part Two evidence is presented in support of the premise that the dismal human condition has always been and continues to be attributable to failed attachment and a myriad of later life negative consequences, especially cognitive developmental delay and poorly acquired emotional intelligence.

Part Two starts with defining in Chapter Four the framework of my analysis of what it all means. To do so requires that I explain the lens, the coloured glasses if you will, through which I see, interpret or understand what I experience in my day-to-day life. My sources of information include reading and watching media presentations of world events. We all have lenses through which we interpret what we experience. My hope is that I can persuade you of the usefulness of my prism, which incidentally is shared by many who are cognitive developmentalists. The good news is that whatever our individual lens may be, it is always environmentally induced and as such can be changed by environmental factors. Hopefully it is this book. The bad news, that which obstructs the human developmental potential, is that many, perhaps most environmental conditions are not conducive to promoting optimal cognitive, emotional or indeed even physical development. While the challenge is formidable, the task of overcoming the obstacles, however, is not impossible. Take your time reading Chapter Four, it is the nexus around which everything in this book revolves.

In Chapter Five I introduce you to a novel, the correct way, I believe, of using the concept of ethics. As a result of recent exposés of malfeasants, outside of the criminal subculture, this concept has received much attention. It is constantly used, and always in the context of some professional, discipline-specific-rule description. For example, people talk about medical, legal, journalistic, social work, psychological, and so on ethics as if standards of practice or rules of conduct are uniquely specific to each. They are not! If they are they should not be. Calling the rules ethical is nothing more than a feeble attempt to make them sound important. When in fact, they are regardless of the description added. The imprecision with which the concept ethic is used has a negative consequence namely that the benefits which would be derived from the real use of the concept are lost. In Chapter Five the argument is made that the concept of ethics represent an activity and as such, it is a verb which implies a specific kind of analysis of behaviours, policies, procedures, rules and laws. The analysis entailed by the activity of ethicing is to determine what cognitive moral developmental perspective is revealed by what we do, and the reasoning which supports our actions. In Chapter Five what was said in Part One is reviewed from this perspective. Hopefully, it will make as much sense to you as it does to me, especially with respect to setting the foundation rationale for the action plan prescribed in Part Three.

Forces which combine and prevail nationally and internationally to maintain the status quo are reviewed in Chapter Six. There are pervasive and insidious forces which, by design and intuition, appeal to our basic, primitive pleasure-seeking propensity. This appeal serves well the market forces and has done so since the beginning of recorded history. The forces appeal to the mother of all sins, greed, whether it is for an ever increasing bank account or possession the greatest number of some brand t-shirt, there is wealth to be had for a few by obstructing us all from thinking for ourselves. In Chapter Six I also discuss what forces are activated against us when we dare to think for ourselves or at least try to do so. Also it is noted that creating and sustaining an under siege regime works incredibly well to obstruct our individual and collective development. There are many primitives who are all too willing to contribute to the siege state as primary actors, the best being the self styled and ideologically motivated terrorists. Then there are those all too willing to capitalize on the real and imagined threat, who justify a myriad of draconian measures all implemented in our alleged best interest. Finally, I discuss our bane, the media, and how they are all too ready to constantly remind us of the siege, keeping us scared and regressed into primitive survival mode, whereby we are unable to think beyond our immediate needs, let alone do something beyond complaining about the state of affairs in our lives.

CHAPTER FOUR
DEFINING THE METHOD OF INTERPRETATION

A Brief History of Interpreting Events

The place to start here is to ask of you a moment of reflection. Consider through what lens you look at most things in life. Do you, for example, mostly interpret world and community current events as the rich get richer while the poor barely survive? Do you see things from the perspective of obligation, responsibility or duty, whether they pertain to military service or paying your fair share of taxes? Perhaps, you look for the positive in everything, ie., what is the lesson to be learned, regardless of how devastating the event? Are you religious in your outlook, and attribute events to God's will and, when events are beyond your ability to comprehend, call them mysteries of faith and be satisfied with it? Some people are conspiracy oriented and approach each situation cautiously: they are always wary of being taken advantage of by others. Others are forever trusting and are unable to see other than the positive in everyone. They expect others also to be trustworthy and honourable. Then there are those who value virtually nothing, have no appreciation of the arts or make any effort to elevate the human condition beyond its base existence. For them mostly everything is "bullshit". Many see the world and experiences as a series of opportunities to confirm their self worth. These are the people who play one-upmanship. They claim to have better children, more expensive houses, faster cars, to go on more expensive holidays, parade their expensive jewellery most of us can't even afford to look at, and the list goes on. Some people actually have a coherent theory of how and why the world is as it is. Not necessarily correct but coherent. There are those who interpret everything from the perspective of basic learning principles. People do that which is rewarded and stop doing that which is not. For them, power is rewarding; the lack of power is not. Dominance over anyone, especially a woman, is rewarding the lack of dominance over a woman is not. Inebriation is rewarding; facing the world cold sober is not. The point is that everyone has a lens, a way of looking at life that was environmentally induced. In other words, we all acquired a lens from people in our lives, most importantly, from the group to which we belong or from the group to which we aspire to belong.

Figuring things out, explaining behaviour and natural events has always been a penchant of human beings. Some, since the time of recorded of history, made it their life long quest. We know such people as philosophers. Their quest has been and continues to be to figure out who we are and why we are here. Neither the search nor any hypothesis about this has ever been definitive. There are and have been in history methods of inquiry and different ideas about these fundamental questions. Some questions, faced by philosophers of the past, have been explained subsequently by science. What has been explained by science could have never been solved by discussion. For example, what is the composition of the moon, or what causes thunder? Then there are other mysteries, or more precisely questions, which, while not amenable to the rigours of physical scientific explanation, are nevertheless worth pondering in order to make better that which is unacceptable. To do so requires a sense of wonder. Because of environmental factors many do not acquire an inquisitive mind. Many are content to be told what to do, what to believe, what to value without any need for reasoned elaboration. For them it is sufficient that the edicts emanate from some sort of authority, not necessarily of a religious kind. Fortunately, for the human species there have been and continue to be curious individuals, some with considerable ability to engage themselves in the wonders of the world. For example, how is it possible for an otherwise relatively intelligent species to have made such a mess of things? Before we can really begin fixing things like global warming, we must first operationally define the problem. I do not mean observing that a significant contributing factor is the burning of fossil fuels. What I mean by defining the problem is explaining why we behave in self-destructive ways rather than not, despite the fact that we now have the science available to explain what was not understood by our ancestors.

My intent here is to stir in you the wonder of childhood lost to the mundane requirements of daily survival. To do so, I recognize that it is first necessary to convince you that the effort is worthwhile. It is worthwhile simply because the discovery of something new, something you have never considered is in itself intrinsically rewarding, like figuring out a puzzle or a really intriguing magic trick. But there is more to be derived than arriving at an understanding. From the understanding comes a behavioural imperative, ie., the knowledge of what to do. While the skill will take time and perseverance to perfect, you will learn that certain actions produce a much desired outcome. The independence which is derived from learning how to drive a car, almost always, is sufficient compensation for the impatient teenager who must persevere with the boring tasks required of him by his driving instructor.

You may be interested to know that the state of human affairs has always been troublesome for some, especially philosophers. To reiterate Campbell's admonishment, "the world is a mess, it has always been a mess". So let me take you on a brief journey of a historical nature about philosophy, a journey which most agree originated in Greece some six hundred years before the birth of Jesus. Before this time mysteries were answered by religious beliefs. The challenge taken up by the Greek philosophers was to prove that such explanations were unfounded.

Socrates, who lived some four hundred years before the birth of Jesus, serves as the ideal beginning point to illustrate the process of acquiring my particular lens through which I see and interpret experience, including world events. Despite his great influence, curiously Socrates never wrote a single line. Nevertheless, many different philosophical schools of thought are attributed to him. For the purposes of our discussion it is noteworthy, as mentioned before, that he was sentenced to death for his philosophical activities. Before delineating what he did which warranted his execution, let's first examine how he did it. First and foremost, according to Plato, his prize student, Socrates never lectured anyone about his ideas as for example how fundamentalist evangelical preachers conduct themselves. He simply engaged people in discussion. In so doing he acted as a midwife to the birth of ideas by those he so engaged. This is a very powerful and effective tactic called the Socratic method. It had great success, and facilitated the youth of his time to think for themselves, to recognize the weaknesses of their argument until they finally came to their own, albeit facilitated, conclusions as to what was right and what was wrong. Moreover, Socrates was not adverse to exposing, in public, the weakness in people's thinking. As time went on, especially the elite considered him to be increasingly exasperating not only because he showed them to be foolish but because he threatened the status quo by facilitating the development of youth. In addition to being accused of introducing new gods, his greatest alleged crime was "corrupting the youth". In other words, he taught them to think for themselves. He was found guilty and eventually condemned to drink hemlock.

As Jesus so also was Socrates executed not only for the sake of his convictions but also for the threat he posed to the status quo. While neither of them wrote down their teachings, both had a profound historical impact, one which persists to this day. Both challenged the power base of their respective communities, the status quo, and both criticized all forms of injustice and corruption. However, it was not their criticism but their initiation of a change process which cost them their life.

Let us fast forward to Emmanual Kant the Prussian, a moral philosopher and historian of philosophical thought who was born in 1724. He was actually the first philosopher to have taught philosophy at a university. In fact, he was a professor of philosophy.

The notion of a lens was introduced first by Kant. According to him, certain conditions govern the mind's operation, conditions which influence the way we experience the world. They are time and space, two innate "categories" which determine how we see things regardless of where we live or how we are raised. For Kant, time and space are modes of perceptions and not attributes of the physical world. Another crucially important idea of Kant is that the mind is not a passive recipient of information. The mind, he said, actively constructs meaning. How often and how well meaning is constructed is determined by environmental factors. Some environmental factors are more conducive to this process of constructing meaning while others can actually obstruct it.

Kant's application of the lens is particularly poignant in his views about determining the difference between what is right and what is wrong. The determining factor he said is reason, an ability which is developmental, as noted above, determined by the quality and quantity of sensory materials with which the individual is presented. Moral law, Kant said, is not bound to any particular situation. It applies to all people in all societies at all times. Such a categorical imperative frees us of the need to figure out what to do in specific situations. It does not matter, whatever you do you would want everybody else to do the same if they were in the same situation. Kant's imperative is never to exploit another to our own advantage. We are obliged to treat every person as an end in him or herself. This is the essence of the Golden Rule. Germain to the content of Part Two is that Kant also postulated that everybody knows what is right or wrong not because people have learned it but because it is born in the mind. From my perspective, whether innate or learned, it is not terribly salient to the issue of how people behave in spite of knowing the distinction. The task for us is to explain why intelligent people who know right from wrong engage in a myriad of wrong behaviours; swindling shareholders of what rightfully belongs to them or releasing toxic chemicals with lethal consequences to the immediate population because it was the financially expedient thing to do.

If you are at all interested in the history of philosophical evolution I strongly recommend Sophie's World written by Jostein Gaarder in 1996. As the friend who gave it to me as a gift said; "it is absolute brain candy for the curious of mind."

The Nature and Nurture Debate

Let us return to the discussion of the influence of the environment on the individual, specifically, how we come to reason and act accordingly, sometimes consistent with what we know to be right and sometimes in opposition to it. What needs to be discussed at this point is the debate about nature versus environment, a debate which, I believe at this time in history, has evolved into an argument about degree and not preference. It also is important to draw your attention to an apparent paradox or perhaps a less than accurate interpretation and/or translation of Kant having to do with knowing what is right and wrong. He postulates that it is somehow innate albeit environmentally activated. As such, I am in agreement that this fundamental ability is environmentally induced through the process of socialization. Therefore, while I'm happy and willing to acknowledge the unique, individual, and innate propensity with which everyone of us is born, environment, from my perspective, is the determinant of how we develop. And I have hard, technological scientific evidence to back me up on this crucially important point. For a quick and readily available reference which cites a myriad of empirical proofs, I recommend to you an Ontario, Canada publication authored by the aforementioned Messrs. Mustard and McCain. The first and recently revised work, Early Years Study reveals with alarming clarity just how powerful environmental forces are not only on the development of a child's psyche but on a child's very physiology.

The literature in support of the role environment plays in development and subsequent adult functioning is extensive. Rather than cite specific studies I urge you to seek out the above mentioned publication. In it there is a comprehensive reference list. My intent here is not to regale you with references but to convince you of what most, if not all of us, know to be true. Environment plays a far greater role in our development than any innate propensity with which we are born. Let us first examine how environment affects on our physical health and well-being and is intrinsically tied to our psychosocial experiences.

Obviously the fact that we are here at all means that our ancestors were supportive of mothers, and facilitated their care giving responsibilities. Without such cooperation, infant mortality rate would have stopped in its track the emergence and survival of the human species. This is environmental factors at work. Similarly, environmental factors were at work prior to the Industrial Revolution when it took some eighteen hundred hours of work per year just to feed and house people adequately. Today, it requires fewer than two hundred and sixty hours of work per year in developed countries to achieve the same results. Because of improved environmental conditions life expectations have increased as well as the overall health and well-being of people in western countries. I don't think there is any denying this.

More precisely, advancements associated with the Industrial Revolution were made at the expense of both the environment and the human organism. According to the literature, much of it referred in the Early Years Study, in the formative stage of life, the brain interacts with the environment and sets neurological pathways that affect health, learning, and behaviour. There continues to be some debate as to just how long the formative stage of life is. Some say that it starts in utero and continues approximately to age six. Others say the duration is much shorter. For example, Elizabeth Randolph, pegs the most crucial time to, more or less, end at the two year mark. The operative term is "crucial", which does not negate the occurrence of life long, ongoing development. If you are interested in knowing how devastating adverse environmental conditions are to the development of a child from a psychosocial perspective, I highly recommend the Randolph publication. Based on my experiences, I am more inclined to agree with the shorter duration view, although I am hopeful that it is longer if for no other reason than a longer time frame may be more forgiving of our initial fumblings as new parents.

To return to the issue of physiology, the brain is composed of billions of neurons, and have the same genetic coding as all of the other cells in the body. How the billions of neurons in the brain become differentiated for their specialized functions is significantly influenced by early life stimulation or experience. Stimulation or experience also affects the development of the, synapses, connections between neurons. Once you think about this, it should be self evident that if we neglect or ignore any living organism it will shrivel up and die even if provided with essential nutrients. Simply put, it is seldom enough to just water the lawn, we need to do some other things for it to thrive.

Vision was the first sense whose development was recognized as being environmentally determined. As early as 1965 researchers identified critical times when environmental experiences influenced the development of a kitten's visual cortex. Kittens at birth cannot see; it takes time for their vision to develop. Now we know what type of environmental stimulation is responsible for their sight to develop. Scientific evidence indicates that the maturation of some visual cortex functions is complete within a few months after birth, while other functions continue to develop in mammals throughout adolescence. Another example of environment interaction with an organism concerns ponies which toiled in mines decades ago. They were bred, born, and lived in darkness all their lives and as such never had fully developed vision.

These experientially derived illustrations have been remarkably augmented by evolving, sophisticated investigative procedures from which we have learned that there are three key pathways to development in the formative stage of life. In order of importance, the sensing pathway determines the development of language, cognition, and the ability to recognize emotional stimuli. There is more to a child's retarded development of speech than his mother's explanation that her ability to speak was slow, too. For both mother and child environmental conditions were not conducive to the development of this pathway. The stress (hypothalamus, pituitary, and adrenal) pathway, also environmentally determined, is involved in the regulation of cortisol. This hormone influences our memory, blood sugar metabolism, heart functioning, and behaviour. Infants repeatedly traumatized by adverse environmental conditions are said to be at a higher risk of developing coronary heart disease, non-insulin-dependent diabetes, obesity, high-blood pressure, memory loss with aging, and mental health problems. The autonomic nervous system is the third pathway determined by environmental conditions and is closely linked to the aforementioned stress pathway.

I hope that all of this is believable, because without accepting the premise that environmental factors are crucially important determinants of development, the importance I place on what we need to do won't make sense. Moreover, the absence of sustained and concerted child development initiatives supports the conclusion that most of us, including decision makers, are either unaware of the literature just cited or do not believe the profound impact environment has on development. Alternatively, some may well be aware and recognize that a concerted focus on environmental conditions early in life will produce consequences later in life, consequences which may disrupt the status quo. I postulate that we could avoid chronic health problems, behavioural and psychological disturbances, if we were to adopt a different approach to child development, however, this would be very bad for business and disruptive to the status quo.

The importance of environment is very well illustrated by recent studies of adopted Romanian children who spent most, if not all of their formative stage in orphanages. Studies reveal that those children who spent their formative stage in an orphanage, developed significant behavioural problems associated with failed attachment, even when adopted into well functioning middle class Canadian families. Conversely, children adopted early after birth were found to develop normally. Nevertheless, couples are still adopting children from orphanages perhaps harbouring hope, albeit unwarranted, that nurturing alone will undo the devastating later life negative consequences to early life adverse environmental conditions.

It is noteworthy that in children a significant, immediate affect created by adverse environmental conditions is elevated sterol (cortisol) levels. This is the body's innate response to stress. Its elevated and persistent presence in the body serves to permanently etch, as acid on glass, a negative experience into a child's makeup. A child who is ignored, denied or refused physical nurturance that is empathic in nature develops a lifelong self-perception of unworthiness. This has significant, concomitant, behavioural consequences as is so vividly revealed by the Romanian adoptees who languished in orphanages well past their formative stage of development and then were adopted.

Before concluding this very brief discussion about environmental influences on development, probably it is important to clarify what may be interpreted or seized upon, by some, as a contradiction when I acknowledge that we are all born with unique innate propensities. Genetic research pertaining to various mental disorders, at least in part, represents an effort to understand the nature of our innate propensities, with what predispositions with which we are born. This research is complex and to fully understand it, you would have to be both a geneticist and a neuro scientist. Nevertheless, despite this complexity, it is markedly evident that there are discernable interactive factors between environment and the organism. Therefore, regardless of whether there is an innate propensity for mental disturbance, the literature is unequivocal that environmental activation is necessary for anything to become manifested.

Nevertheless, the need to absolve, indeed abdicate, familial responsibility prevails. As I was writing this, a headline in the New York, Daily Telegraph asserted in bold print "Kennedy Son Says Alcoholism in Genes". Robert Kennedy, the forty-three year old son of the assassinated Senator Robert Kennedy, candidly revealed his belief that "alcoholism runs in the Kennedy family." Clearly it does but not because of genetic factors, as much as he would like to believe. Environment is the primary, determining factor, and whatever we know about the Kennedy clan represents only the very tip of the iceberg. Suffice it to say, it does no one any good, including the Kennedys, to blame genes.

In the remote event you are interested in exploring the genetic factor, first hand, I recommend to you a comprehensive publication of papers edited by Keshaven and Murray. The same conclusion is reached regarding genetic research into depression. A markedly conclusive report by Caspi, published in Science 2003, is based on Dunedin Birth Cohort in New Zealand. The same conclusions were found to be applicable to Rhesus

Macaque Monkeys. In brief, poor treatment, the absence of empathic nurturance, and exposure to threatening (stressful) situations, during the most crucial formative stage of life, almost always leads to less than effective regulation of the sterol pathways which impact on the serotonin pathway. In other words, children and monkeys, when maltreated as infants, become more vulnerable to mental disorders, including depression. Not only is there a psychodynamic explanation therefore, as to why characterological traits are lifelong, personality features of an individual, there are now also physiological explanations of this phenomenon. This cannot be overstated and, most definitely, should not be overlooked, however, there are decision makers with mandates to implement, who continue to ignore the concrete evidence about the effects of early experiences on brain function and subsequent mental problems in adult life, especially the interaction between experience and gene activation.

The crucial variable about the part nature plays in our development therefore, is that whatever genes we are born with, for the most part, need to be environmentally activated. For those who believe genes somehow cause behaviour, even hair colour and height are not simple traits determined by genes. For example, in the last fifty years Europeans and the Japanese have grown an inch every decade. This is too fast to be attributed to genetic changes. The growth entirely is an effect of environment such as better prenatal, nutrition, and health care.

If you harbour, perhaps secretly, that there is a genetic cure for the human malaise, on the not too distant genetic horizon, you should know that at this time there is no general agreement among scientists as to what is actually a gene. There are, in fact, four or five different definitions. To illustrate the complexity and what has to be resolved before the gene cure will save us all consider: One definition is that a gene is a section of a genome, a sequence of base pairs (ATGC) that codes for a protein. Another definition is that a single base pair sequence (ATGC) can code for multiple proteins. Then there are other scientists who contend that some sections of an ATGC code are simply switches that turn other sections on and off. Yet others are of the view that some sections of a genome lie inactive unless activated by specific environmental stimuli. While still others say that some sections of the genome are active only during a period of development, and never again. While other sections turn on and off throughout an individual's life. Most scientists agree, however, that genes are far more responsive to the environment, both inside and outside the person, than ever realized before. Moreover, the fact that there are multiple gene interactions means that there are billions of possible outcomes. From all of this has risen a new specialization called epigenetic studies. The focus being on how exactly genes interact with the environment to produce what we see. I trust that by now you can see why holding out for a technical (genetic) solution to our various individual and collective woes, including addiction, is more than futile. It is darned dangerous, because such unwarranted hope distracts us from where the answers lie. It is in the environment. To accept this, however, requires taking responsibility for what we create and continue to perpetuate by allowing ourselves to be coopted into the status quo protector status. With all due respect Mr. Kennedy alcoholism may well run in your family but not because of genes. It runs in your family and probably every other family because of family dynamics which are intergenerationally perpetuated.

Mental health problems, maladaptive personality patterns, deviance of all sorts, and poor health are enormous costs in every culture, nation or the human species in general. It would make great sense, therefore, to at least explore the cost benefits of prevention versus reaction to dysfunctionalities. Fortunately, such cost benefit analysis has been conducted by very competent, scholarly researchers. The verdict is unequivocal: Preventative measures are far less costly than treatment of an illness or a disease. Also there is hard evidence available which shows that healthy mothers have healthy pregnancies: the probability of coming to full term increases; and they experience uncomplicated births. As for the new born, their weight is normal and the baby is physically overall healthy. Since the brain starts to develop in the womb it is not at all surprising that avoidance of smoking, alcohol consumption, and other drug use during pregnancy reduces the risk of pre-term births and low birth weights. So does good nutrition and an overall healthy lifestyle. It is of little surprise that prenatal medical care, by itself, appears to have a limited impact on reducing risk factors related to birth and developmental gains. It is a parent's relationship with the infant which influences whether the child grows to struggle with insecurity, anger, and trust decades later. A twenty-five year long University of Minnesota study, (and still ongoing) unequivocally has and continues to demonstrate this powerful force in all our lives. Echoing the seminal work of Hendrix, cited earlier, the Minnesota researchers report a strong connection between how safe and secure young adults feel in romantic relationships and the level of attachment to their primary caregivers as babies.

The researchers fortunately also found that if attachment fails, not all is lost, if there is some significant and timely intervening variable.

The Early Years Study, cited earlier, includes a host of preventative measures with proven and sustainable developmental benefits to a child. There also are sound empirical studies in the field of corrections, studies which clearly demonstrate the cost benefits of preventative measures compared to the enormous financial and social costs associated with reactive measures to the misbehaviour of youths, young adults, and an emerging, aging correctional population. For those interested in a full review of the hard facts, I recommend reading the chapters pertaining to prevention in Developmental Psychopathology and Family Process by Cummings, Davies and Campbell. They distinguish between treatment and prevention. For our purposes the salient point is that prevention programs are aimed at stopping problems before they develop, before a problem or concern escalates into a definable disorder. Moreover, prevention programs can be universal, as opposed to treating a family. Prevention programs can be delivered to everyone, in every state, province and all countries. Examples of preventative measures are the addition of fluoride to the water in many jurisdictions to prevent tooth decay. Then there are examples of home visiting programs for poor, single, teenage mothers, whose children are known to be at risk because of unskilled parenting among other factors. Listed by many as the best known prevention or early intervention program is Head Start; its objectives are enhancing cognitive and social skills prior to kindergarten entry.

I cannot imagine any person, group or even an extreme totalitarian government disagreeing with a complete embrace and implementation of public policy to improve early childhood development. In spite of my lack of imagination in this respect, the troublesome fact is that this has not taken place any where to this time in history. Yet there are wonderful programs in some places but certainly not in all. This begs the question, "Why not?"

The Tri Focal Lens

To return to the issue of the lenses through which I interpret what I see it may be useful to share with you two significant professional experiences. Both occurred at my first job, as a social worker, at a treatment facility for correctional clients. Probably mostly by luck, I was promoted to a management position within a very brief period of time. A significant role of mine, unrealistically expected of me, was to make sound, competent management decisions having to do with the competing claims of the client group and the staff assigned to my unit. A person asserting a right to one thing and another person to a competing something else was a relatively persistent theme on a daily basis. I knew that making decisions of this sort required certain knowledge and skills both of which I was lacking, certainly at a conscious rational level. I was motivated to do something about this, when I had the next significant perplexing experience. It involved cleaning the treatment unit. If it was cleaned better than the other four units in the facility the institutional shift supervisor authorized a special privilege such as ordering in pizza on a Friday night, a particularly sought after prize. On one occasion, a certain resident struggled extensively with his chore. The resident next to his area of responsibility, however, had no difficulty and in fact did an exceptional job. When I asked why he did not help his struggling peer, since the whole unit would benefit from the outcome, the exceptional cleaner looked at me as if I were speaking another language. The very idea I was suggesting clearly was a completely foreign notion. Being perplexed transformed to being troubled; a transformation which served as marked motivation for me to understand how people reason, make decisions, and then act accordingly. Fortunately for me, a mentor and now a long time friend had things to say and I was eager to listen. What I heard subsequently became a synthesis of Kant's views about decision making as to what is the right and wrong thing to do, Piaget's work concerning how children reason at various ages, and Kohlberg's hierarchical invariant sequence of cognitive moral development. Since then and to this day, the lens through which I view the world first and foremost is a cognitive moral developmental one.

This world view is what I use in my clinical practice, program development and evaluation consulting, and how I hope to precipitate a change in the human condition in five generations, to a completely different way of functioning, in a way never experienced before.

Not as a disclaimer, but as a point of fact, it is important for you to know that in academia the work of Kohlberg continues to be much debated. Therefore, I think I should acquaint you with the fundamental aspects of the debate before I explain at length how the cognitive moral developmental lens works. In preparing this section, it became abundantly clear why the cognitive moral developmental field of enquiry has had little practical impact on civilization. The curse of academia is that it has obstructed optimal implementation of the knowledge concerning development because the edict of so called scholarship is to leave no good idea unpunished or at least severely criticized. While initial criticisms of Kohlberg were constructive and served to augment his thinking and those working in the same area, more recent published criticisms in the field of cognitive development verge on the ridiculous. It is, as if so intent on finding fault and finding no substantive ones left to critique, some academics have turned to their creativity to levy criticisms to fulfill the so called scholarly mandate of critical thinking. I for one am less quick to criticise and more apt to search for how a good idea can be applied and where there is a weakness to search for what other knowledge could be applied to complete the idea.

It is the contention of academic developmentalists that the field of cognitive development itself is in a constant state of development. This justifies their musings and highly critical approach, one which does not build upon good ideas but rejects them because of some perceived flaw. The critics replace a bad idea with a flawed idea of their own. This is done quite cleverly most of the time by creating doubt without ever explicitly rejecting an idea outright. In a sea of controversy raised by doubt it is only the most courageous who dare to actually apply and test the implications of their theoretical perspective. Prior to his death, in January 1987, Kohlberg was and continued to do exactly this in a Bronx high school. His work had a significant impact on the lives of many, judging by what some had to say at his memorial service. Admittedly, the foregoing is a harsh critique of the critics but one which nevertheless is justified if for no other reason than the degree to which the various debates have obstructed the synthesis of ideas and their practical implementation in the real world. After all, no original idea has ever been perfect including Einstein's Theory of Relativity. This did not stop, however, significant practical use of his formulation for many decades after he first published it.

From the start, some thirty years ago, Kohlberg's stage theory developmental approach to moral socialization has provoked controversy and heated debate. The function and importance of reason, at the core of the cognitive-developmental approach, has been the most persistently debated. Consistent with the ideas of Emmanual Kant, Kohlberg throughout his work maintained that cognitive moral development requires a propensity to reason, think about or analyse experiences. As Piaget, the Swiss psychologist, so also Kohlberg believed that reasoning is developmental, influenced by experience. Moreover, Kohlberg was steadfast in his conviction that how a person reasons determines that person's behaviour. Philosophers and psychologists of all ilk, however, consistently found fault with the importance given to the function of reasoning. For example, one criticism is that other factors, such as emotion, have been disregarded. I do not see this, to my mind empathy has always been a prerequisite to higher stage moral reasoning, and an evolving ability to relate to another person's perspective or emotional state. Moreover, by definition, decisions made in heightened emotional states are almost always less adaptive than decisions made when emotion and reason are more or less balanced. Furthermore, reasoning compromised by a negative emotional state constitutes a regression to an earlier developmental stage perspective. This requires some further elaboration about emotions and the positive and negative impact emotional states have on reasoning as well as concomitant behaviours.

By definition, emotional reasoning starts and is based on a feeling state which may or may not have any connection to reality. Most often, there is no connection to reality but because the emotional experience is so intense the person concludes that there is a reality, and that what they believe is an actual fact. Some refer to this as a person arriving at an emotional fact through a cognitive distortion. The aforementioned book by Bill Eddy, about high conflict people, has many examples of the distorting effects emotions can have on reasoning. For example, when someone feels abandoned at a time of separation, the feeling becomes a belief of actual abandonment. The belief distorts reasoning, and when a wife is told by her husband that he will no longer pay for utilities, she interprets this as him cutting off the utilities immediately. Similarly, even if a person knows the other is not to blame for a negative event, the intense anger precipitated serves as justification for harming the other person any way. Suffice it to say that the criticism of Kohlberg not giving sufficient importance to emotion when he describes the stage sequence of his cognitive moral developmental model is really a non issue since reason and emotion, while potentially can be antithetical to each other, also always coexist with each other.

Emotional intelligence which is described in the literature as far more determinant of success, success defined as adaptive functioning, than cognitive intelligence, concerns the use of emotion to inform reasoning. For example, being aware of one's emotional state may deter one from making a decision until the heightened state diminishes. As cognitive moral development so also emotional intelligence is environmentally induced. As a developmentalist, Kohlberg, as all other developmentalists did not ignore or diminish other domains, he simply focussed more on moral reasoning.

Feminists have argued that Kohlberg's ideas about moral reasoning discounted, indeed relegated to a lower stage (stage three), the post conventional reasoning of woman because of the feminine emphasis on care and connectedness. The feminist criticism mirrors criticism of Kohlberg's methodology used to ascertain moral perspective through the use of dilemmas, characterized by some, as artificial and too difficult to understand. Most demeaning of all criticisms of Kohlberg's model is that even the most mature, principled reasoner can still be a cold, rationalistic person who is out of touch with the realities of every day life. Perhaps so, assuming that other developmental domains remain stagnant but this assumption is difficult to imagine since rich, diverse, environmental experiences facilitate developmental gains in a myriad of domains and not just moral reasoning.

Not withstanding the criticism of Kohlberg's stage-sequence developmental model, contemporary researchers in the field continue to pursue new investigations. Some address long-standing limitations of the earlier model, while others are pursuing completely different avenues from which to learn about what constitutes the moral domain. Most importantly, there are new initiatives to describe moral behaviour as more than just a function of reason. I count myself as among this group but not at a cost of diminishing the importance of Kohlberg's work. I simply add to it for the purpose of promoting moral excellence and of increasing the number of those who lead their lives by exemplary, principled moral behaviour.

Before concluding this very brief review of the myriad of criticisms of Kohlberg's thirty years of work in the domain of cognitive moral development, I should say that there is merit, of various degrees to most of what everyone is saying. This does not mean, however, that the proverbial stage-sequence cognitive developmental model baby should be thrown out with the bath water. Moreover, while the role or importance of reason is debatable, many if not all critics accept this to be the so called backbone of moral developmental theory. The fact that in interviews most people do not report a conscious reasoning process in making a decision pertaining to competing claims does not surprise me at all. The fact that people report acting on some gut feeling is markedly consistent with my personal criticism of the field. Specifically, my personal and professional life experiences lead me to conclude that there are far fewer people out there who have developed as far along Kohlberg's invariant hierarchical sequence of reasoning than the literature seems to imply. As well, many academics seem to have forgotten the lessons of Kohlberg's early prison work, which revealed that when under duress or siege, as a matter of survival, people adaptively regress to preconventional ways of reacting to situations as a matter of survival. If reason is invoked, it is but for fleeting seconds. Under duress decisions and actions are made on gut feelings, and always in the pursuit of the immediate need gratification to acquire something pleasant or avoid something aversive.

As you can imagine, over thirty years, Kohlberg and others

have described his invariant hierarchical sequence of cognitive moral development in a variety of ways. There has been a zero stage added as well as transitional stages, and some academics do not bother to include the highest stage six, while others say that there are even higher and more comprehensive ways of reasoning about issues of competing claims. To reiterate, methods for ascertaining empirically the stage perspective of an individual remain unsatisfactory for some, but for the most part are accepted for what they are, an evolving approach similar to other methodologies in the social sciences.

To be technically precise, it is not accurate to refer to Kohlberg's stage and sequence as a theory of moral development, or is it accurate to refer to it as his, since he had many scholarly collaborators. Granted it was he who took up the mantle from Dewey and Piaget and developed the framework further. Piaget listened to children's reasoning about game rules and Kohlberg listened to his subject's reasoning about how they solved a moral dilemma. As such, both researchers described, organized, and categorized what they heard. Kohlberg did this for over twenty years, and he reinterviewed his dissertation research subjects every three years. This process does not accurately meet the criteria of a theory, however, Kohlberg and his colleagues did not shy away from explaining their observations once the descriptions of the stages were formulated.

It also is important to note that Kohlberg conducted a cross cultural validation of his stage and sequence description, finding the developmental process to be universal, albeit significantly curtailed in Third World countries.

While the content of stage specific reasoning was found

to differ cross culturally, Kohlberg reported the underlying structure to be the same. The influence of environmental factors, therefore, were said to be paramount.

The importance of this conclusion is crucial since Part Three of this book relies upon this fact.

If you are interested in reading the original seminal comprehensive treatise of Kohlberg, I recommend to you the scholarly chapter in Goslin's handbook published in 1969 entitled, "Stage and Sequence; The Cognitive Developmental Approach to Socialization". The following description of the level and stages, in part, is based on this work but also draws on other descriptions provided throughout the literature. My intent is to try to make it optimally comprehensible.

To reiterate, cognitive moral development occurs in an invariant hierarchical sequence. You cannot skip a stage and each stage is more comprehensive, able to resolve more complex issues of competing claims than previous stages. There are three levels of reasoning, each having two different stage perspectives. The characterization of each stage perspective has been empirically validated as cross-culturally relevant. The degree to which stage development occurs has been similarly cross-culturally validated to be determined by the breadth, depth, and richness of experiences to which individuals are exposed and the facilitation they received through mentoring in their construction of meaning to that which they encountered.

LEVEL ONE: PRECONVENTIONAL REASONING

STAGE ONE: Punishment and Obedience Perspective

What Is Right
It is right to be obedient, to avoid breaking rules backed by punishment. Rules therefore must be obeyed for their own sake and avoiding physical damage to persons and property is paramount because transgressions are punishable.

Reasons for Doing Right
The reason for doing right is to avoid punishment which is meted out by figures of authority who have superior powers. "I won't throw my toys because my mother will spank me ... I want to avoid pain".

Social Perspective of Stage One
The social perspective of Stage One is an egocentric (self-centred) point of view which precludes consideration of the interest of others. At this stage, there is neither recognition that the interest of others differs from the self nor is there an awareness of any relevance between two points of view. All actions are considered from a physical rather than a psychological/emotional perspective without consideration of the consequences one's actions may have on others. The perspective of authority is often confused with the perspective of the self.

STAGE TWO: Instrumental Hedonistic Perspective

What Is Right
It is right to follow the rules only when it is in your immediate interest. It is right to strive and meet your immediate interests and needs. It is right to let others do the same. It is right that all exchanges be equal in kind, and that all agreements be strictly abided by.

Reasons for Doing Right
The reason to do right is to serve your own needs and interests. "If you give me a treat I will pick up my toys ... I will do what you want if you give me what I want".

Social Perspective of Stage Two
Right is relative to each situation and is essentially defined by the path of least resistance and considerations for "what can I get away with".

LEVEL TWO: CONVENTIONAL REASONING

STAGE THREE: Reference Group Perspective

What is Right
Living up to what is expected of you by people close to you or what people generally expect of those in a role as a son, brother, friend, parent, etc. "Being good" is important and means having good motives, and being concerned about others.

Reasons for Doing Right
The need to be a good person in your own eyes and those of others. Desire to maintain rules and that which supports stereotypical good behaviour. "I don't talk in class because my teacher won't like me if I do ... I want to be liked."

Social Perspective of Stage Three
The individual is aware of shared feelings, agreements, and expectations all of which have primacy over individual interests. One relates points of view by putting the self in the other person's shoes.

STAGE FOUR: Social System Perspective

What is Right
Fulfilling the actual duties to which you have agreed. Laws or rules are to be upheld except in extreme cases. Right is also contributing to society, the group or institution.

Reason for Doing Right
Reasons are to keep the institution going as a whole, to avoid a breakdown in the system or the imperative of conscience, to meet defined obligations. "The rules say, Don't swear, so I don't swear ... I will do what the rules say and uphold the society in which I live".

Social Perspective of Stage Four
Takes the point of view of the system which defines roles and rules. Considers individual relation and their place in the system.

LEVEL THREE: POST CONVENTIONAL REASONING

STAGE FIVE: Social Contract Perspective

What Is Right
It is right to uphold rules in the interest of impartiality and because rules represent a social contract. Some non relative values and rights such as life and liberty, however, must be upheld in any society regardless of majority opinion.

Reason for Doing Right
The reason for doing right is to protect the welfare of others, based on a contractual commitment to do so. Laws and duties are expected to be based on a rational calculation of overall utility, "the greatest good for the greatest number". "I pay taxes because it is one of the conditions to which we agree to be part of society and because we benefit from this

agreement ... I will abide by that to which we agree".

Social Perspective of Stage Five
At Stage Five there is an integration of perspective by formal mechanisms of agreement, contract, objective impartiality, and due process.

STAGE SIX: Universal Principled Perspective

What is Right
It is right to follow self-chosen principles. Particular laws or social agreements are usually valid because they rest on such principles. When laws violate these principles, one acts in accordance with the principle. Principles are universal and pertain to justice: the equality of human rights and respect for the dignity of all human beings as individual persons.

Reasons for Doing Right
The reason for doing right is based on a belief that as a rational person one ought to have a personal commitment to universally valid moral principles. "I will disobey the law, if it violates a universally valid principle such as the right to life ... I will act on universal principles".

Social Perspective of Stage Six
The perspective of stage six is that social arrangements are derived from a principled point of view. Any rational individual is believed to recognize the nature of morality specifically, the fact that all persons are ends (autonomous) in themselves and must be treated as such.

From the preceding you can see that there is no one moral perspective. There are at least six ways of reasoning about a moral dilemma, or how to rationalize a decision as to what is an acceptable way of resolving competing claims. The best recognized and most cited moral dilemma is about Heinz whose wife is dying of an illness and a druggist who has the cure which Heinz cannot afford. The question is should Heinz steal the drug. The moral dilemma concerns the right to life versus the right to property. Dependent on your moral developmental perspective a decision and concomitant behaviour can be rationalized in at least six different ways. This is a crucially important point. Most of us tend to think of a moral perspective in a singularly definitive way. The Stage Six perspective comes closest to this idea, although in practice it is difficult to articulate because the majority is far removed from having developed this way of reasoning. My contention is that the majority, that part of the population which falls into the middle of the normal curve, functions at the Stage Three reference group perspective. They do so when conditions are relatively calm but, under the slightest of duress, there is regression to Stage Two instrumental hedonism. It is important therefore, to expand on what is meant by a reference group perspective and then to describe the focus of a regressed Stage Two thinker.

As touched upon previously, a reference group is my gang, tribe, religion, political party, nation, club, race, sexual orientation, culture and so on. Each has its own traditions and some traditions shared with other groups with which it interacts. To be accepted and then to continue to belong requires some degree of effort and awareness. For example, requirements can include a myriad of things such as what values and beliefs you espouse, how much money you have or do not have, how you dress, what hairstyle you sport, whether you adorn your physical body with art, metal objects or not, sometimes where you live, where you went to school or did not, what you do for a living or if you do nothing. By now, you get the idea that gang membership is not easy but also, that it is perfectly normal, an unavoidable behavioural stage consequence in an invariant hierarchical sequence of cognitive development. The fact that the majority of the human species has been stuck at this developmental perspective and concomitant behaviour, however, defines obstructed potential. The stagnation and regression under duress, in my view, has been the singular bane of the human condition.

The trouble with the Stage Three perspective is that it promotes cultural segregation, disdain, and rabid tribal rivalry in the name of which we have and continue to do much harm to each other, sometimes including those in our own gang who do not quite measure up to the tribe's requirements. A reference group perspective also is unavoidable because we are not solitary creatures. Moreover, on our own we are more vulnerable to attack for our individuality, simply for being different. Therefore we seek the comfort which comes from the protection of the group to which we belong. As a requirement of our membership we drink the proverbial Kool-Aid. After drinking deeply the tribal tenets, we are friendlier and more comfortable with our own and less so with outsiders. When trouble comes, especially big ones such as terrorism, we immediately think in terms of us versus them.

Mindful of the need to explain the meaning of what was

reported in Part One, let us examine further what are extracted from us for group membership. Our gang decides when and what to eat at various times of the day. Our gang defines our lifestyle, whether we travel or stay, whether we pursue some quality of life objectives or save for our own and loved ones lavish funerals. Our gang defines what business practices are acceptable, how much we pay ourselves, and to how much shareholders and employees are entitled. Our gang decides when we go to war, against who we wage war, and whom we send to do our fighting for us.

The need for group conformity or cohesiveness, familiar to most of us, is classically illustrated by recruitment, selection, and hiring practices. In spite of the empirical evidence to the contrary, the majority of employers continue to place much weight on relevant experience. In so doing they screen out untold number of individuals with the potential to learn the required knowledge and skills and who have the aptitude to apply their abilities with predictable competence. Instead, employers settle on experience, which may be nothing more than one year repeated ten times in order to ensure that no outsider infiltrates the gang and thereby threatens that which defines it by bringing something new or different to its composition. The same dynamic is at work when you are required to possess the most current idiosyncratic language of the field or when a good idea is met with who else is doing this and, if the answer is no one, you are promptly rejected in the name of upholding the familiar. No wonder innovation is a scarce commodity.

Simply put, gangs create their own reality and gang members learn specific truths from each other. If there is a well recognized leader, regardless of how the status was achieved, this phenomena is especially illustrated. Around the time of writing this, Pope Benedict the XVI declared to all the world that the Roman Catholic Church has always been and always will be the only true Christian church. He was reiterating the second Vatican Council that: "They could not be saved who, knowing that the Catholic Church was founded as necessary by God through Christ, would refuse to enter it or to remain in it". In other words, only Roman Catholics can be saved specifically, I think, this means go to heaven. While it is acknowledged by the Pope and fervent Roman Catholics that only God, and God alone, decides who will spend eternity with Him, clearly the message is that your chances are better if you belong to the tribe of Roman Catholics, as opposed to Anglicans, Presbyterians, and so on. Based on the perspective that only Roman Catholics have possession, and full realization of the truth, clearly there is much value ascribed to having the largest of gangs by enticing others to join it or return to the original fold.

I use the concepts "gang" and "tribe" deliberately because we usually think of these terms in pejorative ways. We usually associate the terms with primitive people who live in Third World countries and in uncivilized regions of the world. Alternatively, we associate gangs with the rejection of all social mores. They live in our midst but act as completely separate and apart from the rest. However, regardless of how sophisticated, well dressed or adorned we may be, our reference group perspective more so than not by definition constitutes a gang or tribe.

From my perspective, our collective deference to authority also can be explained from a cognitive moral developmental perspective. The Nuremberg tried Nazi war criminals, the explanation of what precipitated the massacre of women and children in Mylai, and the Nixon Watergate conspirators essentially justified their actions from a Stage Three reference group perspective. When anyone says, "I was following orders", you can be assured that the person is placing primary emphasis on a reference group perspective. The experiments conducted decades ago by Professor Milgram, a psychologist, in which subjects deferred to the authority of a white coat wearing teacher administering increasingly severe electrical shocks to a much protesting collaborator, had less to do with some innate obedience to authority than it did with the subjects of the experiment who were functioning from a Stage Three perspective. When the experimental conditions were arranged to invoke the Stage Three perspective, subjects behaved accordingly. When conditions were altered, because subjects know the difference between what is right and wrong, they stopped administering the painful shock. Therefore the issue seldom, if ever, is knowing what is right and wrong. Almost always the issue, how we behave, is determined by how we reason, our cognitive moral developmental perspective. It would not matter to a principled individual how white the experimenters coat was nor how authoritative his manner or voice. A principled perspective individual would have said, "Screw you I'm not doing that". While it is true that, indeed, we are trained from birth that obedience to proper authority is right and disobedience is wrong, it is also true that there are many forces which dissuade us from questioning the legitimacy of that authority. Certainly most, if not all, religions count on this and just to make certain persistently and in a variety of ways reinforce the teaching of our parents to obey authority. The efforts of all religions are laced with dire consequences for disobeying, in the case of Adam and Eve it amounted to the loss of Paradise. There also are great benefits to obeying authority as for example was perceived by Abraham, who was willing to stab to death his son just because God, without any explanation, ordered it.

Many play on and take advantage of the reference group perspective to obey authority. It is a significant weapon in the arsenal of marketers and professional sales personnel. The examples are innumerable not the least of which is a curious example of how years ago people were encouraged to ask actor Angela Lansbury, of Murder She Wrote fame, about the benefits of Bufferin. The success of such advertisement reveals less about how a Stage Three cognitive developmental perspective works and more about how many of us are stagnated there and act accordingly. If this were not so, advertisers and sales people would not rely on this approach with such pervasive zeal.

Much of the strife, indeed literal mayhem, which has and continues to define the human condition is attributable to primitive tribal perspectives, whether in war, in religion or business practices. Not only do we fear and distrust others because they are different and live elsewhere, their difference also justifies all sorts of misbehaviour directed toward them. If this does not characterize most of the human species, for most of the time, I do not know what does.

The exception to the reference group perspective is our regression to the Stage Two perspective under duress. In marked survival mode, with less access to our rational abilities, we abandon the safety of the group to become primarily focussed on the immediate gratification of a perceived need. In this context specifically, I am referring to the need to avoid some life threatening aversive event. The structural cognitive developmental dynamics at this stage perspective is the same for those who have not developed beyond it and for those who regressed to it. As well, both are determined by environmental conditions.

It will be useful at this juncture to explore further the Stage Two perspective and concomitant behaviours of people whose primary focus is on the immediate satisfaction of needs. To reiterate, it really does not matter whether the pursuit is for pleasure or to avoid something aversive. What matters is that immediacy is paramount, there is no regard for or appreciation of the fact that decisions have broad and long term consequences, and that whatever is achieved always is fleeting.

To begin, Stage Two has a two sided sense of fairness, a perspective which is lacking in Stage One. While there is acquiescence to parental authority in Stage One, the Stage Two perspective is all about, "What's in it for me?". There is fierce independence based on the belief that everyone is entitled to his own point of view and that it is right to act on your point of view, do your own thing, primarily only looking out for "Number One". The edict is to do unto others exactly as they do unto you, both good and bad. This "tit for tat" perspective is rigid and can sustain efforts to exact revenge. Mean spirited behaviour is justified and there is marked insensitivity to the feelings of others, mostly because empathic skills have not yet been developed.

Once again, we must be mindful of the fact that a Stage Two perspective is an absolutely normal, unavoidable stage in an invariant hierarchical sequence of development. It is a difficult time for parents, and a phase in development which can linger on as a function of not only parental knowledge and skills deficits but also of environmental conditions as, for example, how much is tolerated in school. When children do not develop beyond this stage and in adult bodies harbour the same perspective as the troublesome adolescent there will be considerable misbehaviour of chronic proportions. The same is true of adults who regress to this stage. While there are developmental building-block merits to the Stage Two perspective, the incompleteness of a Stage Two perspective makes life difficult for the person and anyone having to deal with that individual. Consider how familiar are the following characteristics.

From a Stage Two perspective it is all about wheeling and dealing to get what you want and doing only the absolute minimum to get it, failing that, no more than what the other person is putting into the bargain. There is nothing noble or altruistic at the State Two perspective, self interest is right up front. When a Stage Two perspective person fails to keep up his end of the bargain there is an understanding and an acceptance of a negative consequence. Most offenders quickly settle into the sanctions imposed on them for their transgression. The equal reciprocity perspective of Stage Two also embodies a belief in exact revenge. This is the reason why most, if not all, criminal offenders subscribe to the death sentence consequence and act on this belief in reaction to the transgressions of their fellow inmates. Among developmentally delayed, disenfranchised, adolescent gang members, the reason for ongoing and escalating violence is attributable to a Stage Two specific inability to let go of any real or perceived transgression. Everything has to be paid back, every look, push, bump or insult is deserving of retribution.

The Stage Two perspective also is very concrete. It is an outer world, not an inner world. There is not much talk of feelings and certainly no awareness that the other may have feelings or a different perspective on things. Unless you can actually see the harmful effects of your actions, the harm does not exist. From a Stage Two perspective therefore, lying is acceptable because the hurt created by it cannot be seen directly. The same goes for cheating, stealing, and the meanness of which children and delayed or regressed adults are capable.

How much of this very brief description of the Stage Two perspective is familiar to you? I do not mean with having to endure it in your children or the children of others, I mean in your adult dealings with others. How about applying as a lens the Stage Two perspective to what is reported in the newspapers or revealed about the behaviour of some fallen executive, who is found out for his greed and the nefarious ways by which his lifestyle was supported.

What about applying the Stage Two perspective to understanding how conditions escalated on Wall Street that culminated in October 2008 in a need for a staggering American government bailout of the U.S. financial system. To comprehend the enormity of the unregulated, unmitigated, unbridled Stage Two greed of the status quo, capitalizing on the materialistic pursuits of the masses, consider the tax payer funded $700 billion bail out of Wall Street. Consider also the sweeteners to get the bail out through: Congress $140 billion, $85 billion to the insurance giant AIG, and a further Federal Reserve loan of $37.5 billion also to AIG. In a year, the stock market lost somewhere around $8.3 trillion, not vaporized but into the pockets of a select few.

What about applying the Stage Two perspective to understanding how the tenets of the bailout package grew from a mere few pages to the thickness of the New York telephone directory. Much horse trading, instrumental reciprocity, took place to grow it so large. While democracy is based on post conventional reasoning, the greatest good for the greatest number, in practice it is really instrumental hedonism at work.

Probably, quite unintentionally, the conditions of the bail out, as for example government becoming a major share holder of a bank, is an acknowledgement that the naive, child like, preconventional thinking and behaving financiers need external structures to control their problematic propensities. What really amounts to a partial nationalization of the failed banks, given the developmental and emotional intelligence of the players, absolutely is necessary. Moreover, fortunately there is both the will and the means with which to do it. How long this regulatory intervention must prevail will be determined by how long it will take to develop and install in positions of financial authority conventional, ideally post conventional, moral thinkers and doers who also have exceptional emotional intelligence. Our collective expectations and the laws that govern corporations, legally requiring psychopathic behaviours, also will have to change. This will not happen too soon, so the practice of regulating key financial sectors, hastily abandoned not that long ago will have to be revisited. The free market system naturally regulating itself is akin to abandoning all parental responsibility for a child who is at that stage of development where every thought and action is focussed on the immediate satisfaction of hedonistic desires. This is not intended to be condescending nor supportive of some "big brother watching" ideology. Given the very real evidence that shocked and reverberated throughout the world, the need for regulation simply is a reality. Of course all of this begs the questions: "Who will be the regulators?" "Will the regulators be principled or will they also require being regulated?" Regulation need not be indefinite, however, although the recommended initiatives in Part Three will take some time to produce the desired results. Perhaps, contrasting Stage Two and Three perspectives with Post Conventional reasoning will illustrate even more clearly that which is the familiar and that which is encountered very infrequently.

When was the last time you heard a man or woman, who you know personally or someone you know of in your circle of friends or community, being referred to as a person of principle? I think seldom, if ever. Moreover, what does it actually mean to be such an individual? This requires a definition of "principle" a definition which is not surprisingly difficult to do well. First, for our purposes, the concept has to be specifically contextualized insofar as "principled" always is in reference to something. In our case it pertains to inalienable human rights, rights which cannot be given or taken away, and which everyone has simply by virtue of being human. As such, rights are considered to be universal. A principled person therefore does not violate universal rights no matter what the circumstances or who is the person. Moreover, for a principled individual no person is a means to an end no matter how noble the end might be. The best example is the tactics of terrorists. They justify taking and murdering hostages, blowing up buildings and people by proclaiming that they do their evil deeds all in the name of imposing their idea of a better world.

Their loyalty is to the cause not to the people. People become means not an end in themselves. In their disassociation from reality, maturity, indeed adulthood, fundamentalists exchange their innate developmental potential for the rigidity of dogma and the edicts of their pastor, subscribing to a belief that justifies their suffering in life for the promised bliss in an after life.

In contrast to terrorists, principled people are never fanatical, they never sacrifice people's rights to a cause. Nothing is relative, situations do not define what is right or wrong. It is the individual who defines what is right and wrong and acts on this with markedly persistent consistency no matter what. To reiterate, how many people like this do you know compared to the gang oriented perspective of individuals described above and the instrumental hedonism to which such individuals quickly can regress when under duress. What if this current reality could be reversed? How could this be accomplished?

This moral developmental stage and sequence model forms the lens through which I see the world. It explains to me cognitive processes and behaviours of most types of people. I will elaborate on this shortly. Before I do that, I must admit that the lens or glasses through which I see the world, in reality is tri-focal. It is like the glasses of my pilot friend who has a lower prescription to see his instruments on the dash, a middle prescription to see at a distance, and a top prescription to see the instruments above his head. For him, as for me, all three prescriptions are of equal importance, albeit at different times one takes precedence over the other two. So there are the cognitive developmental, the emotional intelligence, and the Early Years development lenses through which I see the world.

As you can see, all are of equal importance, and it is the environment which determines the development of each. For me the question, when assessing an individual, always is, "What environmental conditions prevailed during the most crucial formative stage in an otherwise cognitively intelligent person's life as to obstruct his moral reasoning and the development of his emotional intelligence?" This is a question first and foremost about attachment. When this crucially important life task fails, during the first two years of life, there are dire consequences. Consequences, which are of a physical and emotional nature as described by the Early Years Study cited previously. The time frame is approximately two years because for the first twenty-six months the child interacts with the world (primarily his mother) at a non verbal level. The right hemisphere of the brain is dominant, processing only visual cues and the tone component of speech, both of which are powerful conveyers of emotion. If the right hemisphere functions of the brain are not environmentally activated, by an empathically nurturing parent, it does not develop. If the right frontal lobe circuits are not established the child, later the adult, cannot regulate his emotions and cannot maintain human attachments. According to neuroscientist Norman Doidge, without empathic nurturance during this critical period the child soothes himself and regulates his emotions by learning to auto-regulate, ie., turns off his emotions which causes difficulties maintaining attachments. By the time the left hemisphere of the brain starts its developmental spurt, after the first twenty-six months, processing verbal information, the failed attachment during the previous period begins to manifest itself.

Fortunately, the importance of attachment is well understood by most mental health professionals. Much research has taken place to develop valid and reliable ways of identifying whether attachment has occurred or failed, and what form the failure has taken. The latter determination is important because it has significant implications for intervention strategies, which also have been extensively studied. The good news is that since attachment is environmentally induced, well-defined interventions can have significant remedial effects. Moreover, the earlier the intervention the less time is required to produce better results. The bad news is that when intervention is delayed it takes longer and costs more to help a child. The general rule seems to be two months of intense intervention for every year of life. For intervention to work, according to the majority of mental health professionals who practice in this area, the intervention of the therapist can only be augmented by a foster or adoptive parent who achieved secure attachment as an infant. In other words, for the child to escape the later life negative consequences of failed attachment, he must be removed from the care and control of the inadequate parent and permanently placed with a securely attached caregiver. This is a difficult protracted process and, based upon my experience, reluctantly precipitated by Child Welfare professionals. Often jurisdictional requirement of least intrusive measures also obstruct the timeliness with which definitive action is taken in a child's best interest. The end result is that too little is done too late and the child repeats the legacy to which he or she was destined by virtue of the family into which they were born. When this happens it is a systems failure and a failure which reasonably can be attributed to a cumbersome and ill suited to the task adversarial legal process. To echo earlier comments, it is business in play.

There are many who object vehemently to all of this, labelling the formative stage life task of attachment as deterministic and dismissive of the human potential of both parent and child to change. I agree with this criticism only partially. An adult destined to be an inadequate parent by virtue of a family legacy does not change spontaneously. Without intervention, family legacies are perpetuated, and the exponential growth of dysfunctionality in the human species will, if it has not already, reach a point of no return. With intervention, introduced in a timely fashion, changes can be made and will eventually produce results unlike those we have ever seen.

How our dysfunctional family legacies are intergenerationally perpetuated requires elaboration. Every discussion of this nature must start with acknowledging the unique and specific innate nature of all individuals. This is the "nature component" of who we are. How this is activated, in terms of who they we become, is the nurture part of the equation. As discussed previously, nurture is the most influential part of the equation, probably in all cases. To understand the intergenerational nature of dysfunctionality, it is necessary to identify the key later life negative consequences to failed attachment. As a matter of form, I describe this at some length in every Parenting Capacity Assessment report prepared for courts. The evidence is that the relationship between a mother and her infant constitutes a prototype for all close relationships later in life. Because infancy is a period of rapidly developing social ability, the legacy of an early attachment relationship includes either enhanced, flexible and positive social skills, which mirror the first relationship, or the converse which entails restrictive, inflexible, and maladaptive interpersonal interaction patterns. A significant later life negative consequence therefore, to a failed attachment, is lifelong relationship difficulties most clearly manifested in romantic liaisons.

In his seminal book, Getting the Love You Want, Harville Hendrix brilliantly describes a lifelong quest, mostly at an unconscious level, to satisfy unmet primary needs, during the formative stage, later in life through an adult relationship. Such relationships are doomed to fail because, from the unconscious mind's perspective, the unmet needs can only be satisfied by the primary caregiver who failed to do so in the first place. Alternatively, someone closely resembling the inadequate primary caregiver will do. As such, initially there is intense joyful anticipation. For the very reason attachment disordered individuals are attracted to each other, neither is capable of delivering what precipitated the joyful expectation in the first place. Disappointment quickly sets in, often followed by hostile resentment, much acrimony, and familial turmoil. Can you imagine the fate of a child in this environment? Can you imagine the impact such adverse environmental conditions have on the physical, emotional, and social development of that child? Few, if any, children can escape the destiny of their birth without significant expert intervention.

Another significant later life negative consequence to failed attachment starts off with an inability to trust. Insofar as the development of trust requires an accessible, responsive, and empathically nurturing caregiver, it is no wonder that the ability to trust is thwarted when caregivers are unavailable, unpredictable or abusive. In need of soothing and reassurance, especially in a chaotic adverse environment, only quickly to learn that it is not forthcoming from the external world, the child turns inward and becomes his own inadequate caregiver and protector. This is the genesis of an addictive characterological personality trait or, as I prefer to distinguish it from becoming addicted, it is the making of an addict.

Once again, can you imagine a child in the care of an addict and addicted parent in the most crucial formative stage of life? How likely is that such a parent would be adequately responsive to the child's needs let alone socialize that child through empathic nurturance when preoccupied with the need to escape a constant negative emotional state through mood altering substances? I guess it may be possible but I am certain that it is highly improbable that the child would escape the fate of also becoming an addict and then to become addicted early in life to one or more mood altering substances.

Suffice it to say, attachment, the primary life task during the most crucial formative stage of life, has profound positive and negative later life consequences. Sooner than later the consequences emerge and become well defined as personality disorders: Deficits in empathic and caring abilities, sexual promiscuity, not surprisingly cognitive moral developmental stagnation at the preconventional level or, at best, a tenuous reference group perspective, and poorly developed emotional intelligence. What else could you expect from such adverse environmental conditions? It should be said here also that adverse environmental conditions during the formative stage of life and subsequently are not always chaotic or in the domain of the economically disadvantaged. It can occur in the so called best of families where materialism and status are of primary importance. The best of hired child care providers, and the best of private, residential primary and secondary schools, seldom, if ever, make up for the virtual and persistent absence of nurturing parents. The only difference in such circumstances is how dysfunctional family legacies become manifested. Mostly the manifestations are sophisticated transgressions, committed by well attired individuals, in posh offices, and corporate board rooms.

The importance of attachment at the most crucial formative stage of life admittedly gradually dawned upon me. At first I knew and understood that all the young and adult offenders I worked with came from some sort of adverse background. If it was not immediately evident it soon became so, after some scratching at the surface of superficial propriety. It was not until I started to prepare Court ordered Parenting Capacity Assessments that the profound impact of Early Years became even more evident. Instead of reading scholarly literature, I was experiencing at first hand the intergenerational perpetuation of dysfunctionalities. On occasion, I assessed a dysfunctional grandmother, who begat a dysfunctional mother, who then begat a child deemed to be at sufficient risk to warrant apprehension by a child welfare agency. The patterns became abundantly clear to me and, fortunately for the children, also to the Court. In most instances, by Court Order, they were rescued from the fate to which they would have been otherwise destined. Now and forever more, the lens through which I see and analyse all that is maladaptive in the world, always attributable to people, my analysis goes to wondering what environmental conditions in their youth determined who they became as adults. Instead of vengeful outrage at a twenty-one year old charged with three counts of murder, reported in today's newspaper, I cannot help but wonder about what he was exposed to as an infant and child.

The other lens that makes up my tri-focal conceptual model of the world as it functions at the hands of people, concerns emotional intelligence. Since it too is environmentally induced, it makes perfect sense to me that an attachment disordered individual stuck at a preconventional level of reasoning, in most cases also has diminished or, better said, not well developed emotional intelligence. It also makes perfect sense to me that these marked maladaptive propensities can exist simultaneously with considerable cognitive intelligence. We have all encountered top grade students who are socially inept, who behave in self defeating bizarre ways just as much as we have encountered teachers, professors, people in the clergy and so on, who are also inept and maladaptive in well definable ways. As noted previously, we have, and unfortunately continue to place far too much, indeed unwarranted, importance on cognitive intelligence significantly despite persuasive data to the contrary. To reiterate, give me any day a person with average grades and intelligence quotient and superior emotional intelligence. That person always will out perform the genius in every aspect of life. By the very fact of having superior emotional intelligence that person also will be securely attached and will be a well established conventional moral thinker, if not better.

While a long studied topic, it was Daniel Goleman who first brought to public attention the phenomenon of emotional intelligence. His book is a dense and comprehensive work, at times difficult to read. An alternative book, which is easier to read and digest is The EQ Edge, by Steven Stein and Howard Book. It is important to note that this area of research came into prominence also because of a tool which was developed to measure emotional intelligence. The Bar On EQ-i was first published and distributed through Toronto based Multi-Health Systems in 1998. I used it extensively, mostly to enhance my clinical assessment formulations. Insofar as it is a quantitative tool based on self report, it was to be expected that another standardized instrument would soon follow. An instrument which measures ability and not what you say about your abilities. Both instruments have utility merit but of greater importance for this discussion is the meaning of emotional intelligence, especially compared to cognitive intelligence, otherwise known as your IQ. Simply put IQ is a measure of an individual's analytical, logical, and rational abilities. As such, it is concerned with verbal, spacial, visual, and mathematical skills. The measuring methodology can be culturally and/or educationally biased. It is noteworthy that a high IQ does not necessarily correlate with exceptional academic performance or vice versa. It is also important to note that not withstanding the above comment about environmental activation, it is generally accepted that IQ is an innate propensity that cannot be improved upon through external interventions. In contrast, emotional intelligence is not innate. It is unequivocally considered to be environmentally induced. This good news will be employed well in Part Three of this book.

Before Ruven Bar On, Peter Salovey and Jack Mayer, coined the term emotional intelligence. They define this as "the ability to perceive emotions, to access and generate emotions so as to assist thought, to understand emotions and emotional meanings, and to reflectively regulate emotions in ways that promote emotional and intellectual growth". If you find this definition not terribly informative, I agree with you. When the definition of a concept includes many times the concept, the definition leaves much to be desired. Nevertheless, an increasing body of research supports what we may instinctively believe that there is very much to this idea of an emotional intelligence. To me and many others, it serves to explain why high IQ people can struggle in their personal and working lives. If they are characterized as lacking in "street smarts" or "common sense", it makes a little more sense that upon closer examination these two notions refer to something other than cognitive intelligence. Suffice it to say, high IQ and great grades do not guarantee predictably adaptive autonomous functioning. Emotional intelligence is a far superior predictor of a life of relevance, and getting along in the world.

My purpose here is not to dwell too much on what is and how to measure emotional intelligence. My purpose is to convey to you, indeed to convince you, that emotional intelligence is vitally important to how we function. My greater purpose is to convey and convince you that it is environmentally induced and thereby subject to the influence of external intervention. If indeed, emotional intelligence is comprised of inter and intra personal skills, the ability to manage stress, to be adaptive, and to be stable in mood, then it should be noted that we are not born with these attributes. We acquire these and other abilities through environmental experiences. Some experiences are conducive and others are not to such acquisitions. If we do not see or if we are not taught adaptive stress management, it would seem predictable that we, too, will have progressive difficulties in this respect. The same goes for all the other emotional intelligence indicators cited in the literature. To date, my experience in conducting assessments, for a variety of purposes, supports a working hypothesis that average or better emotional intelligence is indicative of positive environmental conditions during an individual's infancy and childhood. Once a person has the foundations of emotional intelligence it can be improved upon through external interventions such as an online learning resource I once reviewed for purposes of in-service training. In contrast, attachment disordered individuals with marked cognitive moral developmental delays at best reveal some semblance of emotional intelligence. While they can learn information and acquire skills, such achievement hardly is sufficient to predict the competent application of what they learn. Therefore, there is much else to be addressed with dysfunctional, maladaptive individuals before any discernable benefits reasonably can be expected from an emotional intelligence, educational curriculum. These comments are made in reference to remedial interventions only. As a preventive and habilitative measure emotional intelligence considerations are of equal importance to the other two lenses in my tri-focal view of the world. More of this will be said in Part Three.

To reiterate, the three parts of the lenses through which I interpret the world, and the people who impact on it, are probably of equal importance. My awareness of the three and the use to which I put the information developed at different times and hence my personal orientation is first to the cognitive stage and sequence model of moral development, then to attachment, and finally emotional intelligence. In reality, attachment and environmental conditions conducive to its development is primary because it determines most everything else subsequently. Fortunately, all three are environmentally induced, and as the child rescued from a devastating family legacy through external intervention, all of the human species likewise can be saved.

Saving, from my lens, means facilitating instead of obstructing, the human developmental potential. Hopefully I have made the point well that everything, the quality of our relationships, the quality of our parenting, the quality of our very life is defined and determined by our personal development. We can only do that of which we are capable by virtue of our level of development.

I should end this chapter by also acknowledging that there are many simultaneous developmental sequences taking place in an individual's life and all are influenced by environmental factors. My own dissertation, precipitated by the aforementioned first hand experience with an inability to understand the benefits of helping, had to do with the development of social reasoning. Recognizing that there is no such thing as altruism, total selfless action, I described and confirmed a sequence of prescriptive reasoning about why we behave in pro social ways, specifically volunteering. Others like Nancy Eisenberg also described and demonstrated a sequence of pro social moral judgement, June Tapp described the development of senses of law and legal justice while Loevinger described the development of the ego. These and all other developmental domains are determined by environmental factors, fortunately for us all!

CHAPTER FIVE
THE ACTIVITY OF "ETHICING"

The Importance of Concepts

Because we are human our very nature is to seek, identify, and use whenever possible, the path of least resistance. Admittedly this axiom probably applies to every living thing. The path of least resistance also applies to how we speak. Out of expediency, laziness, time constraints, and a myriad of other factors we speak in code. In other words, we use concepts. Whatever benefits come from this, however, do so at a significant cost. The first and most significant negative consequence is a failure to recognize that a concept is not a real thing. It is a made up word to represent something which would otherwise require one or more paragraphs to talk about. So instead of saying: "John is ill-suited by virtue of his personality attributes to his job; he lacks the necessary knowledge and skills to perform well and, as a result, he is in a constant negative emotional state, which is starting to have chronic adverse effects on his mental and physical health, which in his case is manifested by gastrointestinal disturbances, constant flatulence, and weight loss", we simply say;" he is stressed out by his work". The concept being "stress". There are a myriad of concepts in common use today, often differentially used and understood by people in the same conversation. Often concepts also are treated as something real. For example, some think of stress as a condition caught at work, not unlike cold germs spread by a sick colleague. If used in this way, the concept of "stress" creates a medical problem out of a deficiency in aptitude, knowledge, and skill for a particular occupation. While the negative physical symptoms of the deficiency may well require medical intervention, the other indicators (aptitude, knowledge, and skills) cannot be addressed through the administrations of a physician. As you can see, mistreating concepts can have devastating negative consequences, ones which lead us astray, and cause acute disturbances to become life debilitating chronic problems.

Since the English language is alive but not necessarily well, it is prone to constant change, distortion, and some may argue evolution that is inevitable. While evolution may well be inevitable, unfortunately the distortions which go far beyond imprecision, can and do, create a myriad of unintended but nevertheless, serious negative consequences. These can have a systemic ripple-like effect on traditions and practices, both of which have served us well in the past. The best example I can think of is the concept doctor. It comes from the Latin, docere, which means, "to teach". For hundreds of years the title Doctor has been bestowed, by duly accredited universities, on individuals deemed to have made a significant scholarly contribution to their field of study through independent but vetted investigation. The Latin verb docere is then an edict to disseminate the knowledge by writing a dissertation and for many by becoming a professor at an accredited post-secondary institution. Earning a doctorate of philosophy, which is the degree conferred regardless of discipline, has served well those who apply themselves to the rigorous undertaking. Society, too, has benefited much, over hundreds of years, from the contributions made to knowledge by the efforts and sacrifices of scholars. Nowadays, the title Doctor is used with much indiscretion, bestowed upon all sorts of disciplines for learning knowledge and skills without having to conduct vetted independent investigation for the purpose of making a significant contribution toward advancing the knowledge base of a particular discipline.

This observation is not intended to cast aspersions on the work and myriad of benefits derived from the services of physicians, dentists, chiropractors, optometrists, and practitioners of naturopathy or holistic medicine. This observation is simply to illustrate the distortion to which a living language can be subjected, the loss of valuable tradition this can cause and, most importantly, the potential negative consequences which can be created by an absence of clarity in how we talk when we use concepts. I shall illustrate the point further by discussing the inappropriate use of rehabilitation and reintegration in the field of addressing the misbehaviour of criminals. But before doing so, it is imperative that we recognize "ethic" also to be a concept. Unfortunately a concept which is much misunderstood and as such is misused as a superfluous hyperbole to signify the importance of rules, usually applied to professionals. I say "unfortunately" because in its misuse, the valuable activity conveyed by the concept of ethic is lost to us.

My intent in this chapter is to restore, indeed to clarify what eluded many moral philosophers namely, that "ethic" is a verb which pertains to a very specific activity. The activity being, ascertaining what moral developmental perspective is conveyed/revealed by a specific rationale. For example, what Heinz should do about getting the drug from the implied greedy druggist or the Nuremberg defendants' unanimous defence of "following orders" or the Watergate burglars rationalization of their nefarious activities undertaken in to re-elect Richard Nixon.

The activity of ethicing also involves ascertaining what moral developmental perspective is imbued in a particular rule, law, policy or procedure. Most importantly, the activity, is essential in determining what perspective we bring to situations when we are optimally rational, and to what stage we can regress when under duress. Such information tells us how likely we are to abide by professional or other codes of conduct and warns us that under duress we could regress to behaving in unacceptable ways simply to survive a potentially threatening situation. Insight about ourselves of this type, regardless of what we do, can be markedly empowering. Such awareness affords us, first, a better opportunity to control how we behave in all situations and, second, the motivation to pursue with focussed deliberateness the development of a principled perspective. Forewarned is forearmed and we can never have enough insight about who we are.

There are many other examples of ethicing, suffice it to say that when Lawrence Kohlberg interviewed and re-interviewed his original dissertation subjects, when he developed with his colleagues a scoring system to categorize a subject's reasoning about a moral dilemma, when Jim Rest developed a standardized objective measurement tool to accomplish the same results, when June Tapp studied how people develop their senses of law and legal justice, and when I did the same for social reasoning, we were all engaged in the activity of ethicing.

I am not embarking on any fatal semantic silliness. Indeed, my full intent is for you to recognize the importance of this chapter. The success of my purpose for writing this book significantly hinges on my ability to make this significant point crystal clear and to convince you of the benefits that can be derived from the different use to which the concept "ethic" can be put. This is the nexus of this entire book. If I fail, and I must say there are many who would prefer to see this, the concept "ethic" will continue to be relegated to the nonsensical platitude designation currently used, in great fashion, as a reaction to corporate based debacles and transgressions of high profile, nefarious individuals. If I fail, the concept will continue to be used as an unnecessary descriptor. For example, ethical code of conduct, ethical standards of practice, medical ethics, social work ethics and so on, each discipline aggrandizing its rules and regulations by adding the concept, "ethic".

This discussion cannot be complete without, at least, a brief reflection on how the concept of "ethic" has been used historically. By now, it will be clear that I believe it has been used incorrectly but not always and not by everyone. Unfortunately, even the greatest of thinkers, from time to time, used the concept interchangeably with the concept, "moral". While much effort has gone into defining what is moral, comparatively no effort has gone into defining the concept "ethic" or why it is used sometimes as a descriptor, adverb or an adjective, and sometimes as a noun or an object in a sentence. At least I have never found it used as a verb, although there are some vague indications of this use by some. Therefore despite popular belief, to be absolutely precise there are no ethical theories, although there are ethical theorists in all sorts of disciplines. A goodly number have made a career and quite a considerable reputation as "ethical theorists". As far as I can tell, their focus is on what is the right action to take in specific situations. I, for one, always thought this to be the domain, the focus of study, inquiry, analysis or consternation of moral philosophers. Even the subjects of Kohlberg were placed in the role of being moral philosophers every time they were interviewed to determine how differently, from their previous interview, they would rationalize the decision and behaviour of Heinz. The children whom, Swiss psychologist Piaget studied, in their own right, also were put in the position of being moral philosophers as they talked, for example, about the rules of a game of marbles.

At the risk of digressing into mind-numbing academic discourse, and for now mindful of my peers quick-to-critique propensity, I am compelled to cite a specific reference. In 1960 the renowned scholar Mary Warnock published a rather obscure little book entitled Ethics Since 1900. In the preface, she candidly declared that she has struggled with what is ethics and what has been its contribution to philosophy. In spite of this candour, Professor Warnock did not define the concept nor present anyone's definition of the concept throughout the book. She blithely made constant reference to the concept ethic completely unaware of the reader's need for conceptual clarity. The same could be said of E. G. Moore, another scholar, who published in 1903 Principia Ethica. At best he articulated the questions with which he was concerned: What kind of things ought to exist for their own sake and what kind of actions ought we to perform? The answers, if any, he said would define what kind of evidence is proper to support moral judgements; however, he seems to use the concept "moral" interchangeably with the concept, "ethic". Curiously, it is said that the subsequent work of moral philosophers (not ethical philosophers) flowed from Moore's treatise. The examples are many and curious as to how the concept ethic is used most often synonymously with the concept moral.

In difficult constraint of my wanton academic fervour I want to end this discussion with referencing the moral philosopher Immanual Kant. In part, he was very much concerned with rules and respect for rules. He also was concerned with determining what rules should be made and why it is proper and desirable to respect rules. It is no wonder therefore, that scholars with a "thou shalt" perspective such as Rawles, Dewey and Kohlberg have been so influenced by Kant and while focussed on morals, as Kant, they also inadvertently lapsed into using the concepts "ethic" and "moral" synonymously. For example, in describing Stage Six reasoning, Kohlberg speaks of ethical principles and then, absolutely correctly, about universal principles. To the best of my knowledge he never reconciled the inaccuracy of language to which he occasionally succumbed.

The Importance of Belonging and Other Preconventional Penchants

Notwithstanding the lapses of Kant or perhaps inaccuracies in the translation of his work, which would not be unusual judging by some significant distortions of what Sigmund Freud actually wrote, and the lapses of Kohlberg, while not explicitly stating so, moral philosophers and Kohlberg implied that the activity of analysing how people decide is "ethicing". My contribution is that I am simply stating so explicitly here and, in order to make my point, I will demonstrate the marked utility of the activity of "ethicing" by explaining all that was reported in Part One. You will recall that in Chapter One, three topics were discussed, each topic including references to those raising the alarm and references to those downplaying the crisis proportions of our global circumstance. Global warming out of control, first world consumerism, and the rapidly emerging energy crisis were the topics of discussion throughout which my hope was that you might ask: "How can we be doing this to ourselves?" The stage-sequence developmental lens through which I view the world provides a rather simple, answer, however, the solution is not so simple. But more of this later. Agreeing with and signing declarations such as the Kyoto Accord are necessary but markedly insufficient conditions to precipitate sustainable comprehensive change. You will also recall that I chose to believe deliberately, based on a clear rationale, in the social activists cited. My rationale to believe was described as "prudent conservatism", based upon the potential horrific consequences to our world, if indeed, time proves the activists negative predictions to be correct. In this discussion, it is also important to acknowledge that some people, especially in First World countries are starting to do the right things. The operative word is "starting", as for example, by replacing incandescent light bulbs with high efficient, low energy, florescent bulbs. Even though, there are other encouraging examples, on the whole, we continue to be markedly reliant on carbon based fuels and Third World countries are intent on catching up to us at breakneck speed . Most poignantly and alarming to me, is the number of SUVs on a Volvo dealership lot I saw the last time I had my car serviced. Few, if any, of us have any remotely justifiable reason to own such contraptions, even if they are hydrogen fuelled. The manufacture of huge vehicles such as Hummers is enormously energy-consumption costly. So what is going on? I hope you can at least hazard a guess or the answer that we are running with the herd. Our gang, our tribe or the gang/tribe to which we aspire to belong values things which contribute to global warming. The concrete signs of our membership and the requirements of our tribe are to avail ourselves of as many amenities as possible, all of which consume carbon based energy during their manufacturing and in their use. If this reference group perspective is raised to the conscious level of our awareness, we become threatened that some external force will cut us off from the herd. We do not want to hear about it because we know that on our own, without membership in the tribe, our instinct tells us, we are vulnerable. The same instinct precipitates regression from the reference group perspective to the instrumental hedonistic reciprocal orientation which characterize Stage Two preconventional level reasoning and behaviour. The satisfaction of our immediate need, for belonging, becomes paramount. Damn the Kyoto Accord, damn the torpedoes of global warming and full speed ahead! "I must, indeed, I will belong and no Al Gore or David Suzuki will dissuade me otherwise", is the unconscious mantra of the majority. Besides, from their moral developmental perspective, they cannot really understand let alone attend to the broad and long term consequences of their actions. How is this reasoning and behaviour any different from the Easter Islander who cut down the very last tree, as so eloquently described by Jared Diamond? It does not! Once you strip away the superficial content of time and technology, the dynamic is identical. Not similar but identical. The underlying structure is: "This is what my tribe does. I am a member of my tribe and I want to continue to be a member of my tribe, and if you try to stop me I will work even harder to do that which my tribe requires of me". Of course, there is more involved in tribal membership, such as beliefs, values, and lifestyles. To reiterate, do not be fooled by the content or the visual manifestations of tribalism. It is the underlying structure of reasoning and concomitant behaviours which are at the basis of our potentially rapidly encroaching demise.

Well intentioned, well informed, and truly responsible activists seem not at all aware of the human condition component in the equation of what they advocate. Concerted and sustained effort to do that which we must also requires addressing the human condition. Not just here and there by disconnected groups but everywhere by everyone if we are indeed going to change what now presents itself as an inevitable and close to irreversible tide.

We are as a species not mad nor bad. We simply are stuck where the majority has been and continues to be stuck since the beginning of recorded history. We are stuck because of a myriad of forces. Forces, well recognized by those all too willing to exploit them to meet their own ambitions and affiliative requirements. Frequently, even the exploiters lose sight of their affiliative needs and regress to the instrumental hedonistic perspective. The difference between this small group of "haves" and the "have nots" is that the "haves" always are in a better position to get more.

Explaining Part One

In Chapter One, I discussed consumerism and its myriad of devastating environmental and social consequences. Why is it so prevalent in First World countries and why are most, if not all, Third World countries in feverous pursuit of it? Because all of us, with great effort, much purpose, knowledge, and well honed skills are consistently enticed and persuaded to buy into the importance of having stuff. We have been afforded and we willingly consume the poisonous elixir that materialism is the answer to: "What is my purpose? Why am I here?" Although well entrenched, the enormous success of marketing materialism, a direct appeal to our Stage Two perspective, need not prevail. To shift, perhaps even revert this paradigm, it first will be necessary to understand the basis of its huge success.

In 1984 psychologist Robert Cialdini first published: Influence: The Psychology of Persuasion. It has been reprinted many times and I suggest this book to you as mandatory reading, as an antidote to the insidious infection perpetrated on us all by marketers. In a comprehensive manner, Cialdini, relying on a number of excellent sources, vividly describes the deliberate ways in which we are influenced to behave in specific ways, mostly by marketers or sales people who want us to purchase or do something specific of their bidding. The first significant weapon of influence described by Cialdini pertains to 'reciprocation'. The primary focus of this strategy is based on the human propensity "to repay, in kind, what another person has provided us." Cialdini is in fact describing the primary structure of Stage Two instrumental reciprocity. By virtue of this propensity we are said to feel obliged to repay favours, gifts, invitations, and the like. Not surprisingly, because of the cross cultural nature of cognitive development, as described by Kohlberg, there is no society which does not subscribe to this rule.

While Cialdini explains the phenomena of reciprocity as a manifestation of cooperation we know it also to be indicative of Stage Two reasoning. In the beginning, our ancestors invoked the rule of reciprocity for survival through the cooperative sharing of food and skills in the tradition of obligation. Cialdini's observation of human behaviour describes both the need for co-operation, (Stage Three), and the pursuit of immediate gratification, (Stage Two), through specific, time-limited, reciprocal arrangement with someone else. You do for me and I do for you an action of equal value. Applying this phenomenon is so effective because it resonates especially well with our preconventional way of reasoning, void of appreciating at a conscious level, let alone acting on, that there are broad and long term consequences to our actions. Knowledgeable about this phenomena and skilled in the behavioural application of its imperatives, sales people are markedly successful in persuading us to buy stuff simply because we believe ourselves to be obliged to do so, often for no good reason at all. Let me illustrate how this works by an example provided by Cialdini. In 1985 the impoverished people of Ethiopia sent five thousand dollars of relief to the people of Mexico. Reportedly, officials of the Ethiopian Red Cross had decided to send the money to help the victims of that year's earthquakes in Mexico City. An investigation of this curious incident revealed that in 1935 Mexico had sent aid to Ethiopia when it was invaded by Italy. Simply put, time and destitution did not erode the drive to act on obligation. Of an equally global stature, is the practice of giving free samples. In part, it is intended to familiarize us with a product but even more so to invoke the obligation response. We experience this most often in the supermarket, when we buy something we had no intention of purchasing only after we could not refuse the sample. The consumerism described in Chapter One therefore, to a large extent, is a function of appealing to our base pleasure seeking, (Stage Two), propensity by encouraging our cognitive developmental regression and by appealing to those of us who primarily function from this stage view of the world. Suffice it to say, there also is mixed in for good measure an appeal to our Stage Three reference group perspective: "I must have that to belong".

Another significant weapon of influence described by Cialdini is known as social proof. This dynamic is described as being in effect when we are trying to determine what is the correct thing to do using as our benchmark, our reference point, the behaviour of others. This human propensity is said to be a convenient shortcut for determining how to behave and makes us vulnerable to get caught up in the agenda of others, as for example at work. I screen for this when designing and conducting staff selection procedures, especially when there are work culture issues which need to be curtailed. But more to the point of our discussion about consumerism, this propensity, which by now you recognize to be a Stage Three reference group perspective, makes most of us vulnerable to the manipulation of profiteers who market their wares using knowledge about how most of us function in the world. Since most of us are imitators, it is understood in the profession of sales that we are persuaded more by the action of others than by any proof of the virtues of a product. It is no wonder therefore, that salespeople spend a disproportionate amount of time telling us that a product is the "fastest growing" or "largest selling" item as opposed to how well it is made, how long it will last or how much better it is than the product of a competitor.

The principle of social proof reportedly operates most effectively when we are observing the behaviour of people just like us, our gang, our tribe, or the gang or tribe to which we want to belong. The behaviour of such people affords us the greatest certainty as to what to do in general and in specific situations. This fact is not lost on product designers, marketers or salespeople. Witness the similarity of clothing among our rebellious teenagers. Just how these boys keep their low worn pants from falling down or tripping them up has always been beyond my understanding of the physics of gravity. Whatever they do must be worth the price of abiding by the social proof of their peers.

There are many other powerful weapons of influence articulated and explained in various ways by people such as Cialdini.

Regardless, the appeal always is to our preconventional moral developmental perspective or at best to our earliest conventional stage, namely the reference group orientation. As long as we are developmentally stuck, as long as we are prone to regress under duress, we will continue to be slaves to materialism as it is practised in First World countries. While most, if not all, of us agree that this is ultimately going to contribute to the demise of us all and in the process continue to rob us of a quality of life for which we have the potential, we nevertheless continue to be seduced by the hollow promise of the happiness afforded us by a new refrigerator, high definition television, new sound system or an SUV. Raising our consciousness about all of this is necessary because if we remain stuck at the Stage Three reference group perspective, not much will change in the structure of our reasoning and ultimately how we behave. The only changes will come in content, in the form of "new and improved". This is the product we must have because everyone, who is anyone, especially in our group has it or is buying it.

We concluded our discussion in Chapter One by examining what is being said about the energy crisis. As you will recall, I referred to Rifkin's argument that the energy crisis is real and that it is inevitable. Most others who have examined this issue have said likewise. Moreover, it is simply intuitive that we will run out of something we cannot renew, and that the rate at which we will do so is hastened by the Chinese and Indian rapidly escalating enamouration with motorized transportation. The impact of all of this on global climate also is a significant factor. So why are we still purchasing gasoline-guzzling SUVs, eight-cylinder powered, air-conditioned automobiles. Why do we continue to rely on coal-fired electrical generation, even though we grumble about the price of fuel? Notwithstanding the exceptions to the norm, once again, the root of the problem lies firmly grounded in the human condition. From our innate pleasure seeking propensity, aided and abetted by our Stage Two instrumental hedonistic perspective, we want what we want and we want it immediately with only, at best, lip-service to concerns about the big and long-term consequences to our individual and collective actions. Moreover, our reference group approves of our behaviour by behaving similarly and we can all, with very little effort, justify what we do by some logical explanation, one which makes sense if the reference point is how we and our gang see things. Once again, Stage Two and Stage Three, interchangeably are at work and will continue to influence energy consumption until it is too late. Unless we break out of the constraining cognitive developmental perspective which dominates our reasoning and behaviour, the warning of the likes of Rifkin will continue to fall on deaf ears. At best, we will agree with Rifkin and expect everyone else to act responsibly but then invoke: "I deserve the monster truck, because I always wanted one, and because I worked so hard for it, besides if it was so bad to have one, the government should ban their sale just like marijuana".

You might well react to this explanation as simplistic, not applicable to everyone. Granted, it is not applicable to everyone, but it is the majority who has shunned the Smart Car in North America, and it is some market researcher who caused the dealership, where I have my Volvo serviced, to stock their lot mostly with the large, SUV type models.

Well then, if the masses won't heed the warnings of fossil-based energy depletion, that fuel will become unaffordably high as it runs out, that we will suddenly grind to a halt and some of us freeze to death in our palatial, grand room, adorned homes because we ran out of heating fuel, why does the industry not do something about this problem? You will recall from Chapter One that the industry is made up of two parts. One part manufactures the fossil burning vehicles and the other the fossil based fuels. Neither is willing to risk initiating change and, as such, the required developmental funds are lacking. Most, if not all of us, believe that the manufacturing industry, with some effort and cost, has the potential to design and produce on mass, for example, affordable hydrogen fuelled vehicles and electrically powered engines. Perhaps, even small enough hydrogen fuelled generators that could be placed in each of our homes, condominiums or apartment complexes. After all, the human species is capable of great technological creations. Similarly, most, if not all, of us believe that the fuel manufacturing industry, with some effort and cost, has the potential to produce affordable and readily available hydrogen to run our various power generating machines. You will also recall from Chapter One that both sides are afraid of taking the first step, lest the other side does not follow suit. Let us say that Vancouver based Ballard Industries received the financial support required and in short order put on the market an affordable hydrogen fuelled engine that could be installed in every make of car. That would be fantastic for all of us in many ways including severing our reliance on oil. Therein lies a significant obstacle, insofar as there are many powerful forces whose interests are served by our addiction to fossil fuels. But we all know this by now. Notwithstanding this reality and how it may impinge on Ballard Industries, what would happen if they were able to overcome all obstacles and efforts to curtail the development of the hydrogen fuelled power plant? Simply, there would virtually be no market for it because hydrogen fuel would not be readily available. This is the very salient point which Rifkin makes in his book. Business is business, based on well defined rules of reciprocity. I give you something in return for something of at least perceived equal value. Does this sound at all familiar? Is this not the major feature of Stage Two instrumental reciprocity? It is! As long as this focus prevails, progress with respect to developing and using alternative fuels will be painstakingly slow. Moreover, the instrumental reciprocity of Stage Two is far removed from the Stage Four reasoning that one must engage in sustained behaviours from which society can benefit. Any corporate or educational initiatives to promote so-called socially responsible behaviour, at best, are well intentioned but ultimately can be described as rhetorical posturing designed to seize the opportunity for a new business venture while remaining oblivious to the realities of the human condition. Without attending to the cognitive developmental limitations of the majority, the University of Toronto's Institute for Corporate Citizenship will be nothing more than yet another opportunistic business venture reacting to a need from a corporate perspective.

At this juncture I am compelled to clarify that my intent is not to single out the automobile industry or the oil companies. It is just an easy example to which the majority can relate. In truth, automobiles in Canada reportedly produce only twelve percent of the country's total greenhouse gas emissions. Other sources such as home and hot water heating and especially industry are responsible for most of the other percentage of greenhouse emissions. Automobile industry executive Reid Bigland even contends that burning one chord of fire wood produces more greenhouse gas emissions than ten modern SUVs will do in their lifetime. As such, the auto industry arguably has been doing its share to address the problem of greenhouse gases, albeit mostly with respect to decreasing the toxicity of fossil fuel emissions but not the consumption of fossil fuels. While very encouraging and reason for considerable optimism, the problem with the production of greenhouse gases from all sources remains the same, namely, our collective need for immediate gratification perspective supported by respective reference group values, beliefs, and concomitant practices.

In Chapter Two, we went from broad global issues to examining how groups contribute to the exponential growth of problems which threaten all of us. Global warming, consumerism, and the energy crisis, to various degrees are precipitated and exacerbated by corporations, more precisely the corruption inherent to the very essence of this business entity. From my perspective, any business entity, any political party, or any religious group is a corporation. By definition, their sole purpose is to advance their self interest and to do so at any cost. Their respective ends justify whatever means are employed. Defrauding pensioners of their life savings, promising then reneging on promises in order to get elected, and waging holy wars are all justified means to advance the interest of the group. The requirements of membership are extremely well articulated not only in behavioural terms but also, in some cases, by even prescribing what you can and cannot think. As so well said by the late comedian George

Carlin, if you thought about committing a sin downtown save your bus fare because you have already done so, just by thinking about it. Does this sound at all familiar? It should because this is the essence of Stage Three reasoning and all concomitant behaviours. Yes, there are exceptions and thankfully so, for without the exceptions, there would be no hope. But first we need to face the unabashed reality that tribes, regardless of how each dress, what type of building each live in or what alternative concepts are used to represent them, exist no more or less as they have always. As long as the requirements of membership are fulfilled, sanctuary in numbers is assured. There is much comfort in this, especially insofar as the pursuit of immediate pleasures is not as risky as when done with the sanction of a group as opposed to when it is done as a sole, pleasure seeking individual operating from a Stage Two perspective.

It is noteworthy that in an invariant, hierarchical sequence of development earlier perspectives are not lost. Earlier perspectives are simply incorporated into successive ones which, by this very process, makes each subsequent perspective better capable of successfully negotiating increasingly more complex circumstances because there is more to draw upon. This is significant because it serves to explain the human component in the misbehaviour of corporations. After all, it is people of each gender, of all races, and ethnic origins who make up the rules of membership in each type of corporation. The rules may be made up by one or many, and these rules are then accepted by those who want to belong. What reference group affiliation accomplishes therefore, is to provide Stage Two individuals with the sanctuary of a legitimized group. As pointed out in Chapter Two, the psychopathic propensities of individuals are even mandated by laws, to do whatever is necessary to make a profit, albeit with at least some semblance of propriety. This pervasive persistent undercurrent only boils to the top when some individuals profit more than others especially if it occurs in the same reference group. When Stage Two instrumental reciprocity was violated the Hollinger board of directors became incensed and had their chief executive, Lord Conrad Black, investigated, charged, and eventually convicted of malfeasance. From my perspective/lens Lord Conrad Black was no more guilty of greed, opportunism, obscene consumption, and lavish lifestyle than to what his board of directors aspired. Perhaps, some may have even been his equal. His mistake was to violate the conditions of instrumental reciprocity so blatantly as to draw attention to himself. This example is no different from the decades, old sociological analysis of the black market in the now defunct Communist Soviet Union. Everyone was doing it, and officials did not interfere until someone's conspicuous extravagant behaviour raised the ire of a neighbour. Once informed upon, sanctions were imposed and the social order of black marketeering was restored. The order being: "Do it but be quiet and be subtle about it". I believe this has been the lesson for all corporations and their chief executive officers. Do it but not so flagrantly and, for pity's sake, do not draw attention to yourself, Lord Black of Cross Harbour indeed.

While the loss of life savings of corporation defrauded shareholders by out and out criminal behaviour is undeniably a tragedy the route to this destination is seldom talked about. There is an apparent conspiracy of silence about the greedy falling victim to the greedy, the only difference being that some greedy people may have a greater opportunity than others. Little mention is made in the media that high yielding investments also come with high risks no matter what the product or business in which the investment is made. I learned this lesson decades ago from a prisoner I met, on the unit I managed, who was convicted of a series of frauds. All he had to do, he said, was to play on the greed of others. While probably everyone knows the adage, if it is too good to be true it is, no one acts on this knowledge consistently. Remember, another feature of Stage Two instrumental reciprocity or hedonism is an undeveloped ability to recognize that there are broad and long term implications to action. Primary focus is on the here and now. In short order, the thinking is: "I can double my money!" The prospects of these seem especially to be more appealing to those who see their time as running out, specifically pensioners.

No discussion of corporations and the instrumentally greedy hedonists who manage them would be complete without reference to the global financial crises precipitated, on New York's Wall Street, in the fall of 2008. As mentioned earlier, the magnitude of the greed is equal to and revealed by the magnitude of the bailouts provided by the various governments world wide. From my perspective, this financial debacle is nothing more than further evidence of the global developmental deficits that have and continue to afflict the human species. Sadly, much will be written about the global economic crisis in the months and years to come, mostly to satisfy our morbid, macabre curiosity about fatalities. There will be little, if any, analysis provided that will point us to the need to facilitate the development of our children to become the principled financial leaders which are so clearly needed to manage every size and type of business.

Corporate corruption therefore, at least from my lens, is rather straightforward. It is attributable to Stage Two perspective individuals hiding out in particular types of reference groups (tribes or gangs) which legitimizes, indeed require of them, instrumental hedonism. This arrangement could not exist without the other half of the equation which is comprised of the equally greedy masses, albeit with far less opportunity to realize their individual need for immediate gratification. Admittedly, the paradigm I just described is infinitely more complex and has been subjected to all kinds and levels of academic analysis. To what avail is difficult to ascertain since it continues as I write and as you read this. No wonder, as the axiom goes: Greed is the mother of all sins. This is all that we need to know. I only add that greed, the pursuit of immediate need gratification, in denial of reality and lacking in the ability to recognize that there are broad and long term consequences to actions are the hallmarks of preconventional reasoning.

In Chapter Two, political corruption was examined from both a serious and satirical perspective. It is always a part of some discourse everywhere because its existence touches all of us. I believe everyone is a political pundit, some better than others, most better than the talking heads on television. However, from my lens what is seldom, if ever, talked about is that political ideology is really nothing more than subterfuge, something offered up to us, only to distract us from the reality that we are only exchanging one gang or tribe for another, each comprised of individuals whose primary focus is on the immediate satisfaction of needs. Among political gangs or tribes, the need seems more to do with power and prestige, as opposed to money. Instead of appealing directly to our greed, political gangs approach us indirectly with the promise of rescuing us from a life of drudgery by delivering to us a vastly improved quality of life. I say, "indirectly" because the promises always boil down to something monetary such as reduced taxes, more taxes but relief from other costs, better wages, more employment, and the list goes on. Whereas, the greed factor of corporations is enshrined in law, the Stage Two, short term, immediate here and now need for gratification is similarly prescribed for politicians by laws pertaining to elections. In most countries and jurisdictions, elections are held after a predetermined period of time on a specific date. This precludes anything but the most esoteric long term planning since almost immediately after being elected the campaign for re-election starts. How the masses or those who vote, expect to be rescued by any political gang or tribe is strictly a function of cognitive developmental delay aided and abetted by some semblance of a reference group perspective. The thinking is: "My tribe says that if I value this, believe that, and behave in these ways, things will be good for me. Perhaps not this time, but certainly the next time, and in the interim I have a tribe to hang with, to identify with, and if I should ever need to rely on, they will be there for me". Most of us never want to test these beliefs.

To underscore the point of political tribalism, reflect for a moment, on the paintings that depict the authors and signatories of the American Constitution and the British North American Act which established the Canadian provinces as a Confederation. Both documents are held out to be the quintessential examples of democracy, the greatest good for the greatest number. As long as you were a white male of European descent, primarily British. To reiterate an earlier point, I see no women nor persons of colour in those pictures depicting the glorious beginning of the two neighbouring countries. Curiously, no on talks of this very much or the rampant racism that is only now subsiding, I hope, in the United States of America and most other First World countries.

Both political and corporate corruption, therefore, constitute an equation, one which incorporates an implicit collusion between like-minded individuals. It is an arrangement of instrumental reciprocity hidden in the bosom of a reference group perspective. For both sides of the political equation, at least from a monetary perspective, it is not nearly as lucrative as what goes on between corporations and those who invest in them. Nevertheless, the system prevails and in spite of past, current, and future tinkering with it, it will remain more than less the same, unless the human condition is recognized for what it is and is addressed. Without concerted initiatives to address the pervasive cognitive developmental delays which shape the actions of politicians and those who elect them, any tinkering with the system will only change the content. The underlying structure will remain the same as it has since the beginning of recorded political history. By structure, I mean the allocation and prioritization of emphasis in the political system.

A brief digression is warranted here to acknowledge that there are always exceptions to how people conduct themselves even within one of the worst blights on the human condition, the profession of politics. The political exception, in 2009, appears to be President Barack Obama. He probably is an exception because of one, singularly important factor. President Obama presents as a person of principle. As such, there is a genuine quality to him and everything that he says. He appears to be the principled type of individual required at the helm of every institution, industry, and nation. Only time will tell how President Obama will lead and how he will cope with the paucity of available principled resources in his circle of advisors, nationally, and internationally. Nevertheless, he too is good reason to harbour hope for sustainable change through well defined thoughtful efforts. Not efforts to stimulate the economy by bailing out mismanaged and corrupt corporations but efforts that are recommended in Part Three which will have sustainable positive consequences. Even on this account, there is good reason for optimism judging by President Obama's already identified and articulated need for a nation wide focus on children. A focus not only on their education but on promoting their optimal developmental potential. I hope what I heard him say, was not wishful interpretation, but what he actually meant. Time will tell.

As innately pleasure seeking organisms in constant pursuit of pleasure and the avoidance of pain, all human beings have been drawn to the promise of religion since one of the mythological sons of Adam and Eve made a burnt offering to God. Any subsequent offering, regardless of kind has always taken place with an expectation of a return. To join a religious tribe then and now makes perfect sense. The evolution of what is expected also makes sense. At first the expectation was tangible, rain for the crops or healing from an illness. Since these consequences were intermittent and random other benefits had to be derived. The most logical and the most consistent with the human condition was and continues to be group affiliation. There is safety in numbers and much sanctuary in being part of the tribe. There is little effort required, especially of thought, since everything is clearly prescribed as well as the negative and positive consequences to compliance. How much easier could it be to be told to endure the hardships of life because there is promised eternal bliss after death. All of this makes sense, especially for those who need to feel secure and protected in the reference group tribe.

The tragedy of religion, from my lens, is best illustrated by the rise and distortion of Christianity. Most other religions have similarly been corrupted but for the sake of clarity let us stick with Christianity. As declared previously, it is irrelevant who Jesus was or if indeed he ever existed as a historical figure. For me the idea of a Jesus and the idea of his message will suffice. The message will still suffice even if it was crafted at the Council of Nicea in 325 A.D. at the behest of Constantine. The message is very simple! It is based on recognizing the innate developmental potential of humankind and that it is being obstructed from developing by a myriad of social forces. Development was just as obstructed then as it is now, except all organized religions have joined the ranks of the various forces which prevent us from reaching our potential. The Roman Catholic Church best illustrates the point that all religions in essence are nothing more than tribes or gangs and, as such, have their individual unique trappings, including club houses which reflect what the gang is all about not unlike the club houses of other gangs, including outlaw motorcycle groups, such as the Hell's Angels. Just check out St. Peter's Basilica the next time you are in Rome and see for yourself the quintessential club house of this gang. As a matter of fact the synagogue in Florence, Italy also is not too shabby nor is the great blue tiled mosque in Istanbul, Turkey. So what happened? It was Constantine who seized the opportunity to profit from something happening that was very positive. Probably, he did not see the inherent danger of the Christian movement continuing and flourishing as it started out. If he did, he deserves greater credit for having the intellectual insight to recognize that the masses actualizing their potential would be impossible to subjugate to his rule. At the least, he saw an opportunity and capitalized on it but, in order to do so, he understood the need to impose interpretations from which he could benefit. Fast forwarding to 2001, it would not be outrageous to draw the parallel to the Bush administration's war on terrorism and everything which ensued from the 9/11 attack on the World Trade Centre Towers. There are many other historical examples of political figures capitalizing on current events to advance their personal lust for power, influence, and financial gain. Instead of facilitating the developmental potential of human beings, Christianity, because of Constantine's political hand, has evolved into nothing more than another gang or tribe, one which subjugates its members with the promise of eternal salvation in the afterlife. Until then you must abide by the rules, which periodically are changed by the Pope who is, we are told, a representative of God on earth. As such whatever he says, in a specific context, is infallible. A nice arrangement and probably an envy of many politicians.

When you peel away all the rhetoric, when you peel away the pomp and ceremony which surround events such as the Congregation for the Doctrine of the Faith, one of the various number of Vatican Counsels, what you discover is simply a reference group doing its thing. To call it for what it is, is considered to be a grievous offense, by those who have drunk the Kool-Aid . From my lens, what should be considered as an even greater, grievous offense is the distortion of the original message and thereby the wanton squandering of an opportunity to advance the lot of the human race. To reiterate, Christians are not alone as organized entities capitalizing on the preconventional needs of human beings and invoking a concept of a God to create a powerful and rich tribe composed of a small elite and privileged management group who dictate to the masses. Can you imagine what would happen to the practice of all religions if the masses were no longer obstructed from developing their cognitive developmental potential? It would be the heaven on earth, without the managers (clerics), for which we have the potential of which Jesus spoke as is believed by some religious scholars such as the aforementioned Anglican Bishop, John Shelby Spong and Albert Nolan.

For the sake of argument and to make my point further, let us accept for the moment that, indeed, Moses, Elijah, Jesus, Mohammed and all the other prophets actually had direct contact, spoke with, God All Mighty or a representative such as the Angel, Gabriel. As such, each was conveying, first hand, God's directives to the human race. As the all-knowing and infinitely wise Father, He knows more than Kohlberg and his ilk about the very real fact that we can only understand directives, notions or reasons at our current developmental stage perspective or, at best, just one stage above. But the heavenly Father clearly was unaware of this empirical fact because the message of each prophet, Jesus included, reveals a post conventional principled perspective. So who made the mistake in how the messages were formulated? Was it the heavenly Father? I think not! Was it the prophets? Absolutely! It took the self serving Constantine to rectify the problem. His solution was to corrupt the principled message of Jesus to which very few could relate, and articulated it from a Stage Three perspective to which most everyone could relate. Some two thousand years later this scenario prevails, virtually unchanged. Insofar as similar corruptions define most other denominational histories, I for one cannot, even remotely, consider any religion as conducive to human development. On the contrary religion is a detriment to it.

In Chapter Three, the misbehaviour of criminals was examined. Since the debacles described in Chapters One and Two really are perpetrated by people, not the corporation or an entity, it made sense to conclude Part One by examining what is reported or said about individuals in certain categories of misbehaviour. Starting with criminality serves to illustrate further the tri focal lens through which I see the world. Having started my professional career working in a prison, then consulting to prisons, and continue to be involved to this day at one level or another, has served to validate and reinforce the benefits of this world view. What I learned very quickly was that, regardless of the facade with which every offender came, it took very little scratching at the surface to discover adverse environmental conditions during the youth of each and every criminal I interviewed and/or assessed. With little or no exception, it would not be unreasonable to characterize offenders, in addition to a number of related conditions such as fetal alcohol syndrome, first and foremost, as attachment disordered. This failed, formative stage life task is intergenerationally perpetuated and almost always becomes manifested in criminal activities. The transgressions start early in life, that is almost always lived in adverse environmental conditions created by inadequate parents. Needless to say, environmental conditions also are not conducive to cognitive moral development, and the unfortunate child is left behind by their mainstream peers in this and other spheres of development, especially pertaining to emotional intelligence. In contrast, their mainstream peers achieve the reference group perspective whereas, the unfortunate child is stuck at a Stage Two emphasis on immediate needs gratification, unable to connect with others beyond a simple reciprocal exchange.

The Stage Two stuck child never feels integrated and finds the company of similar youth comfortable since they, too, are in constant pursuit of immediate need gratification. This state is inconsistent with the social propriety expected of us all and, sooner than later, the child finds himself in trouble with the law. Unfortunately, this is a rather predictable sequence of events. The sequence is attributable most importantly to environmental conditions, ones which delay or impede development. The criminal who either breaks into your home through your basement window or squanders your stock dividends on an extravagantly lavish lifestyle are both at Stage Two, satisfying an immediate pleasure seeking need. The criminal has never been a part of mainstream society and therefore is in need of integration. Similarly, the criminal has never developed a conventional social perspective and cannot be described as having lost it and thereby in need of rehabilitation. What the criminal really needs is habilitation, that is to say, he must develop a cognitive moral developmental perspective which is antithetical to violating the rights of others. The criminal also needs to be integrated once habilitation has occurred, since he was never nor did he ever feel himself to be part of the community in the first place.

Violence probably is now the most frequently reported criminal activity. Not a single weekend goes by without at least one, but mostly more, young men killing other young men. Notwithstanding the innate propensity for competitive aggression, as seen from my tri focal lens perspective, violence also is environmentally induced, initially through inadequate parenting and subsequently by conditions in our communities, conditions which exacerbate an exponentially growing problem. Seldom is the reality of inadequate parenting identified when violence erupts or results in a loss of life. At best, there is talk of single parenting but never of irresponsible, ill-conceived, and unplanned procreation by people who would be inadequate parents whether rich or poor, living in high style or in the ghetto. Witness the parenting of Hollywood's rich and famous as reported daily in the supermarket tabloids or on television.

The prevalence of substance use and abuse and, most importantly, the crimes committed to afford the drugs also is a manifestation of failed attachment, subsequent later life negative personality trait consequences, poorly developed emotional intelligence, and cognitive developmental delay that can foster a pervasive denial of the problem. In the oral phase of development, which coincides with the most crucial formative stage, the child learns about life by putting things into his mouth. It is at this time that the child develops a sense of himself by ingesting and then metabolizing the empathic nurturance of primary caregivers, although one caregiver will suffice. If there is insufficient empathic nurturance to ingest and metabolize a void remains. This emptiness is experienced as a constant negative emotional state, one which is the essence of an addictive characterological personality trait. The life enduring nature of this and all other traits is now further explained by the previously described empirically based Early Years studies. Specifically, there are physiological correlates to the psychodynamic explanation, described above. Suffice it to say, the prevalence of addiction, and the huge underground economy this has spawned, indicate that we are in considerable trouble. The genesis of these troubles are the environments created by inadequate parenting during the child's most crucial formative stage in life.

Lest you think addicts consume only illegal drugs you should know that this is only the tip of the iceberg. I once knew an addict who drank at least a case, twenty-four or more, cans of Coca Cola a day. I have known several addicts who drink as much beer or the equivalent of whiskey or wine every day. Simply there is no limit to the ingenuity of people with respect to what they can become addicted in order to escape their constant and pervasive negative emotional state.

From my lens, the exponential growth of obesity is another manifestation of being an addict. In 1990, obesity in America was negligible. By 2007, fourteen percent of Americans were judged to be obese. The abusive ingestion of food is no different from the abusive ingestion of any other substance. This abusive behaviour is an attempt to achieve relief from pervasive, negative emotional and physiological states. The only difference is that eating disorders are not illegal and food is readily available, especially in the United States, in great proportions at relatively affordable prices. As such, there is a pervasive institutionalized promotion of this pathological behaviour. Furthermore, we do not need expensive and questionable surveys to tell us how pervasive obesity is among the population. It will suffice to simply scan any public gathering to see for ourselves just how fat we are becoming as Tonight Show host Jay Leno is so fond of saying. Obesity is a very objective indicator of how prevalent inadequate parenting is and how adverse are the environments to which children are exposed during the most crucial formative stage in life.

Admittedly, acquiring an addictive characterological personality trait and then becoming addicted to one or more things is a far more complex process than the above discourse conveys. My intent is to elaborate on this devastating social problem in a forthcoming book. Here, my point is to define its origins as attachment related and its exponential growth to environmental factors, factors which impede human growth and development at all levels. As such, the war on drugs has and will only continue to foster better deception tactics in an enormous underground industry, one which is simply responding to a need. As long as the need continues, as long as the intergenerational perpetuation of various dysfunctionalities remains unaddressed, there will be a demand for drugs. The same can be predicted about other addictive substances and behaviours including obesity, gambling, sex, and let us not forget, the twenty-four or more cans of Coca Cola consumption mentioned earlier.

The behaviour of groups in the legal profession, health

care, and journalism, was examined in Chapter Three. By now, it should be clear that each of these professions represents a reference group. As such, membership, affiliation or acceptance is determined by compliance with requirements. In other words, each profession has implicit and explicit rules for conducting its respective businesses. Their respective behaviours are codified which then normalizes, within the group, what the professional is doing. Exceptions, those who violate the codified practices become marginalised or exiled by the group. Violations can entail blatantly pursuing immediate gratification of pleasure needs (eg. sexual impropriety with clients by a health care professional) or behaving positively from a broader social perspective, able to reason beyond what the group prescribes and thereby breaking rank. These positive exceptions in professions are the ones who acknowledge that the emperor has no clothes, such as Thomas Szasz of the Myth of Mental Illness fame. For the purposes of this Chapter, an analysis of how one becomes eager and willing to drink the professional group Kool-Aid is more salient and therefore requires elaboration.

Those who excel professionally, those who exemplify what their profession does and stands for, first and foremost found their niche. They are a good fit because they have the aptitude to do, well all the good and bad things activists say about each of the three groups being discussed. Aptitude, as you will recall is a combination of innate propensities and are activated by very specific environmental conditions. Remember the illustrations concerning testosterone levels? Even those with levels higher than the norm can be taught to exercise control over concomitant behavioural propensities. Those who can and do engage in the negative aspects for which each of the three professions is criticized do so, to a large extent, because of environmentally activated aptitude.

The next component in the making of a professional is the extent to which a neophyte can be socialized. If the aspiring professional is stuck at a reference group perspective, attributable to rather impoverished environmental conditions, socialization will be much easier than for someone at the Stage Two or Four cognitive moral development stage perspective. The socialization is very deliberate and occurs mostly in the field, although the foundation is well established through the course work required by each profession. The question: "How can they behave in the ways activists criticize each of the professions?" can be answered with a simple response: "Because that is what that professional group does." Perhaps a humorous anecdote about a hiker and a rattlesnake will serve to illustrate the point. The story goes that a rattlesnake requested from the hiker a favour, to take it across a rather heavily travelled road. The hiker refused the request and cited the known practice of the rattlesnake to bite and poison whoever comes in contact with it. But the rattlesnake was quite persuasive promising not to do that which it was widely known to do. He told the hiker that it will need him to bring it back across the road when he returns from his hike. Eventually the hiker capitulated to the snake, picked up the snake, took it across the busy road, and put it down at which instant the rattlesnake immediately bit him injecting its poisonous venom. The hiker's dying words were "but you promised" to which he barely heard the response from the rattlesnake "but this is what I do".

While some may intend the negative characterization of the

three professions to be an act of reciprocal unkindness, that is not the intent here. The intent simply is to acknowledge that each of the three professions discussed simply does what it does because of what it is. Each is a business, first and foremost, and each has its current well defined ways of doing business. Whatever is done within the professional group is normalized by the group and in very powerful, albeit mostly implicit ways, is approved by it. To expect anything different is tantamount to the naive gullibility of the hiker who soon enough suffered the consequences of his foolishness. Explicit codes of conduct and standards of practice generally are profession-specific and really entail the blatantly obvious. To add the descriptor, "ethical" makes neither more important and certainly does nothing to curtail professional conduct especially that which garners significant monetary rewards. For example, physician specialists in psychiatry, will continue to use the non scientific method of diagnosis and rely on medication as the primary strategy of intervention; lawyers will continue to fan the flames of acrimony charging for every conceivable thing they can; and journalists will continue to pursue a bias simply because negative sensationalism sells. Journalists, especially in the news media, will continue to "dumb down" their work to an average of grade five reading abilities. Thereby, they appeal to the lowest common denominator and significantly contribute to forces that obstruct development. The so called requirement to "dumb down" also is an unconscious, but very real, recognition that preconventional reasoning and ideas are what the populace can relate to the best. Perhaps all of this is a huge exaggeration and rightfully can be accused of over-simplification as well as disregarding all the good apples among the few rotten ones in the barrel. Regardless, I think I have made the point, that the misbehaviour of professional groups can be attributed to adverse environmental conditions early in a child's life and subsequently obstruct development especially in the domain of moral reasoning. This has been and continues to be the case unless we do something about the root causes.

Chapter Three concluded in an examination of the abhorrent behaviour of individuals. My intent was to underscore, establish as firmly as possible, that experiences in the first two years of life are the most important time in every individual's development. When things are bad, unless interventions of a colossal order are introduced, invariably later life negative consequences will emerge. Instead of giving in to our morbid curiosity about what Jeffrey Dahmer did, how Paul Bernardo and his wife lured little girls into their perverse clutches or exploring the bizarre propensities of personality disordered individuals, especially psychopaths, my intent is to redirect attention to where these psychopaths come from. What degree of inadequate parenting and what degree of adverse environmental conditions produced and continue to produce such human aberrations? Without such understanding most everything we do in reaction will be, as it has been, inconsequential. At best our reactions serve to make us feel empowered momentarily against the frightening and the mysterious. We lock up forever a Paul Bernardo and exclaim with great satisfaction: "Well that's that". Those unsatisfied with this feeble reaction demand execution, but to date, to the best of my knowledge, no one has demanded to really know where he came from. How was a Sesame Street, Teletubbies-watching, Elmo-cuddling, vulnerable infant, hungry to ingest empathic nurturance, systematically turned into a monster capable of atrocities most of us cannot even imagine?

I hope to have made the point that Professor Hare's position on the etiology of the condition known as psychopathy is extremely disturbing. I refuse to accept that these adults simply were innately difficult children who can come from the very best of families, and who are absolutely immune to parenting and socializing efforts to curtail their rapidly emerging, profound pathology. As you will recall, my position is that as much effort as has been exerted to describe the personalities and behaviours of individuals who meet the diagnostic criteria of psychopathy should be exerted by experts, with a psychosocial bent, to examine the gestation and formative years experiences of these psychopaths. Clearly, whatever they experienced as infants had profound physiological and psychological developmental effects. The challenge is to operationally define the, "whatever".

Apart from the condition of psychopathy, the etiology of other personality disorders or disturbances is not at all mysterious. There are clear links made in the literature between failed attachment, adverse environmental conditions, and a variety of later life negative consequences. Most researchers cite personality disorder as a sequella, explaining that a failed attachment with a primary caregiver sets a tone for all subsequent relationships in life as well as the nature of internal dynamics including disregulated emotionality and an inability to sooth oneself, especially during stressful times.

Whenever I conduct a Child Welfare precipitated Parenting Capacity Assessment, my primary emphasis is on contextualizing the parental behaviour of the person being assessed. This is the essence of a psychosocial perspective through which much is revealed, most often about the obstructed development of a primary caregiver and the destiny from which a child must be rescued. Poor prenatal conditions, inadequate parenting, adverse environmental conditions to which an infant is exposed, invariably are predictors of a host of later life negative personality and behavioural consequences. I say invariably because if there are any exceptions, I have never seen one and I have never been told of one. Good intentions, expressed in court, to be a better parent, while necessary simply are insufficient, to look favourably on primary caregivers who seek and constantly expect to be rescued by their advocate lawyers. Such caregivers recognize no part they play in their problems as parents. Since they play no part, for them it is logical that their acrimonious relationship with a child welfare agency is absolutely caused by others. Others must change therefore, not them. Such a perspective does not bode well for an infant, a toddler or an adolescent in their care. And so the well-defined pattern passes from one generation to the next.

A brief digression is warranted here. When a child is apprehended by a child welfare agency, the decision to do so, almost always, is for a good reason. Unfortunately, in far too many cases the apprehension of the child is the only constructive event in the total process. Since the apprehension is adversarial, it is protracted. Well intentioned but misinformed and often poorly trained child welfare agency staff also contribute to protracting the process. Their unfounded optimism about a parent's timely rise to meet the onerous responsibilities of parenting most times is disappointed. This results in many months lost, while waiting for a parent to change. The accumulative consequence is that the apprehended child completes the most crucial formative stage of life without appropriate intervention. Even when the child's status is finally determined, intervention is in short supply and difficult to access. The hue and cry therefore, by many, is that child welfare agency intervention does not work. In response, I say, the entire process is flawed and the myriad of its shortcomings are exacerbated by the adversarial process. Fortunately for children at risk, there are better models of responding to their needs than those based on the English adversarial process. They exist in places such as France and are worthy not only of mention but examination with the view to adopting their best practices.

It is not difficult to see that environmental conditions created by inadequate parents also are not conducive to cognitive moral development or to the development of, at least, average emotional intelligence. Therefore, to reiterate an earlier point, while my main lens is a cognitive moral developmental one, it is really the attachment life task which sets the pattern for everything which follows the formative stage. While it may be possible for an attachment disordered individual to become a conventional or better moral thinker and to have better-than-average, emotional intelligence, I believe this to be highly improbable especially if the child is not rescued from the environment to which he was born or there is no significant, intervening variable to alter the fate to which the child is destined.

Most alarming about attachment is that the incidents of such cases are exponentially growing. In my own career, I have seen more than a few times, three generations, as many as seven people embroiled with a child welfare agency. How many times this occurs at a state, provincial or national level is unknown. I do not believe this is a palatable survey to conduct because it is still politically incorrect to explain our deplorable human condition as attributable primarily to inadequate parenting and the adverse environmental conditions created by inadequate parents. It is easier to blame poverty, obstructed access to education, insufficient minimum wages, prejudices, and the list goes on. Through my lens, current explanations and a reluctance to articulate the family/parenting etiology of the human condition problem, has little to do with being correct. Through my lens, it has everything to do with maintaining the status quo, a historically pervasive force to which we have all inadvertently contributed. As the personality disordered individual always finds a negative enabler, according to Bill Eddy, the status quo makes unwitting co-conspirators of us all.

To illustrate further the developmental and environmental lens through which I interpret the world, I will digress and return briefly to the much-debated bible of physicians specialists in psychiatry, the DSM-IV. From my developmental lens, the various DSM-IV labels represent nothing more than ways in which individuals act out the effects of the adverse environmental conditions to which they were exposed, especially as children. The family history of a certain type of so-called mental illness does not represent an innate or genetic disposition. The so-called mental illness represents a pattern of behaviours which was modelled for the child by significant others. Children are keen observers and students of what we do. If I behave, as defined by the DSM-IV, in ways associated with bipolar affective disorder, the possibility is significant that later in life so also will my offspring. Not so curiously therefore, there are familial patterns of acting out, precipitated by adverse early life experiences. While behaving is innate, and we all act out, how we act out is environmentally determined.

I want to conclude this chapter on ethicing by reiterating that every one of us must become experts in conducting this activity. First, we must apply it to ourselves, to ascertain our dominant cognitive moral of developmental perspective and thereby vulnerability, if any, to violate our personal standards by which we want to live. Next, we must apply the activity to the code of conduct and standards to which we hold ourselves as workers, regardless of what we do for a living. Much benefit can come from this to ourselves, the people in our lives, our communities, indeed to the entire human condition. Doing this will serve to better define where we are, what is our starting point and that to which we must aspire.

CHAPTER SIX
STATUS QUO

Insidious Forces At Work

The risk in writing this chapter is being perceived as paranoid-delusional. It is especially risky because the idea conveyed by such a designation includes a rather firm belief that there are actual people plotting, implementing, and monitoring various ways by which to maintain the status quo. When, in fact, there are not. But I put to you, is history not chock-full of verified conspiracies? It was a conspiratorial group of Roman senators who plotted the assassination of Caesar, and Brutus did the dirty deed. Benedict Arnold, the infamous traitor in American history, also was a member of a conspiratorial group as was John Wilkes Booth, who performed the dirty deed of assassinating Abraham Lincoln on Good Friday, 1865. Volumes could be written about the various conspiracies throughout the ages, and probably has been, but we frown at the idea of it still going on. Especially, the status quo protectors, who characterize the very idea as too fantastic and argue that sinister plots cannot be kept secret. In response, I say they can and there are many very current ones to serve as salient examples not the least of which are the events of September 11, 2001. Granted, however, the forces which serve the status quo are profoundly more subtle and more pervasive and span the entire globe. The singular goal is to keep most, if not all, of us in our place.

The other risk in writing this chapter is being perceived as profoundly misinformed about the degree to which such things as information, prices, the engineering of products and so on are deliberately, often maliciously manipulated by, who else, those who benefit from the status quo and therefore are guardians of it. But let us also not forget that every one of us, at one time or another has been an unwitting protector of the status quo for a variety of reasons, mostly of an unconscious nature. It is imperative therefore, that the unconscious, abstract, and obtuse be brought into the light so it can be examined and, from the knowledge gained, finally conquered.

So what is the status of the human condition? It is everything which has been discussed, analysed, and explained so far. It is the general malaise of the human condition by which a disproportionately small group benefit. While the victims of our miserable history are not the status quo many certainly are its protectors, often surreptitiously, who are co-opted into participating in the process of maintaining it. Religion promises an afterlife and eternal salvation. Those who rule the great capitalist dream, promise that success is there for the taking if we are willing to work hard for it. Failing that, there is always the lottery and with a winning ticket you, too, can become one of the privileged few and just in case you might win, do not mess with things, leave well enough alone. Such thoughts have run through the minds, probably of every one of us.

Before elaborating on how the status quo is maintained, not unlike a homeostatic balance whereby in any system all forces are directed towards restoring that which has been disrupted, let us start by putting to rest the myth of lotteries as the road to happiness. Admittedly, you cannot win without a ticket. This is the only truth there is about this social phenomenon. Everything else is mostly a desperate creation of our making. The very fact that I purchase a lottery ticket reveals a self-created myth that I will be the one out of fourteen million who wins the jackpot. While possible, it is highly improbable. Statisticians such as Jeffrey Rosenthal point out that we are a thousand times more likely to die in a car crash on the way to the store to buy the lottery ticket than we are to win it. Said differently, if we purchase one ticket a week, on average we would win the jackpot fewer than once every 250,000 years. Nevertheless, someone always wins, a fact which accounts for the billions of dollars spent on lottery tickets worldwide. The forces of status quo maintenance are well at work and provide feint hope of a huge, financial windfall, one which will allow us to live happily ever after. Was the system deliberately perpetrated on us to curtail our displeasure of life's hardships? No one will ever know. What is known, however, is that gambling of all kinds exists; it is sanctioned by virtually every government and despite the laws of probability working against us all, the lottery business is alive and well. My point is that strategically the lottery/gambling system is a relatively easy way of appeasing the masses. But even for the winners, access to the elite remains as unlikely as having won the jackpot.

There is no denying that there has always been a small group of virtually anonymous elite. Not the rich and the famous showcased by Robin Leach in the years gone by television series or the ever increasing number of media programs currently feeding into our voyeuristic perversion to know about celebrities. I am referring to the virtually unknown powerful, fabulously rich few who keep it in the family and have much vested interest in maintaining the status quo. For example, in Canada this distinction belongs to Paul Desmarais, one of the key players in the life insurance industry through his Power Corporation. Interestingly, most Canadians are said to be unaware of the breadth and influence of this corporation, nationally and internationally. To illustrate the insular and closely guarded nature of this power base it is noteworthy that Mr. Desmarais has been joined by his sons in the family business with their own respective resumés of corporate influence. The daughter of former Canadian Liberal Prime Minister Jean Chretien is married to one of the Desmarais sons. The very next Canadian, also a Liberal Prime Minister, Paul Martin, was hired by Mr. Desmarais in 1974 to be President of his Canada Steamship Lines and then in 1981, Mr. Desmarais made him spectacularly rich by selling the company to him and a partner. Former Conservative Canadian Prime Minister Brian Mulroney also has a close relationship with Mr. Desmarais, who at one time was characterized as being Mr. Mulroney's mentor. Former Ontario Conservative Premiers, William Davis and John Robards, have sat on Power Corporation's national advisory board. John Rae, brother of Socialist former Ontario Premier

Bob Rae, and a one time key advisor to Jean Chretien, was listed as Power Corporation's Vice President, Office of the Chairman of the Executive Committee (Paul Desmarais). I would say this is a pretty elite and impenetrable group not likely to welcome into its fold the lucky lottery winner or the nouveau riche upstart who, against all odds, broke through the status quo barrier.

The American elite landscape is not dissimilar. Bill Gates and Warren Buffett are merely the public faces of the anonymous fabulously rich and powerful small group of elite. Their club is as exclusive with even greater national and international influence on business and government than Mr. Desmarais. The American elite operate through financial institutions, most notably the Federal Reserve system. If you are interested in those who deliberately manipulate the economy, indeed, world affairs, and how they do it, I strongly recommend you read any of the works of G. Edward Griffin. Much of his writings can be accessed on line.

My point in drawing attention to the mostly anonymous protectors of the status quo is to impress upon you that we might as well forget they exist. They are hardly going to be amenable to even giving any thought, let alone relinquishing their power and finances, to support initiatives,ones which will advance the human condition from where it has been stuck virtually forever. This would mean displacing the status quo with a new order, an order into which they cannot fit.

If we cannot work with them we must work around them. To do so requires, however, further exploration of how various factors constantly are in effect to maintain the status quo.

Marketing To Our Greed and Developmental Deficits

For most of the time, most of us are under one siege or another. Our jobs are being taken off shore, teachers are threatened with the loss of their jobs if the "three R" marks of students don't improve, prices fluctuate so much and so fast as to impede planning, and education, especially for the lucrative professions, is increasingly further from our financial reach. No sooner do we pay off our debts, retire, and expect to live the quality of life we dreamed of, then discover that our financial means are being eroded by escalating property taxes and consumer prices. While it is not all gloom and doom, the fact of our collective problems serves as proof that our potential in most, if not all, spheres has been thwarted. Under siege, from all sides, for most of the time, most of us are in survival mode. Under fire, in harm's way, it is difficult to think let alone do something about our personal and collective malaise. We just want to survive the day and recuperate enough to survive the next day. This is a powerful process which serves well the status quo.

Paradoxically, while in survival mode, we are still falling for the old, carrot and stick enticement that money, property, and stuff will bring us happiness. Even though we have all heard and most of us believe "you can't buy happiness", this does not stop us from working long and hard for money. This singular focus obstructs most of us from really examining our lives and, if not subverting the status quo, at least opting out of the rat race. We do what is expected of us not what we prefer, and we believe that we really have no choice. The idea of having no choice indeed is true as long as we want to maintain the status quo, i.e., our wealth and materialistic pursuits.

The power of the status quo forces is so profound as to discount empiricism which reveals the contrary. It is of no surprise that survey results reveal that money spent on stuff, tangible status symbols such as bigger homes, luxury cars, and fancy holidays, does not increase our sense of happiness still, we persist in these pursuits fervently. Moreover, whenever I ask someone to define what is happiness to them, invariably their response is a blank stare followed by ramblings about money. The trouble is that there is some truth to this, and it is this truth which makes out of us all status quo apologists. In 2007, an Associated Press poll found that people who make more than seventy-five thousand US dollars a year are far more likely to say that they are satisfied with their lives than those who make twenty-five thousand US dollars a year or less. Nevertheless, while the average income in the United States has more than tripled in the past fifty years, average life satisfaction has remained the same. Some speculate that you get used to earning more money so, after a while, it does not cheer you up as much as it did at first. The eventual discontent then reignites the whole process all over again, always punctuated by brief periods of satisfaction which rapidly dissipates and are replaced once again by discontent. All of this, I believe, is proof of the status quo mantra doing its job, playing to our conscious and unconscious minds that you can indeed buy happiness.

To reiterate, money can and does play a part in our subjective sense of happiness but in a very limited way. There are, in fact, happiness researchers such as Ed Diener, a Professor of Psychology at the University of Illinois, who tells us that people in poor countries who become richer, indeed, gain substantially in happiness because, with money, they are able to meet their basic needs for food, shelter, and health care. Once average, annual income in a poor country reaches a certain level necessary to meet basic needs happiness plateaus, and rise very slowly afterwards, even if the economy booms.

Richard Easterlin, Professor of Economics at the University of Souther California in Los Angeles, says that money, beyond meeting our basic needs, does not proportionately make us happier because we do not know how to use it well. For example, researchers report that a good family life is worth more than money. I cannot imagine anyone disagreeing with this. Nevertheless, instead of wisely applying our surplus wealth, that which is beyond the requirements of our basic needs, as noted above, we pursue more and in the process of doing so neglect our spouses, our children, in essence our quality of life.

We need not look too far to see alternatives to the North American lifestyle and what impact this has on a national happiness quotient. Specifically, with respect to the family, it is noteworthy that restaurants in Spain close for lunch so staff can go home and have lunch with their families. It is noteworthy that virtually in every European country employment comes immediately with as many paid weeks of holidays as is provided in North America after a decade or more of employment by the same organization. These and other differences contribute greatly to family life. Instead of building the family, in which every child is shaped for the rest of his or her life, the status quo in North America has contributed greatly to what many health professionals refer to as "the breakdown of the family". According to Gabor Maté, family physician and author of Hold Onto Your Kids and Scattered Minds, western society is not family friendly, and as a result, "we are not giving our kids enough of our quality time and we are paying the price". The addicts he works with in east Vancouver are the product of what he calls the "crisis in child development". At least, in part, this is attributable to status quo co-opted parents who are described as busy and stressed out because of their work schedules, which make them unavailable to their children. Many children are put into day care where says Maté, "the ratio of children to staff is not high enough for children to be properly nurtured". When children lack close parental contact they are said to miss out on precious one on one time with their parents. As a result, children look to their peers for love and attention. Unfortunately, from peers, children cannot obtain the unconditional love which would be forthcoming from a competent parent. These circumstances, according to Maté, have contributed to increases in child mental health problems as well as violence and use of drugs among youth. To cope, children shut down emotionally and pretend or actually come not to care. When emotionally shut down, boredom becomes more prevalent. To alleviate their pervasive negative state, they act out in a variety of ways. They use and abuse drugs as well as engage in high risk, dangerous and often violent activities. In this respect, Gabor Maté is of a kindred mind insofar as he, too, believes we are victims of a culture which measures success in monetary ways. In other words, we are victims of having been co-opted to support the status quo. While he does not specifically say that the breakdown of the family is an intergenerationally perpetuated phenomenon, he does call it a "crisis in child development". He identifies the devastating consequences of failed attachment, as occurring during the most crucial formative stage in life. As well, although Maté certainly is not adverse to who have been politically incorrect, he is less than specific about what I believe to be a significant contributing factor to parents being co-opted by the western pursuit of financial success. Specifically, the ease with which we are manipulated is due to our adult inadequacies, related to failed attachment, cognitive moral development delay, and less than an optimal degree of emotional intelligence. At this time, therefore, even if families were to spend more time together, probably it would not be quality time and, as such, it would not alleviate the exponential increase in what is happening to many of our children. Nevertheless, try we must to foster the family, since it is in this context that each new generation is shaped to become the adults who either perpetuate the old dysfunctionalities or play a positive part in creating a new order in the human condition. As such, I am not in complete agreement with Maté's characterization of circumstances as a crisis, one which conveys some recent event which has disrupted the normal course of events. Quite to the contrary, I believe that the normal course of events has been always the obstruction of development and the maintenance of the status quo, accomplished by putting the majority of families under siege.

While someone like Easterlin advocates national initiatives to facilitate better health and family lives, as for example, by doubling the number of national holidays, status quo protectors such a Bill Beach, economist at the Heritage Foundation, a conservative think tank in Washington, opposes having any national holidays at all. He says, "should we be getting into the business of telling people not to work? People might want to work. Work is not necessarily an unrewarding activity". The implicit concern conveyed by Beach is that people not under siege, free to use that for which they have the potential, can be and have been disruptive to the few who benefit disproportionately from the way things are.

Under Siege

The notion of humanity under constant siege bears further elaboration insofar as I believe it to be a significant factor in obstructing our collective development. Consider, for example, the media proselytized war on drugs, on behalf of the government. I believe it first and foremost to be a strategy of distraction. Not unlike the illusionist who distracts our attention from the magic trick, the war on drugs serves to distract us from the root of the problem. Specifically, focussing on the environmentally induced characterological addictive personality trait individuals who demand it. Without addressing the very source of the problem, the demand always will be there, and there always will be ingenious individuals or groups who will respond to this business opportunity. Being at war is pretty serious business which demands a virtual singular focus. It is not unlike the adage that when you are up to your butt in alligators it is difficult to remember that you are there to drain the swamp. In other words, at war, it is difficult to recognize the real problem to be one of demand not supply.

A distraction such as the war on drugs also creates side effects, much appreciated by the protectors of the status quo. To wage the war is expensive. The war diverts funds from where it is truly needed such as better education, better developmental opportunities, and better access to health care services. These adverse environmental conditions precipitate a sense of being under siege, as we worry about our children and what if we fall ill. Consider, the Centre for Uniform Drug Law estimates the war on drugs to cost the United States some forty one billion dollars a year. As such, the war on drugs adds approximately two hundred dollars to the taxes of everyone, not to speak of the hidden costs in wasted resources and economic disruption. Put differently, the funds expended on the drug war could buy every grade school child in the United States a brand new lap top computer every year.

Some status quo conditions serve international interests while others serve the interests of a specific nation or group. The war on drugs serves mostly an American status quo interest and, as such, considerable international initiatives are exerted to co-opt other nations to follow suit. I am specifically reminded of a documentary, some years ago now, prepared by the 60 Minute program on the legalization of drugs in the Netherlands. In a markedly transparent manner, the practice was demonized by showing most probably a very fringe group of drug addicts/users in a park setting. The group was conspicuously misbehaving and was offered as examples of how conditions can degenerate when laws are removed from the arsenal of agents of social control, such as the police. The documentary completely neglected to reveal that drug trafficking is virtually non existent in the country, that people do not have to commit crimes to obtain the narcotics to which they are addicted and that the jails are not overpopulated by people serving drug related offenses such as possession of marijuana. Another example of a national initiative to break from the status quo American agenda is the introduction of a Bill in 2003 in Canada to remove criminal penalties from the possession and cultivation of small amounts of cannabis for personal use. A concomitant, extensive analysis as to the pros and cons of the Cannabis Reform Bill revealed that decriminalization of cannabis probably will not lead to a long-term increase in the use of the substance. Nevertheless the Cannabis Reform Bill was blocked, at least in part, in deference to American interests. Perhaps the greatest obstacle to this forward thinking effort in Canada was the country's sharing of a border with the United States. Among a myriad of interests in maintaining the war on drugs for the United States is its aggrandized propaganda of it being the promised land as opposed to a place of great inequalities, subjugation, discrimination, and pervasive, adverse environmental conditions which obstruct and intergenerationally perpetuate developmental deficits in its population. Deficits which are revealed by a broad spectrum of addictive propensities which include cannabis use.

Those who toil in the genetic explanation milieu, I believe to be inadvertent status quo protectors also. They not only promise an eventual, easy solution by altering some gene structure but also protect our collective delusion that an addictive characterological trait has nothing to do with failures in parenting, failures in family functioning or failures in creating developmentally conducive environments for our children. Even if there is eventually found a well defined inherited genetic cause of drug abuse, who cares? It is still environmentally induced. Would it not serve us all better to divert genetic research concerning addiction to environmentally focussed strategies with which to prevent the activation of an inherent propensity, if indeed it is ever unequivocally proven to exist? It would serve us but not the preservation of the status quo.

The prevalence of Aids in Third World countries is an epidemic particularly effective in creating a siege mentality and thereby serves to curtail initiatives to disrupt the status quo. Current statistics reveal that some thirty-eight million Africans have Aids and more than twenty thousand die of it each year. One country, Botswana, has a forty-four percent infection rate. This epidemic is fuelled by two capitalist, profit driven forces. One is the sexual recklessness spread by pop culture, and the other is the Christian condemnation of condom use. Both forces are status quo protectors. Any ember of hope for a better quality of life in most Third World countries is quicky doused by survival concerns created by conditions which could be alleviated albeit at a cost to the status quo.

War, the actual killing of each other, by its very definition is the essence of being under siege. Contextualizing, rationalizing or justifying war as a cause against terrorism intensifies the under siege mentality. Our efforts are focussed narrowly, living life one day at a time. This works for maintaining abstinence if you are a member of Alcoholics Anonymous but not for improving our lot in life. There is another complication to all wars, namely the cost which is diverted from everywhere else from which the human condition could benefit. The recent cost estimation of the war in Iraq is six billion dollars a month. This is a staggering amount which could more than pay for universal health care for all Americans. Of course, then there are the losses of lives to which everyone virtually reacts the same, justifying the loss of life by justifying the war. It is the rarest of parents or communities which react with intellectual integrity as to the real reason a life was lost, to maintain some small elite group's sense of the status quo and thereby advance their power based on wealth. When the charade which justifies the Iraq war crumbles, when the anti-war movement grows exponentially, as was the case with opposition to the Vietnam War, life-sustaining positive events are precipitated. Such historical incidents, as rare as they may be, give good and sufficient cause for optimism. For this to occur the challenge is to understand and then to put into motion forces which disrupt the status quo. Of equal, if not greater importance, is the challenge of maintaining the momentum of change. Unfortunately, the Vietnam anti-war movement could not sustain itself once the war was over. Despite the fact that the positive energy of the movement could have been well utilized in a variety of other causes, tragically, it simply fizzled out. The few who remain, the few intent on attacking the status quo, simply have not been enough in number to accomplish anything as significant as ending a senseless loss of life through the barbaric, primitive practice of socially sanctioned mass killings.

All social institutions by definition are bureaucracies and the very engines which work to maintain the status quo. There are impenetrable procedures created by bureaucrats, procedures which force us all into compliance. Just try to skip one step in a series of prescribed requirements and see how far you get. Try to be innovative, try to think outside of the box, try to purport when seeking employment that your work experience in one area is related to another, try to argue for an initiative no one else is doing, try to argue: "No we are not doing it but we should be". Just try any of these and see how far you get with formal social institutions. In contrast, the familiar is comfortable and acceptable, perhaps with the slightest of a twist. Compliance, the more eager the better, is warmly encouraged and patience has been and continues to be elevated to the highest of virtues. Above all, play along and do it without even the slightest hint that you aren't playing along, and you will be hailed as the greatest of team players. Thus, the status quo is maintained and life goes on as it has since the beginning of recorded history. Content changes but the underlying structure remains the same.

My boomer generation was afforded anomalous opportunities, I believe, simply because the status quo maintenance forces were in a disarray after World War II and remained to be so for at least two decades. In part, the duration of the disarray also can be attributed to sentiments of gratitude to soldiers returning from the war. For example, they were afforded educational opportunities they would have never had in their socio-economic strata before World War II. This gratitude lingered on to my generation. Regardless of our immigrant working class status - living on the wrong side of the tracks - most of us not only completed high school but a majority went on to complete post secondary degrees. A goodly number went into professions. The sons and daughters of labourers became lawyers, physicians, engineers, accountants, social workers, and psychologists breaking out of the status quo to which they would have been assigned by virtue of the family to which they were born. Needless to say, this loophole in the system has been effectively closed. While a considerable number continue to pursue post-secondary education, an equally goodly number also drop out of high school and become unskilled and unemployable, and rely primarily on social assistance. Since they procreate young, their numbers are growing exponentially. Those who complete a post secondary degree do so at a great financial cost to the their families and/or start their working lives with student loan debts relatively far greater than that which my generation had to contend. For everyone but from the highest economic strata, financially a professional education is out of the question. One year of law school tuition is in the neighbourhood of twenty-five thousand dollars, one year of medical school tuition is in the neighbourhood of twenty thousand dollars. The cost of both is rising along with everything else. The same escalating costs apply to all the other professions, making them out of the reach of the majority just as it was before World War II. The forces of status quo maintenance once again are functioning optimally returning us all to historical times, before there was a discernable middle class. But there are many other variables at work now than there were before, or are there? Will the forces which protect the status quo eventually implode on themselves? One can only hope. Alternatively, the challenge is to finally subvert, conquer, and change beyond the point of no return the stagnation of the human condition.

To illustrate what is possible when people are not constantly under siege, consider for a moment, an example, at least one interpretation of events which resulted in a break from the status quo, a historical event which exemplifies the human potential to reflect, analyse, interpret, and then set out a well defined plan by which to improve the human condition. I am referring specifically to the creation of the Communist ideology. It was conceived and articulated by two German citizens Karl Marx and Frederich Engles. They were two men not under siege. In fact, they led a privileged life afforded at least, in part, by the work of Engles as a manager of English cotton mills. If you have never read the Manifesto of the Communist Party you probably should. It is no more evil than the original message of Jesus. The intent is to replace the existing social and political order status quo, with a different order, an order that is based on egalitarianism. The major difference between the original Christians and the Communist ideology is that the latter was blatantly militant whereas the former pursued change through persuasion. Both movements, however, failed to understand the human condition and the pervasive status quo maintenance forces. Both ideas quickly became distorted/corrupted to serve the immediate need gratification of its quickly emerging elite. The elite group justified its actions from a reference group perspective as opposed to the post conventional level of reasoning on which Christianity and the Communist ideology were initially based. There are other examples of what people are capable, if not under siege, which combine to justify the optimism that the plan in Part Three will indeed come to fruition, albeit in five generations.

I hope to have made the point that the obstacles to freeing and thereby actualizing the human potential are formidable. They come in a variety of shapes, mostly subtle often disguised as paternalistically well intentioned. The protectors of the status quo can be academics intent on identifying how many and what kind of angels can dance on the head of a pin; well intentioned authorities who insist on telling us all that problems are complex and require lengthy comprehensive investigation before any effort at remedy can even be contemplated; bureaucrats who require absolute compliance with procedures or gun toting conservatives willing to shoot and kill in the name of God anyone who threatens the status quo, especially those who have a plan or anyone actually doing something specific. The tale bearers, social activists discussed in Part One, at the very least, all expose the status quo forces. Those who oppose the social activists, as for example, the "Nay sayers" about global warming, in contrast are all deliberate or inadvertent deniers that status quo forces even exist.

Before concluding this chapter, I need to acknowledge that while I am not predisposed to abide by rules simply because they exist, I do recognize the need for rules, standards, and prescribed procedures. As time consuming as some rules may be and as little transparent sense some appear to make, for the sake of orderliness, fairness, and completeness we cannot coexist without them. The antithesis of the status quo therefore is not anarchy, the wanton pursuit of immediate needs, concern only about what I can get away with. Instead, the antithesis of the status quo is a systematic, well defined and purposeful plan to foster the optimum growth and development of each and every child. For it is not our genetic, hereditary makeup, which obstructs us but environmental conditions of our own making which rob us of that which is there for all of us, literally, just for the reaching.

PART THREE

THIS IS WHAT WE NEED TO DO!

PART THREE

PREAMBLE

Before we embark on any journey there must be a drive, a desire or need to do so. The impetus may be entirely voluntary and based upon the pleasing anticipation either about the process of getting there or being there or both. This can apply to a much needed and earned holiday or a self-initiated desire to lose weight, get into shape or to gain control over a debilitating dysfunctional propensity. Alternatively, a change process can be externally driven, such as attending the funeral of a relative on another continent; bad news after an annual physical, a diagnosis which forces us to do something about our lifestyle or a spouse taking a stand: Either we change our ways or the relationship is over. Whatever the source of the impetus to change, there is no journey without some reason to do so. The entire premise of Part Three also is drive determined and is based on answering for ourselves the question: "Why Bother?" Why not let events take their inevitable course? Why not let economic, social, and environmental factors culminate in their inevitable conclusion? If it entails the demise, indeed the extinction of the human species, so be it. After all, the human experiment, beyond some notable exceptions, has been rather a disaster. Moreover, we probably are not going to be able to adapt quickly enough to conditions of our own making. It is unlikely that we can adapt our respiratory system to function on carbon dioxide as opposed to oxygen. It is unlikely that we can adapt our finely balanced, physical makeup to function in conditions of extreme heat or cold, nor are we likely to evolve gills so that we can live underwater after all the polar icecaps and all the glaciers melt. As the end nears, our suffering will exponentially increase, but we won't be there to experience the pain. It will be the suffering of future generations not ours. So let the next generation worry about it, which in practice, albeit not in rhetoric, is what has been happening from one generation to the next for millennia. For all the talk about leaving a better legacy to our children and grandchildren, nothing is more than rhetoric as evidenced by all that was reviewed in Part One. Even as I write this, there is another report of David Suzuki saying to another audience that businessmen and politicians are forgetting the environment as they make economic decisions, thereby they treat economics as the source of everything. He is reported to have said that: "Instead of looking at the next quarter report, let's look at the next generation". In the same presentation he also chastised society's reliance on technology to produce cleaner emissions and fix polluted sites. Some may say that Suzuki is just beating the same old drum because he has no new material to say or that his talks are now redundant since we all get it and change is in the making. Personally I could not disagree more! While increasingly more people are recognizing that we are in trouble there are not enough objectively measurable processes in place. Most discernable so far are articulated good intentions.

By these comments, I do not wish to discount or in any way diminish existing and continuing initiatives. Certainly, modern cars spew far less pollutants into the atmosphere than cars did a decade ago. Some industries have increasingly better scrubbers on their toxic pollutant emissions and there is a growing acceptance of recycling procedures to name just a few good changes. Therefore, it is not all doom and gloom. Moreover, the positive initiatives serve as concrete evidence of what we have the potential to do. I agree with Suzuki's ongoing message and share his fear that we cannot, must not, rest on the laurels of some change since it is so easy to stagnate in complacency. I also cherish and honour the tenacity of all activists. By what they say and do, they are not only raising consciousness but also creating, cognitive conflict. This is an essential but not quite sufficient state of mind without which cognitive development cannot occur.

The question remains, however, how can we become proportionately mobilized to act when our cognitive developmental perspective remains stagnated as described in Part Two. If not in pursuit of immediate need gratification, at best, we are acting according to the membership requirements of our reference group. To sustainably do that which we must, to fully comply with, for example, the Kyoto Accord, requires post conventional reasoning from which we are far removed. Exploring the existential question, "Why bother?" therefore, is futile, let alone expecting an answer, which will serve as an impetus for sustainably concerted actions.

A viable solution to the impasse created by our collective

developmental malaise is to accept the reality of the human condition and to work with it. The reality is that the majority can relate to a reference group perspective. An example of applying this fact will serve to illustrate how it can work to bring about a significant, sustainable, and desired change.

In Canada, some two decades ago, a law was implemented concerning young offenders. One of its requirements was to segregate young offenders, eighteen years and younger, from adult offenders. Whereas their marked propensity to act out was curtailed previously by older offenders, this influence was lost when the young, markedly dysfunctional males were grouped together. Administration crafted rules, enforced by enhanced staffing levels, simply were insufficient to curtail what adult offenders were able to accomplish in the previous system. Violence among the young offenders became rampant. When victims were placed into protective custody the size of the protective custody group quickly grew and violence emerged among them. We quickly realized that creating an ever increasing number of protective custody groups was not only impossible but would not have solved the problem we were trying to address. Necessity being the mother of invention, or in this case, serving as an impetus for desperate correctional staff to try an innovative approach, we invoked the dynamics of a reference group perspective. Simply put, we played on the developmental reality that group membership, through compliance to group norms, is paramount to young people in a far more immediate way than it is for adults. Group membership was important not just for the victims of violence but also for the perpetrators, the dominant youths in our residential secure custody facility. We made and implemented strictly the rule that any transgression would garner a negative consequence for the entire group. All privileges, including weekend passes, movie or pizza nights, excursions, and so on would be lost to everyone, regardless of how important or planned in advance. While the process was far more onerous in practice, the abridged version should serve to illustrate how social science knowledge can be applied in a practical way. Suffice it to say that all violence, quickly abated, and we were able to sustain the gains by applying the tenets of the reference group perspective.

On a much broader scale, the same tactics can be applied with equal success. It requires grass roots, community initiatives, whereby we deliberately articulate and act upon beliefs and values, which will advance and not curtail the human condition. As such, we cannot look to government regardless of its ideology or to business or organized religion to do the right thing. First we must look to our respective reference groups to advocate for initiatives conducive to promoting the optimal development of our children. Eventually government, business, and religion will respond to our respective reference groups but it will take at least one generation of better developed youth before you can reasonably expect support and buy in from the institutions.

That which is advocated in Part Three requires the educational system to get the ball rolling. I have agonized over this much but have not been able to find an alternative agent of change. In many respects I am not surprised by this since our advancement as a species, as shabby as we may be, primarily is attributable to education, specifically literacy. Many consider the greatest invention of all time to be the Guttenberg Press invented in the year 1436. This invention precipitated unbridled dissemination and access to information. Third World countries are even less functional than First World ones primarily because of continued illiteracy and markedly curtailed access to education other than indoctrination into religious and/or cultural ideologies. To get the educational system involved in the change process, however, will be a formidable undertaking because it is a significant, inadvertent status quo protector and because it is politically influenced, in some jurisdictions directly and in others at greater arm's length. Nevertheless, there are various local governance influences, especially on pre and elementary school systems. There are volunteer and elected, community representatives who govern or oversee educational organizations, and it will be through these groups that change gradually can be precipitated. My optimism in this rests with my often quoted Anthropologist Margaret Mead: "Never doubt that a small group of thoughtful, committed citizens can change the world; indeed it's the only thing that ever has". Whereas she was counting on a group, to change the world, I am advocating for several grass roots group initiatives.

To reiterate my introductory comments, it will all start with individuals asking themselves: "Why aren't we doing this?" and then talking with others in their reference group until the entire group adopts the idea of promoting the optimal development of every child as a fundamental principle to which the group subscribes. Eventually, in such groups, membership will require believing and valuing this principle.

Perhaps this is a personal limitation of mine, but I can't imagine anyone objecting or disagreeing with the goal of promoting every child's optimal development. I can, however, imagine the most staunchest of status quo protectors paying lip service to the idea and then continuing to do the same things, their rationale always couched in the position that further study is required to determine what really defines optimal development and how do we really go about promoting optimal development without indoctrinating our children with values which are reference group or situationally based. I also can very easily imagine, since I have seen it in the professional journals, academics aiding and abetting the status quo protectors by their well-socialized and practised propensity to argue the minutest of details from every which perspective and to debate how many angels can really dance on the head of a pin. I do not intend to sound cynical or derogatory to any or all such groups. I believe that they all believe, as individuals and as professionals, that they are behaving responsibly, indeed wisely, are promoting caution lest we go astray. But we are astray, stagnated in the development of our optimal potential. How much worse can it be? We have done it all: The Christian inquisitions, the burning of witches in Salem, Nazism, and whatever new human debacle is lurking in the wings at this very moment. I say again: How much worse can it be?

However, there are justified reasons to be optimistic since not all of us are developmentally stagnated. There are many principled people amongst us who quietly go about doing the right thing simply because it is the right thing to do. Often they do not draw attention to themselves because they reason and behave in a principled manner and not for attention or notoriety. Sometimes, however, circumstances bring attention to principled post conventional thinkers and doers, and thankfully so. Without such circumstances, which reveal to what we should aspire, the very idea of post conventionality would remain an abstraction. But it is not an abstraction because if there is one Nelson Mandela, if there was one Mahatma Ghandi, one Martin Luther King, one Mohammed, one Jesus or one Buddha, their very existence proves the possibility. Having established that something is possible the challenge is to have more of it. Admittedly, this is easier said than done. But why can't we have ten, a hundred, a thousand or ten thousand Nelson Mandelas, Ghandis or Buddhas and others such as they? Why can't we have most of the human species achieve optimal emotional intelligence, the post conventional perspective, and act accordingly? Perhaps we could reason and behave even better and in ways beyond our current abilities to define. I believe we can! The challenge is to create circumstances which are inconsistent with the current and past conditions, conditions which have persistently curtailed the innate developmental potential of us all. Admittedly, to precipitate an exponential increase in the number of principled individuals amongst us will not be an easy undertaking. This brings us full circle to the question: "Why bother?" Perhaps the simplest answer is, "Because we can we must".

Part Three begins by delineating the anatomy of deliberate change. It is intended to be a recipe anyone can follow. As all recipes it is not carved in stone. It can be modified as long as the underlying structure of the method is maintained and as long as the underlying structure of the method can break through the insidiously pervasive successes of the status quo protectors. Chapter Seven therefore, begins with the vision followed by a delineation of key objectives through which the vision will be achieved. Instead of speaking in parables, in the language of the Old and New Testament, the Koran and the Torah, Chapter Seven is intended to be conceptually and operationally practical. Within our everyday abilities to do. Simply put, and something to which many can relate, Chapter Seven is a modern, strategic plan to achieve the vision of the prophets. This is grandiose only if you believe ambition, forward thinking, and a desire for a better life for your children and grandchildren also are grandiose. No one believes such a thing, so Chapter Seven operationally defines the vision and the objectives through which it will be achieved.

Chapter Eight identifies the initial key actors in the change process. As alluded to earlier, the initiative must come from grass-roots activists who are assembled into many small groups each comprised of thoughtful, committed citizens of the kind whom Margaret Mead described. The chapter concludes with describing the basic conditions required to get the change process started and to keep it going until the process acquires a sustainable life of its own. Once a certain momentum is reached, the change process will accelerate exponentially and will no longer be the initiative of a few but the will of the majority.

In the interest of practicality, Chapter Nine concludes this work by describing, in preliminary detail, a five-generation long critical path. Approximately a hundred year endeavour. Hopefully, it will require less time, but in the grand scale of things a hundred years is not long at all. The notion of a critical path draws extensively on the work of Buckminster Fuller who, in 1947 worked with Brazilian business interests to implement a fifty-year industrialization plan. In 1997, reports revealed that the plan achieved at least 80% of what it started out to do. In my books, an 80% mark in any subject or endeavour is commendable. Moreover, the reported grade evaluation underscores what can be accomplished with focussed, time targeted effort. Unfortunately, for the human race most, if not all, herculean, seemingly impossible efforts have been exerted on technological tasks. It is time to try our hands at changing the human course with as much deliberateness and commitment as that with which John F. Kennedy marshalled the technological forces of the USA to land human beings on the moon and return them home safely.

The greatest challenge in writing Part Three was not to bore you to death with mundane detail. It also was a challenge not to repeat what has been said earlier. Most importantly, while the recipe for change may lack an element of excitement about it, I hope this will be compensated for by the absolute doability of the task at hand. All it requires is the will to get it started.

CHAPTER SEVEN
THE ANATOMY OF CHANGE

The Vision

Throughout my career I have facilitated the development of numerous strategic plans. By definition, the intent of each plan was to achieve something. Sometimes the goal was vague and at other times with help it was specific. The impetus behind these plans ranged from addressing something aversive to actively responding to changing environmental conditions. Almost always, which seems to be the human way, action was precipitated by some degree of pain. If the pain subsided the strategic plan was placed in abeyance until the pain intensified again. It is too bad that we have to be virtually in excruciating pain before we decide a change is necessary. But that is the way it is, at least for now. Suffice it to say, as was reviewed in Part One, there is enough global pain to serve as an impetus to embark on a transformation. The task therefore, is to define the change, to what.

Whenever I facilitate a strategic planning session my first task always, and I do mean always, is to define and differentiate between a goal and an objective. The need to do so invariably is signalled by people talking simultaneously about multiple goals and objectives as if these aims were synonymous. They are not!

For a plan to succeed there must be one, and only one, goal. Some people call it a vision and some a mission. Regardless, there is only one goal and that goal cannot be achieved directly. The goal only can be achieved indirectly, specifically by successfully accomplishing a number of related objectives. The importance of understanding this specificity cannot be overstated. Furthermore, it cannot be overstated that most people, at least in my experience, the point initially is lost. Considerable time and effort is required, in each instance, to reach a shared understanding about this. Only then is it possible to create a viable plan, one which will produce the desired outcome.

Our first task therefore, is to define operationally what is our vision for the human race. Fortunately, we don't have to do this onerous task ourselves. It has been done for us many times and by many people who we refer to as prophets. For the sake of brevity, I chose the message of Jesus to illustrate this. I could just as well have chosen Mohammed, Buddha or for that fact the I HAVE A DREAM speech of Martin Luther King or the song IMAGINE by John Lennon. But let us just examine the message of Jesus, mindful of the fact that whether he really existed or not or if he is God or not, is quite irrelevant. What matters is the message!

In Part Two, Albert Nolan was provided as a very useful

reference for understanding the message of Jesus in the context of the language of the time. Three passages from Isaiah (29:18-19, 35:5-6, 61:1-2) make reference to a variety of ailments such as being deaf or blind and being cured in the "kingdom" of God. The ailments, in the context of the time, were simply different ways of describing the poor and the oppressed. Therefore, the healing, the restoring of sight and of hearing, the bringing of joy and so on, Nolan contends, were different ways of describing liberation from oppression. The message of Jesus was that of hope, based on the innate developmental potential of human beings. The message of Jesus was that of good news because it was hopeful and encouraging, in today's language, motivational to action. Nolan and other scholars, are emphatic that the hopes articulated by Jesus originally had nothing whatsoever to do with heaven. Certainly not as a place of happiness and rewards in the after-life. In fact, for the Jews and Jesus there was no thought of people going up into heaven after death. The Christian belief in heaven originated after the death of Jesus, largely at the hands of the Constantine commissioned Architects of the Council of Nicea. It was a powerfully convenient way of appeasing the oppressed masses. It invoked the Beatitudes attributed to Luke (6:20-21) in which it is written:

> *Blessed are the poor*
> *because yours is the kingdom of God*
> *Blessed are you who are hungry*
> *because you shall be satisfied*
> *Blessed are you who weep now*
> *because you shall laugh*

The good news of the "kingdom of God" was news about a future state of affairs on earth when the poor would no longer be poor, the hungry would be satisfied, and the oppressed no longer miserable. According to Nolan, the Christian conception of a heavenly after-life is attributable to a mistranslation of Luke (17:21) "the kingdom of God is within you". Today all serious scholars and translators reportedly agree that the text should read: "the kingdom of God is among you or in your midst". Alternatively, the misconception may well have been deliberately created by the authors of the Council of Nicea. Regardless, the point is salient to the task of formulating a vision statement for humanity. Before doing so, let us consider further the message that life can be markedly different, void of oppression, here on earth.

Most references in scripture to the "kingdom" is as something that is yet to come. The "kingdom" will not be something within a person, it will be something within which a person can live. There is therefore, a pictorial image of the "kingdom", one which depicts a place, a community, a walled city with a gate or simply a house where a festive meal is taking place. According to scholars such as Nolan, the fact that the "kingdom" is based upon a pictorial image of house, city or community leaves no doubt that the promise is of a politically structured society of people here on earth. The concept "kingdom" as used in scripture, according to religious scholars, is a thoroughly political notion. Nothing which has ever been attributed to Jesus' sayings, even remotely, suggests that he might have used the concept "kingdom" in a non-political sense.

When Jesus reportedly said, "My kingdom is not of this

world" (Jn 18:36) scholars contend that this did not mean that the "kingdom" is not or will not be, in this world or on this earth. Similarly, when Jesus and his disciples are said to be in the world but not of the world, the meaning is that although they live in the world they are not worldly. The meaning is that they do not subscribe to the values and standard of the world at the time. The values of the "kingdom" are different from and opposed to, the world in which Jesus lived. To interpret the notion of the "kingdom" as something floating in the air somewhere above the earth or as an abstract entity without any tangible social and political structure is simply said to be wrong.

The message of Jesus, therefore, is said to be a liberating admonition to overthrow the Satan, the power source of evil in all its shapes and forms. As Jesus and his followers understood it, at their time in history Satan ruled the world. Theirs was a perverse and sinful generation, a world in which evil reigned supreme. This was evident in the suffering of the poor and the oppressed. It was evident in the hypocrisy, heartlessness, and blindness of the religious leaders and in the merciless avarice and oppression of the ruling classes. Jesus condemned all the political and social structures of the world, as it was in his time, as all evil. I daresay he would evaluate similarly current conditions while steadfastly holding on to his message that the potential to realize the "kingdom" here on earth exists, as it has always done so, prevented only by the myriad of obstacles to our cognitive moral and emotional intelligence development. To reiterate, therefore, what really matters is the message. First and foremost the message, of all ancient religious messages, is the potential quality of life available to us all here on earth, during our lives. It is there but for the development of our potential, which clearly is much easier said than done. Very little has changed since Jesus condemned the world of his time as evil.

This, then, brings us to what is entailed in this "kingdom" of which Jesus spoke or in today's language, what is the vision to which we should commit ourselves. Continuing with the Christian reference, suffice it to say that in the "kingdom" wealth is diametrically opposed to the idea and, thereby, also its puerile, Stage Two driven, pursuit. Truly the pursuit of wealth and prosperity as the song goes "cannot buy you love" or a quality of life void of the need to do evil. By which I mean the oppression of others to advance your pursuit of wealth and possessions. To define something by a list of what it is not, however, only is marginally useful. Therefore, let us examine how the "kingdom" was described beyond the political entity referenced above, and then let us look at some modern descriptions of what we ought to be striving for.

Consistent with the message that there will be no place in the "kingdom" for the rich, Jesus asked for a total and general sharing of all material possessions. The best example of this message is the so-called miracle of the loaves and fishes (Mk 6:35-44). It is noteworthy that the incident was interpreted by early Christians as a miracle of multiplication although this is never explicitly written anywhere. Instead, it is said by religious scholars to be a remarkable example of sharing. When those in attendance ceased to be possessive about their food and began to share, they discovered that there was more than enough to go around. The same was discovered by the first Christian community in Jerusalem when they divested themselves of their respective possessions and shared the proceeds according to what each needed. Jesus, however, did not idealize poverty. His concern was to ensure that no one would be wanting because of the avarice, greed, and conspicuous consumption of a few.

In the "kingdom," in our vision of the future, there will be equitable sharing and as such no poor or rich. To give up surpluses and to share also requires trust in others to do the same. Not unlike the prisoners dilemma non-zero-sum game paradigm mentioned in Part Two the best, most mutually beneficial strategy is to co-operate but to do so requires trust and the belief that others will do likewise. In the "kingdom" there is sharing, trust, and co-operation by all for the benefit of all.

In the society in which Jesus lived, money was second only to prestige. Everyone had a place on the social ladder based on ancestry, wealth, authority, education, and virtue. It was paramount to know your own place in the precisely detailed hierarchy of the community. Jesus absolutely contradicted this elitism. For example, his criticism of the Scribes and Pharisees was not of their teachings but of their life consumed by the quest for prestige and admiration. When asked, "Who is the greatest in the kingdom?", Jesus offered the child, not as an image of innocence, immaturity or irresponsibility but of littleness. In the society of the time along with the disabled, children were totally excluded, they were insignificant and lacked all status and prestige. This is said to reveal that Jesus valued humanity not status or prestige, since humanity is inclusive whereas status or prestige is exclusive and antithetical to sharing and unqualified co-operation. In this context Jesus gave the same value to women as to men.

The "kingdom" as described by Jesus also embraced the collective. Not the collective of the Stage Three reference group perspective described in Part Two but the all-inclusive solidarity of the human race as defined by the principled cognitive developmental perspective of post conventional Stage Six reasoning. This is said to be a significant departure from the Old Testament perspective of "love your neighbour," a perspective which was restricted to kin or at best the reference group. Jesus extended one's neighbour to include one's enemies, in other words, all people, a notion completely unheard of in his time. He was asking for the group solidarity of the family to be replaced by the more basic solidarity with all human kind. Pretty revolutionary thinking at the time and probably is true currently from the perspective of many. Hopefully, by now, you are beginning to see that I am taking this process in order to articulate a modern expression of the vision for the human race. Let us continue, however, for a little longer before concluding with the goal we set out to define in this chapter.

The last but by no means the least aspect of the "kingdom" concerns power. Society and power are inseparable since by the very definition of society, there is a delineation of who has power over whom and who can decide what for whom. The message of Jesus was clear that in the "kingdom" power will be totally different from power as it existed in his time. At the time of Jesus, the power of evil was manifested in domination and oppression. The message of Jesus was that in the "kingdom" power will be derived from service and freedom. Instead of power being served because of domination that is afforded to it, in the "kingdom" power will have influence in the lives of people by being of service to them. Moreover, Jesus, according to the scholars, saw the use of Hebrew law as a means of oppression used by Jewish leaders such as the Chief Priests, Elders, Scribes, and Pharisees. Not that he was opposed to the law as such, he was opposed to the way people used the law. This harkens back to the earlier discussion about the futility of trying to control human behaviour by passing more laws. Then and now, the law was and continues to be a burden rather than a service to human kind. In the "kingdom", power, authority, and law, according to the message of Jesus, will be purely functional. They will constitute the arrangements (Social Contract) which are necessary if people are going to live co-operatively together. Consistent with post conventional principled reasoning, in the "kingdom" described by Jesus, every kind of domination and every form of slavery will have been abolished.

So let us review, the "kingdom" here on earth described by Jesus as being within our potential to achieve. Instead of embracing a capitalist, unbridled pursuit of materialism, the "kingdom" will be defined by sharing. Instead of pursuing at all costs prestige in the "kingdom", all humanity will be equally valued. Instead of aligning with either our nuclear or extended reference group, in the "kingdom", the good of all - the collective - will be the concern of everyone. Instead of being subjugated to the power of elite individuals or an expanding array of laws, in the "kingdom" both will be put to the service of the people. Indeed this sounds like heaven because it is so appealing and because it seems so unobtainable here on earth. But is this really so? Probably not on both counts. It is probably not appealing to everyone, certainly not to the majority of cognitive developmentally delayed individuals. As you will recall, one cannot relate to reasoning more than one stage above the perspective of the individual. As such, the message of Jesus was and continues to be lost on most people. Hell, damnation, fire, and brimstone are what preconventional thinkers can relate to, nevertheless, the message was given by a principled person. The structure of the message is consistent with post conventional reasoning. The appeal was not to preconventional thinkers but to those who could relate to it. We can only guess that Jesus intended to stir their leadership into action and to deliver the masses, not out of the allegorical desert but out of the evil of their time. From my perspective, the gift of Jesus, indeed all of the prophets, to the human race was their insight about the human potential. Their unqualified belief and vision for the human species has been articulated superbly by at least two, incredible modern visionaries, Martin Luther King Jr. and John Lennon of the Beatles. Specifically, I am referring to Reverend King's I Have a Dream and Lennon's Imagine. I believe that both encompass, in modern language, the tenets of Jesus' "kingdom" and the ideals of Stage Six, principled reasoning about justice. If you have not read Reverend King's speech, delivered on the 28th of August, 1963 at the march on Washington for jobs and freedom, I urge you to do so. If you read nothing else, I have recommended so far, read only this. To spur you on, let me quote the last phrases;

> "All of God's children - black men and white men, Jews and Gentiles, Protestants and Catholics - will be able to join hands and sing in the words of the old Negro spiritual: "Free At Last! Free At Last! Thank God

Almighty, we are free at last!"

John Lennon's lyrics echo the same vision, especially regarding the abandonment of the mystically created, fanciful idea of a heaven in the clouds. His song begins;

> *"Imagine there's no heaven*
> *Its easy if you try*
> *No hell below us*
> *Above us only sky*
> *Imagine all the people*
> *Living for today"*

Lennon continues the song in, two more verses, by lyrically voicing the conditions of the "kingdom", sharing, the collective good, and living in co-operative harmony:

> *"Imagine there's no countries*
> *It isn't hard to do*
> *Nothing to kill or die or for*
> *And no religion too*
> *Imagine all the people*
> *Living life in peace*
> *Imagine no possessions*
> *Wonder if you can*
> *No need for greed or hunger*
> *A brotherhood of man*
> *Imagine all the people*
> *Sharing all the world"*

Protectors of the status quo have and continue to characterize the modern language used to described the "kingdom" as the musings of dreamers and idealists who have little appreciation of reality. These same people also subscribe to a distorted interpretation of Jesus' message, a message which has to do with an afterlife, and in so doing obliterate the message of hope and potential on earth. By presenting to you I Have a Dream and Imagine as our vision for the human race, I have probably alienated a major segment of the human collective who subscribe to racial and religious intolerance as well as those who insist on the literal and distorted interpretation of scriptures. This leaves now a far smaller grass roots initiative to embark on the journey we must.

So far, I have not stated why the preceding has particular appeal to me and why I selected deliberately this strategy to articulate the vision for the human race. Clearly there is a direct correlation between the tri focal lens through which I interpret events and how I see the world as described in Part Two. Of equal importance, beyond the appeal of the message, is that there is a well defined behavioural prescriptive to the message. In other words, the ideas embody in them what one must do to achieve that of which one is capable. Simply put, the challenge is to have, at any given time, the majority of the human species reasoning and behaving from a post conventional, Stage Six principled perspective. To reiterate the theme, if there was one Mahatma Ghandi, one Martin Luther King, Jr., one Nelson Mandela, one Jesus and so on, the challenge is to have hundreds, thousands, indeed millions of such principled individuals who will comprise the majority of people as opposed to the minority status that they currently have. To me, the idea is appealing because it is doable. But it will take time, and probably at least five generations of purposeful, deliberate, and developmentally facilitative administrations to our children. The greatest efforts are expanded prenatally and during the most crucial first two years of their life. The remainder of this chapter, therefore, focuses on the objectives and concomitant actions through which the "kingdom" on earth will be realized.

As an introduction to the objectives it is important to explain that before optimal parenting is realized prenatally and during the most crucial formative stage of life, certain prerequisite conditions must be achieved. Moreover, the intent is not to inculcate the populous with any specific ideology, values or systems of beliefs, although, admittedly, this can be a very fine line on which to balance. The intent is to optimally promote all aspects of human development. To do so will require simultaneous initiatives, some remedial and, eventually, all preventative. Prevention best accomplished by positive, well-informed parenting of all our children.

I have chosen to begin with remedial initiatives intended to curtail the exponential growth of maladaptive dysfunctionality attributed, indeed caused by, inadequate parenting. Beginning with remedial initiatives is easier since many good interventions already are being done. The challenge is to promote the practices everywhere and perhaps to promote their more competent performance. It is always easier to do more of, and to do better, that which is already in the human repertoire than it is to initiate something completely new. Admittedly, there is virtually nothing which needs to be done, even of a preventative nature, that is not already being done by some people somewhere. Therefore, it is really a continuum of activity which I will discuss, starting from the more familiar and moving to the less familiar of initiatives. Since everything which needs to be done, of a preventative nature, is already being done, albeit to less than an optimal degree, there is much justified cause for optimism. The challenge is in the doing, and the devil is in the details. Once convinced to take certain action, human ingenuity can be incredibly creative in solving obstacles.

The two categories of objectives I propose, by no stretch of the imagine are all inclusive. You are welcome, indeed encouraged, to identify more. The activation of the objectives I have proposed must not be linear, that is to say sequentially implemented. Simultaneous action is required, invoking a critical path strategy, that will be discussed at length subsequently. For now, the focus must be on children. Numerous objectives must be activated at the same time to ameliorate the adverse conditions in the lives of children in order to prepare the youth of today to be the better parents of tomorrow. The operative terms are "simultaneous activation" of both categories of initiatives, although the largely preventative measures will require some prerequisite foundations to be established.

Remedial Strategies

Remedial strategies are required to engage our youth and the troubled adults in their life. Engaging our youth should occur in elementary and secondary schools. After that efforts such as pre-marriage and parenting courses produce diminishing results. For example, while there is no systematic data collection about the efficacy of pre-marriage courses, most of us know experientially that people marry and that marriages break down regardless of what objective input couples might have received prior to their wedding day. In a pre-marriage course, with a ceremony date set, most people are in a euphoric state harbouring great and pleasant expectations impervious to what a pre marriage course leader might have to say. In contrast, children in elementary school and even in high school can be very curious and receptive to information about relationships, especially their demise. Children's receptivity always is determined, as you will recall from Part Two, by the presentation of information no more than one stage removed from the cognitive developmental perspective through which they interpret experience. For elementary school children, this means that new information is presented from a Stage Three, reference group perspective and for high school children from a Stage Four, social perspective. The goal is to create cognitive conflict to which they can relate and, of equal importance, resolve by actively creating new meaning and better, more comprehensive ways of reasoning about life, especially relationships.

The focus at both educational levels must be on what constitutes competent parenting and how to choose a compatible procreation mate. Building knowledge and facilitating developmental gains in these two domains is markedly incremental. Even more incremental is acting on what is learned. Some educational systems, however, do incorporate these two areas of knowledge into their curriculum. I am aware of parochial school systems focussing on these two areas from grade one to the end of high school. I am not aware, however, of any widely published outcome studies. Nevertheless, I cannot imagine such efforts, even if poorly done, not producing at least some discernable positive outcome.

> **RECOMMENDATION** 👍
> Every school everywhere in every grade should have in its core curriculum the elements of competent parenting and how to choose consciously a compatible procreation partner.

Now, more so than ever, there is a proliferation of excellent parenting books. The strategies are not value laden and they do not proselytize a particular ideology. The parenting strategies are derived from understanding what environmental conditions promote optimal physical, emotional, psychological, and cognitive development. I hesitate to offer examples because the list can be onerous to create. Nevertheless, there are some seminal works about which everyone should know, such as that of Barbara Coloroso and Thomas Lickona. Their work and that of others can inform and elaborate on the recommended parenting curriculum. The twelve-year parenting and relationship curriculum among many other topics should include empathy training. Such training is essential to establishing a secure attachment with a child during the most crucial first two years of life.

There are several empathy training programs for children. One with which I am particularly familiar is Roots of Empathy. Its aim is to reduce aggression through the fostering of empathy and emotional literacy. The program is aimed at children aged three to fourteen years. In addition to reducing aggression, the program also is conducive to later life empathic nurturing. This is essential to establishing a positive attachment as discussed before. As part of the program, children observe a loving parent-child relationship. This models for them competent parenting. Empathy also is a prerequisite to successful learning. According to some studies, the academic success of students is corelated with an advanced ability to communicate with others and to recognize that others view the world differently. When identifying elements of emotional intelligence, empathy plays a significant part in its composition. In brief, Curriculum Canada, the country's leading standards agency, highly endorses the six hundred and thirty-nine page 'roots of empathy' curriculum divided into nine themes.

In the same vein, a study by the University of Washington's Social Development Research Group demonstrates long-lasting effects from a program which teaches impulse control in elementary school. The program involves not only the teacher and students but also their parents. The program focusses on teaching children how to get what they want without resorting to aggressive behaviours. A key element in the program is empathy training, i.e., learning how to recognize the feelings of others. The more social skills with which children are provided at an early age, the more functionally adaptive they will be later in life. These programs should be universal; they should be part of the core curriculum in every school.

While the innate propensity to behave co-operatively can be lost forever if not activated environmentally at a critical time, this does not mean, however, that remedial initiatives cannot produce beneficial results. For example, years after school racial integration, close examination revealed that desegregation is more likely to increase prejudice between blacks and whites than to decrease it. Instead of the the well-intentioned but horribly misinformed tactic of creating a melting pot, children were found to gather ethnically and to separate themselves, for the most part, from other groups. Furthermore, inter-ethnic interaction in the harsh, competitive, academic environment does not lead to greater liking but, in fact, continued exposure under unpleasant conditions was found to create less liking. In response to this unintended result came the idea of "co-operative learning". The tactic is simple: Replace competition of classmates with co-operation. The idea came from Turkish-born social scientist Muzafer Sherif, who investigated inter-group conflict at boys' summer camps. The solution to escalating discord and hostility among the boys instigated by the experimenters, as part of an experiment, was simple and effective. The solution, in fact, was not unlike the best solution of Anatol Rapoport to the prisoner's dilemma game. The Sherif group constructed a series of situations in which co-operation was necessary for mutual benefit. After a number of conjoined efforts toward common goals, the competitive hostility among the various groups of boys disintegrated. This is not unlike the initiative described earlier in which I was involved in controlling the acting out behaviour of young offenders when they were required by law to be segregated from adults.

From the discovery of Sherif regarding the behaviour of boys at summer camps came the "jigsaw classroom" developed and tested by Elliot Aronson and his colleagues. The essence of this method is to require that students work together to master the materials scheduled for an upcoming examination. The students were organized into co-operating teams and each student was given only one part of the information - one piece of the puzzle necessary to pass the examination. As such, everyone needed everyone else to do well. In this milieu, students became allies rather than enemies.

In subsequent studies, especially in desegregated classrooms, the jigsaw approach to learning precipitated significantly more friendships and less prejudice among ethnic groups than traditional teaching methods in the same schools. In jigsaw classrooms everyone benefits in a variety of ways. Fortunately, the positive findings of these early experimenters had legs of longevity. Co-operative learning has been the mainstay of many professional schools, especially schools of business and medicine. It also is present in both primary and secondary grades and is constantly evaluated and fine tuned. Nevertheless, co-operative learning is no silver bullet which will save the day or solve all of our social woes. It is, however, clearly a powerful strategy when combined with other tactics. It will, indeed does, go a long way to facilitating the development of our children to become functioning adaptive adults. Jigsaw-learning programs also should be universal. They should be a significant teaching strategy in every school.

There are a myriad of courses, scattered everywhere, which challenge our elementary and secondary school students to reflect on crucial social issues. Their beliefs and the values are instilled in them by social forces, not the least of which, are the media. The cognitive conflict precipitated by many atypical, educational experiences of this kind is to choose between quality rather than quantity of life and to define what constitutes quality and quantity. Such efforts are intended as antidotes to persistent efforts to convince us that we must consume to have a good life; that we must spend our money, and that we must not think about things which do not have a commercial or monetary connection. Instead of offering an alternative value system, such efforts are in fact challenging our youth to think for themselves, to figure out for themselves what is really important rather than being told or pressured into joining one gang or another. From my perspective, such anomalous efforts are developmentally stimulative and also should be a part of all primary, and secondary, educational curricula.

More to the point, it is noteworthy that among most scholars, the importance of moral education is unequivocal. There are many programs in effect, whereby developmentally conducive interactions are shaped intentionally by educators to promote an adaptive sense of self and a sense of the other. The focus is not only on the differentiation of "the self" from "the other" but also on the different needs, interests, and welfare of the self and others (empathy), differences which must be balanced and actively furthered within and through interaction. How this balancing and enhancement is best achieved in any given instance is the object of moral education. Such education is best accomplished when the class is part of a greater school milieu referred to as a "just community" or "participatory democracy". More will be said of this later. Here, I refer you to the work of Dwight Boyd, Clark Power and many others who write about moral education and who teach the teachers who do it.

By now you will be aware that there are many developmentally conducive, educational programs in effect throughout most of the world. To list them all would not only be an extremely formidable undertaking but for our purposes not necessary. Eventually, somebody, some group of people will have to do this, however, if for no other purpose than to select the most effective, empirically proven approaches designed to facilitate optimally the cognitive developmental perspective and emotional intelligence of our children because this will make them in turn better parents. You may rightfully wonder after reading that there are many developmentally conducive programs why they have had no discernable effect on the human condition. I know that they all have had a positive impact albeit not yet wide spread. This impact has not yet reached a critical mass. The very purpose of this book is to hasten the process of reaching the critical mass that will produce the discernable impact on the human condition so overdue.

The quality of our relationships also is a significant determinant of how we function and behave at any given time. As children, the quality of our relationship with our primary caregivers is paramount, as discussed in Part Two. Then, it is our relationship with our peers, evolving to the selection of a romantic partner, the person with whom we choose or inadvertently procreate. This phenomena of romantic attraction requires some further elaboration. It has been my personal experience that during special anti-violence retreat days, students were extremely interested in my workshop entitled "When Romance Turns to Abuse". The two hours allotted were never enough. When the room was filled to capacity there were more who wanted in, and, when our time was up, they always wanted to discuss the topic further. The workshop content was fashioned after the seminal work of Harville Hendrix whom I referenced earlier. Interest in the content I attributed to the novelty of talking in a systematically rational way about something important to the pubescent students. It would not be unreasonable to argue, therefore, that the topic of relationships be a part of an educational curriculum from grade one to the end of high school.

The romantic love of which Hendrix talks is relatively unique to the world. It also is relatively new even to the western world starting sometime around the 16th Century. Prior to this the dominant form of marriage was the arranged one and based upon economics, politics or social position. This form of marriage, in fact, remains numerically dominant in the rest of the world and is followed by the slave marriage arrangement in which the purchased spouse usually is a woman. Of course, this is not to say that love-based relationships have and do exist in all cultures. The question that is salient, in reference to raising children, is the relative benefits of love or arranged-based marriages. From the lens through which I view the world, love based marriages are more conducive to promoting the optimal development of children. This is so because a marriage based on love and mutual selection requires freedom of choice and gender equality. Nevertheless, as Hendrix so aptly points out, this principle is hardly sufficient since the selection of a partner, in a love based situation, is arranged by the unconscious, a force far more insidious and powerful than any cultural or patriarchal perspective. When the unconscious judgement about the object of affection is wrong as to the person's ability to satisfy specific, unmet emotional needs, joyful anticipation quickly turns to disappointment, then to resentment, and even to hostility. Parents in such states have their emotional, empathic nurturance capabilities compromised, if indeed they had any to start with. Of equal importance, they cannot create an environment which is conducive to promoting the optimal development of a child because they are under duress and focussed on their own unmet emotional needs. For the sake of generations of children yet to be born, it behoves us also to improve the abilities of each new generation to select better a romantic partner and then, most importantly, the partner with whom to procreate.

With our primary grade-school children we should start by exploring values and why we like and dislike certain things, including people. The exercise of raising their consciousness, encouraging thinking, and deciding for themselves can nicely serve as a segue, in high school, to the topic of romantic attraction. While it will be some generations away before a love based choice will be easier to make, with a better probability of success, current choices can be improved vastly by introducing an element of rationality. In better love-based marriages, children will fare better in a myriad of ways. For instance, we can expect a decline in the number of diagnosed cases of so called attention deficit hyperactive and other childhood disorders. When children are nurtured better, when their parent-created pre and post natal environments are better, because the relationship between their parents is better, specific necessary conditions for positive attachment to occur are achieved. All of these factors combine to reduce and eventually eliminate the occurrence of children acting out their emotional turmoil in increasingly more troublesome ways. This will then stop the drugging of children with Ritalin, an achievement which will benefit even greater their children and their grandchildren. Intergenerationally, not only dysfunctionalities are perpetuated. So are good things perpetuated. Therefore, the recommended focus on relationships and attraction should also be a universal part of all school curriculum.

Making children aware of the profound unacceptability of abuse is yet another recommended remedial intervention. Not just aware of the unacceptability of physical abuse but every kind of abuse, including but not limited to emotional and psychological abuse both of which can take the form of either assault or neglect. Diminishing the occurrence of abuse will positively affect progressively each subsequent generation until the time comes when no one will accept abuse as the norm in relationships.

This recommendation is remedial because there are many such programs available and in use already. Of particular excellence is the phoenix whicht rose out of the death of a daughter. Donna Spears of Oakville, Ontario, created the Spears Society as a response to romance turning violent. Her daughter, in her teens, was kidnapped by a spurned boyfriend who then murdered her. This event followed the murder of my best friend's (Jessie Smith née Edwards) parents by her sister's also spurned boyfriend. The synergy created by these events culminated in the production of a film: Monica's Story, and an accompanying manual for focussed discussion by high school students. When the Spears Society closed, the educational tool was handed over to the Canadian National Film Board for distribution. It is readily available, literally for the asking. While it has been used widely both nationally and internationally, it should be used in every high school, not once but every year until every child has seen it from each of his and her invariant hierarchical developmental perspectives and participated in discussions about it.

Before addressing remedial efforts with adults, I would like to address possible criticisms of the previous discourse. I believe that there is much cause for optimism about positively impacting the development of our children. Just as the messages of Gore and Suzuki about climate are of hope not doom so also is my message. To illustrate this point, I want to give you some examples of extraordinary children. Extraordinary because of their achievements, what they achieved is attributable more to the environment in which they were raised than to their cognitive intelligence. The salient point is that cognitive intelligence accounts for success minimally. As discussed in Part Two, the greater determinant of success is emotional intelligence and cognitive development, which include a number of variables such as empathy. Moreover, and this is the point, everything which makes up emotional intelligence and promotes cognitive development are environmentally induced. The examples, therefore, are not of superior cognitive intellect. The following examples really are of young people who, securely attached to their primary caregivers during the most crucial formative stage of their life and subsequently, lived in an environment, created by their parents, which was conducive to their optimal development. Another cause for optimism is that there are many such children out there. Unfortunately, their good news most often is perceived as not worthy of media coverage. Some have made it into the papers, however, and serve as evidence in support of Part Three.

There is Andrew Lambert and Peter Martorellie, two McMaster University students in Hamilton, Ontario. Both reportedly enjoy an active social life including drinking beer and watching Sunday afternoon football. In fact, they say that they spend as much time socializing as they do studying. Martorellie is pursuing an MBA and Lambert is in the Mechanical Engineering program. Both are twenty-one years of age and both are repeat winners of the Provist's Honour Roll. That means they achieved a 90% or better in all their classes since starting university. Incidentally, there were thirty-seven others, albeit not repeat winners, of this award. While the achievement of the two is truly remarkable, what is even more important is that there are people out there who give cause for optimism. What if these two kind of boys became the majority rather than the minority in universities?

Then there is Kayla Cornale, a so-called, whiz kid from Burlington, Ontario. She earned a scholarship to study sciences at Stanford University and was selected from seven thousand nominees from eighty countries to be one of eighteen finalists in the 2007 CNN Heroes; An All-Star Tribute. As a finalist she won $10,000 and won another $25,000 for inventing and refining a patented learning system which teaches autistic children language through musical tones. The impetus for her invention, Sounds Into Syllables, was a young autistic cousin. Kayla was in high school at the time. Most assuredly Miss Cornale is blessed with considerable innate cognitive intelligence which, however, also needed environmental activation to begin the actualization of its full potential. The need for activation was discussed in Part Two. But more importantly if she only has high cognitive intellect, while necessary it would have been insufficient to achieve what she has done at such an early age. Her success, the success of every other nominee and the success of every other similar young person, from the lens through which I view the world, is primarily environmentally determined. An environment, which was created by parents or a parent, was at first conducive to attachment achievement and subsequently to cognitive moral development and the development of superior emotional intelligence. Every so-called whiz kid is as much of an example of intergenerational perpetuation of a family legacy as is every acting out, troubled underachiever.

The importance of environment needs more elaboration since the plan is to have each successive generation create progressively better environments for their children. While environment is clearly necessary, this, too, is insufficient, since what also matters is the aptitude of parents, to perform the onerous task of promoting the optimal development of their children. Without aptitude for the role of being a parent, taking a toddler to the opera, a concert, to the zoo, or building a vast library of information for him is good but not good enough, as demonstrated by the analysis of Levitt and Fryer of academic performance data collected on 20,000 children from kindergarten through the fifth grade. Their data includes demographic information, interviews with the students' parents, teachers, and school administrators. Their conclusion is that parents do matter a great deal with respect to how children perform. What matters, however, is who they are not what they do as parents. From the perspective of Levitt and Fryer, the emphasis on child-rearing techniques appear to be highly overrated since who a person is determines whether he seeks knowledge and skills, what knowledge and skills he seeks and then most importantly how he applies what he has acquired. Specifically, the results of Levitt and Fryer speak to an individual's aptitude to be a parent. Fortunately, those with an aptitude for parenting invariably, by definition, create and sustain environments which are conducive to optimal development. When, in five generations the minority of the Kaylas, Andrews and Peters become the majority business will not go on as usual. This will mark a total disruption of the status quo, characterized by the current materialism, consumerism, the destruction of the environment for immediate gain, corruption, and greed. A proliferation of such young people growing into adulthood and perpetuating their legacies intergenerationally will bring us remarkably closer to what all the prophets said we have the potential to achieve here on earth.

Simultaneously to attending remedially to our children, it is necessary to attend better to the adults in their lives. Especially adults who are responsible for the exponential growth in the dysfunctional maladaptive population which is rapidly approaching a worrisome mass and may one day consume us all if not curtailed. Admittedly, this comment verges on blaming the victims of corruption and if nothing else, in most circles, meets the criteria of being politically incorrect. Be that as it may, it is an undeniable, statistical fact that there is an exponential growth in dysfunctionality, in poverty, in unemployability, addiction, and various other behavioural disorders in the adult population. To various degrees and with various levels of competence, there are programs to address their needs. Most probably all are necessary but, once again, insufficient if a significant developmental component is missing.

> **RECOMMENDATION** 👍
> Each and every adult focussed program, whether aimed at addressing illiteracy, poverty, criminality, addiction, perversion, aggression, violence, abusive behaviour or mental illness, however it is defined, should incorporate a significant focus on habilitation and social integration.

In one way or another troubled adults have influence over the lives of our youth. Some of those who are troubled come to the attention of authorities who feel compelled to help them. Such helpers with very few exceptions are well-intentioned but most often are ill informed. Often they also forget some of the fundamental basics of their training. Namely, the first task is to evaluate the person's awareness and/or acceptance of a problem. Without accepting the presence of a problem, efforts to be of assistance to individuals at best is compromised and at worst is a waste of limited resources. When little changes in the cognitive developmental perspective and concomitant behaviour of such adults, almost always they compromise, to various degrees, the positive, developmentally conducive experiences of their children. To focus on reducing the stress of an inadequate parent by teaching relaxation techniques may be helpful to the parent in the short term but does nothing to address the underlying reasons for that parent's distress.

The first step in the Alcoholics Anonymous twelve-step program best illustrates this point. In spite of the reality of alcoholics' troubled lives, the first obstacle to change is accepting that they have a problem. In the social sciences, this is referred to as being in a state of denial. For the majority this can be understood best as the creation of a pleasing fantasy by a cognitive developmentally delayed adult. Functioning from the cognitive developmental perspective of a child, the troubled adult can pretend with much success and for an indefinite period of time. This developmentally delayed propensity is especially enhanced when the individual is placed under duress and regresses even further to an earlier childlike way of thinking and behaving.

Most criminals and addicts manifest this dynamic. As such, they are not in need of rehabilitation or reintegration as discussed in Part Two. They need to be habilitated so that, at a higher stage of reasoning, they have more difficulty, or cannot, sustain their self-created, pleasing fantasies about themselves, their circumstance, and especially their abilities to parent. This is a prerequisite to accepting a problem and doing something about it. Once a problem is addressed, brought under control, the next task is to facilitate integration, since throughout their lives they have always felt themselves alienated from the mainstream of society.

Parents who are in a protracted, adversarial, legal conflict with a child welfare agency are almost always first and foremost in a state of denial, mainly because of their cognitive developmental delays. All they would have to do is to admit to having a problem, one which put their children at risk and necessitates their children's apprehension by the state. To address and bring their problems under control would require less effort, time, and difficulty than the protracted, adversarial, legal process, a process which for most of them, fails to achieve the vindication they fantasize is owed to them. Of course the problem is that they cannot admit to the existence of one, let alone more than one. Of equal importance, those who counsel them, more often than not, fail to recognize and act on the habilitative needs of their clients. The entire process negatively affects the apprehended children because their status remains unresolved.

The strategy to habilitate adults is remedial because it seeks to repair damage which was done. It also is noteworthy that such efforts are taking place in several locations, albeit clearly not everywhere. Also, I am absolutely heartened to read some of the literature about therapeutic communities in which talk is of habilitation and integration. This is evidence that at least some mental health professionals are beginning to abandon the medical model of rehabilitation and reintegration, although it has been slow in coming. Nevertheless, change is in the air, and I don't think we will regress. The challenge is to propagate these changes so that we can learn from the efforts of others how best to habilitate troubled adults and then integrate them into the mainstream of society from which they always were alienated. Effort with adults can only add to all the various habilitative efforts with children.

Anything insightful or inspirational which is targeted at adults invariably is habilitative in focus and challenges the individual to a higher level of reasoning and behaving accordingly. Anything which challenges materialism, consumerism, and advocates finding meaning promotes maturity. By maturity I mean the ability to see beyond the immediate here and now and to recognize that there are broad and long term consequences to what is done. It is seldom articulated in this way probably because mental health professionals or authors neither want to risk turning off their readers nor risk being politically incorrect. They do not want to risk being perceived as too simplistic in their formulations about the malaise of the human condition. Inadvertently, by being cautious, inspirational professionals, especially authors, are playing to the guardians of the status quo who do their job by confusing us all with their insistence on complexity. After all, complexity requires further research, scientific debate, exploration into various possibilities; all of which takes time and the allocation of much financial resources.

This is very reminiscent of what we are told by Griffin, as referenced in Part One, about the cancer research business. Just because a solution is simple it does not make it wrong. And even if a solution is simple the doing is hardly ever. With respect to adults, the doing pertains to knowing about and having the skills with which to work towards habilitation and integration, in addition to whatever else is being focussed upon. There is much written about this by a variety of authors referenced in Part Two. To reiterate, the therapeutic community literature is especially worth exploring because of its emerging, non-medical perspective as is made evident by reference to habilitation and integration. As well, what Lickona has to say about methods for raising good children I have found quite useful when working with adult groups of offenders and individuals. The point is we are doing it already. We just need to do more of it.

If, indeed, we are doing most of what needs to be done what is it that we are not doing that we should? What are the innovative, anomalous objectives through which we will also have to reach the goal referred to earlier as the "kingdom"? At first this was very much a perplexing question, probably because I too was co-opted to look for something complex or profound. This markedly distracted me from seeing the obvious.

Innovative Strategies

The most important innovative strategy will be an incredibly hard sell, let alone implement in a timely way. Sell and implement, however, we must. We should have started yesterday.

To persuade you, to sell you on the idea, I have borrowed from Cialdini's elaborations on the most successful tactics used by what he calls compliance professionals (a nice term for sales people). The strategy is to invoke the sales tactic of social proof. It is a simple strategy, one which takes advantage of our Stage Three, reference group perspective. Most of us determine what is correct and decide whether we should or should not do something based on, in part, what other people consider as correct. From a Stage Three perspective, a behaviour is more correct in a given situation if we see others perform it. More often than I care to remember, after a carefully researched and crafted proposal presentation of a proposal the first response from the executive decision maker was, "Who else is doing this?". In other words, the phenomenon of social proof is the path of least resistance to decision making. Our behaviour in this respect is neither negative nor positive. It is what it is, and how it is used determines its value. I intend to use it positively.

Consider the medical attention given children pre and post-natally and until they reach some magical age when they enter the ranks of how adults get treated. Consider also the types and numbers of pediatric specialists. Consider how many jurisdictions have specialized children's hospitals and the fact that almost every hospital at least has a pediatric wing. Consider what we are willing to do and pay when our child is sick. Consider what we are prepared to donate and approve when it comes to flying a child from some remote area of the world to have an unsightly or lethal tumor removed from his face. These examples are all very familiar to every one of us.

Now juxtapose the above examples to the previously referenced Early Years Study and the unequivocal fact that the most important time in an individual's life is the first two years and, perhaps, a few years after.

I suppose pediatric care is a service which we use where money and the cost of expertise is no object because of our primary drive to procreate and the value we place on a new life. This explanation also helps with respect to the "money is no object" approach we have to post-secondary and graduate education, especially of service professionals such as physicians. They may become the saviours of our infants' lives, we reason.

But what about the quality of their lives? What about the quality of their development? What about the quality of their environment? Because we remain stuck on life, not its quality, the answer is that these matter far less. Admittedly, we have made advances and some cultures more so than others but the reality of most children is that after a mother's maternity leave expires, and should both parents be working, the child is left with a babysitter or a live-in nanny. Some children are shuttled to a set of grandparents or the grandparents come to the child. As soon as possible, the next phase is day care, where many children are accepted while still in diapers. Even more shocking is that in many day-care centres, children are dropped-off at 7 a.m. and picked up at 7 p.m. Even if a parent is off from work, the routine is maintained, probably because the parent is in dire need of rest.

Now, consider what we expect, and pay for, from the caretakers of our children after the first year of their lives. Most often grandparents are paid nothing, and we expect from them no more than what they gave us when we were infants in their care. We pay, very little for the services of a nanny and an early childhood educator compared to medical pediatric specialists. Often, a nanny is from another country seldom if ever with any or sufficient training. Those who come with training, such as an English Nanny, at best bring knowledge and skills equivalent to a graduand of a two-year, community college, early childhood, education program. These young, college graduands, to whom we entrust the stimulation, development, indeed, the very lives of our vulnerable children, are paid slightly more than minimum wage in most jurisdictions. We pay elementary school teachers considerably better; we give them winter, spring and a considerable summer break. High school teachers enjoy slightly better pay with the same benefits as the elementary school educators.

The pay scale and benefits of university educators, compared to the early childhood educators reaches a ridiculous disparity. The primary responsibility of university educators is to disseminate information and to teach some skills to young, fully formed people. At least people well beyond the most important formative stage of life bringing with them a myriad of later life consequences formed by their childhood experiences. This is of little concern for most university faculty who are preoccupied with their own research and fully or partially paid sabbatical (time off). I do not particularly care about what we pay university faculty or the various perks which come with their chosen career. I take issue, however, with how educational finances are distributed because the rationale is of a status quo maintenance nature.

> **RECOMMENDATION**
> Financial and educational resources should be gradually reversed so that the best trained and the best paid are our early childhood educators who take over the facilitation of a child's development from a primary caregiver after the completion of the most crucial formative stage in a child's life.

This is not a nonsense, pie in the sky ambition, especially if the plan is to have it implemented gradually, by each better developed generation. As generations evolve and become capable of higher stages of reasoning, the preconventional perspective which focusses only on life and not its quality will be replaced by a far more comprehensive view as to what is important in life and what initiatives are worthy of support.

This is also a two-part recommendation, one being much easier to implement than the other. In France, and the province of Quebec in Canada, there is an advanced perspective about the care of children. This is evident in policies and procedures both of which affect child care. It would not be a huge stretch to rationalize extending maternity leave by a year or more until the end of the child's most crucial formative stage. The government-funded maternity leave would guarantee future savings. Borrowing a few paragraphs from the Early Years Study should be sufficient to make this argument and to justify the cost. Of course, the remedial strategies should have some impact on the stay-at-home parent. What good would it be for an inept parent to stay at home for two years with a newborn infant?

The second part of the recommendation will be far more difficult but not impossible to achieve. The task will be progressively less obstructed by progressively better developed, emotionally intelligent generations.

The first task is to change the qualification criteria of early childhood educators. It should reach toward the requirements of a pediatric specialist. The operative term is reach toward. To begin this paradigm shift, it will be necessary to provide the student, early childhood educator, with far more knowledge than possible in a community college and far more time to assimilate what is learned. A four-year specialized, university program is ideally suited to accomplishing this task. Once knowledge is acquired and assimilated, the next obvious requirement is skills development. A community college or technological-institute, two-year program is ideally suited for this task.

After six years of post secondary education and training, it will then be necessary to pay our early childhood educators according to the importance of their work and the degree of expertise required to perform it. "But where will these funds come from?", is the anticipated refrain of the status quo protectors. In addition to the gradually accrued savings from diminishing numbers of troubled children and adolescents, at least some of the funds can be derived from a different formula for funding our universities. Most are already significant, entrepreneurial enterprises, ones which should be fully encouraged, but differently funded. Instead of direct tax-based payment, universities should be classified as special, non- profit entities allowed to hold unprecedented tax exempt savings, ear-marked for staffing and supporting their entrepreneurial activities. Additionally, staffing and research should be derived from grants and donations, a practice which already is well established in many jurisdictions. In fact, in most jurisdictions, universities and their entrepreneurial initiatives enjoy non-profit status. This, some contend, give them an unfair competitive advantage in such areas as the development of new drugs by university laboratories. In this paradigm shift, faculty whose primary interest is education, should continue to be tax base funded, at least in part. They can hone their skills as educators, and the researches can be freed of the burden, of having to deal with those troublesome and demanding students who invade their research sanctuary from the Fall to the Spring of each year.

I do not, for a minute, believe the preceding to be outlandish ideas or myself to be foolish for admitting having them. While not often, paradigm shifts have occurred in history and continue to do so to this day. However, delineating the details through which change can be realized, at this time, is not nearly as important as selling the idea. My intent is to stimulate ideas not to prescribe a formula. Admittedly, the devil will be in the details of implementing this proposed principle. Nevertheless, when the change begins and how it progresses will assuredly take many shapes until it culminates in attending, in mind and deed, to the quality and not just to the lives of our children.

There is another marked innovation required in order to achieve the vision given to us by the prophets. The innovative, objective really is a way of comprehensively implementing the remedial strategies. It is derived from my personal experiences as a social work clinician in a prison setting. Regardless of how effective a group or individual therapy was, the inmates left the room to return to their residential units housed in the larger institution. The majority of their time therefore, in spite of the daily intensive, intervention models, was spent on the residential unit and in the greater institution. This reality quickly became obvious because gains in therapy were being eroded outside of the meeting room. To counteract this, we introduced in the residential units and in the whole institution a therapeutic community. This was no easy task but one which had to be done. My experiences working in prisons are not, if at all, dissimilar with what happens in our preschool settings, in elementary, and high school. Even if all, and more, of a recommended, habilitative curriculum is implemented at each phase in our educational system, there are mitigating conditions outside of the classroom which will diminish the gains students make inside. Therefore, discernible, focussed, and well informed action is required.

> RECOMMENDATION 👍
> From pre school to the end of high school, each and every facility should be operated as a therapeutic community whereby all procedures and all activities support classroom curriculum by being conducive to optimal development of cognitive moral reasoning and emotional intelligence.

All schools must be run like therapeutic communities simply because by definition the fundamental tenets of this approach are habilitative. While the idea may be objectionable to some, on the basis that the children do not need therapy, they are going to school to learn how to read, write, and count. On closer examination, very few will object to the idea of schools also promoting the development of their children. This will require, however, some effort to convince inadvertent status quo protectors, especially of the ilk who are concerned that their children will be inculcated with the values and ideologies of someone other than themselves. I suppose that in some respects, the recommended strategies are threatening for the very fact that, indeed, an ideology is being advocated, (if one can call promoting optimal development to be that). Of course, from my lens, promoting development is neither an ideology nor a value system. It is functional, that is to say, life sustaining as opposed to the path of destruction we have been hurdling upon, as discussed in Part One.

Briefly, let us examine the basic tenets of what constitutes a therapeutic community. For a thorough discussion and as an ideal reference, I heartily recommend the work of George DeLeon on this topic. However, you will have to extrapolate significantly from his work to discern the relevance or applicability of the approach to a school setting. More to the point and easier to extrapolate, is the early work of Kohlberg and his colleagues in a woman's prison setting. They called the strategy The Just Community Approach To Corrections. In their 1974 manual, they presented both the therapy and the practical implementation of such a community at the Connecticut Correctional Institution at Niantic. Around the same time, I also modelled a prison based program on their approach and enjoyed significant, measurable success over a three-year period. Subsequently and for over sixteen years, I have been primary consultant to two residential facilities based on the model, although we call it a Participatory Democracy. It also is noteworthy that Larry Kohlberg built on his prison experiences by chartering the idea of just community schools, the activity in which he was passionately engaged prior to his death in 1987. There is also the Association For Moral Education founded for the purpose of fostering communication, co-operation, and research among professionals who are concerned with advancing both theory and practice in the field of moral education. Doctors Ann Higgins and Clark Power, Kohlberg's colleagues, have done much in the field of implementing and evaluating the just community approach to participatory democracy in high school settings. The innovation in the above recommendation is to structure all school settings, including pre elementary, on this model.

To tweak your interest in this method of structuring all schools, a brief review of how all this is done may suffice. It is demanding but not impossible. It requires effort but the payback is many-fold. It is a novel way of resolving competing claims but not entirely unfamiliar and, therefore, a part of our existing cognitive and behavioural repertoire.

In a therapeutic community and participatory democracy, the focus is on development and not on controlling behaviour through discipline and punishment. Discussion and disagreement is encouraged and role-taking is an essential element of what and how things are done. Decision making also is required from everyone and active discussion is the primary tool for resolving issues. The discussions are structured and facilitated in small groups and as community meetings. Exile from the community is the tactic of last resort, and zero tolerance is defined as a criteria for invoking individual and collective responsibility, activated through reflection and dialogue in groups of various composition and size. From a practical point of view, peer relations and relations between students and staff, inside and outside of the classroom, always are structured to be optimally conducive to development. The aforementioned cooperative strategies to foster learning skills ideally fit into this milieu and model of education.

Clearly there is much more to creating a participatory democracy in a school setting. Moreover, there is no rigidly prescribed format to follow, albeit certain conditions do have to be satisfied. Well-informed creativity should always prevail as long as the focus is on the students' development. The very process of resolving that which obstructs is developmentally conducive in the just community educational setting. Furthermore, as in the prison settings described earlier, so also in just community education settings, bullying and violence are eradicated.

As you will appreciate by now, to find something innovative to do, as an objective through which the vision set out in the beginning of this chapter will be realized, requires some far reaching. Far reaching simply because there is little new under the sun. This is a good thing because it feeds into the earlier discussed tactics of compliance strategists described by Cialdini. If someone already is doing something somewhere, it is easier to persuade someone to do something similar here and now. I do believe, however, that engaging pre and elementary school children in methods to which high school children are exposed, is very much out of the ordinary and would go far to achieving the five generation plan envisioned in this work. Of course, how you engage younger children requires tactics which are mindful of the developmental perspective through which they interpret experiences. Fortunately, children are ripe for development because they are innately curious, explore, test their environment, and observe intently what we do around them. Children are not only interested in how inanimate objects work but also how they should behave as individuals at any given time. This curiosity is either fostered or not in a child's environment. If it is fostered before they attend preschool and in preschool, so much the better. These children will be voracious consumers of the recommended curriculum and milieu in which it is delivered. If their innate curiosity is not fostered, if their spirits already are broken before they attend preschool programs, it is still not too late. It will be far easier to begin fostering their moral and emotional development in pre and elementary school, even high school, than to start with them as adults in some therapeutic, correctional, halfway house facility.

You should know that the preceding ideas concerning cognitive moral development and the development of emotional intelligence abilities are very much evidence-based as are the ideas and practices of therapeutic communities. Simply put, each is capable of being measured. In fact, the quantitative evaluations have been essential to building knowledge as well as skills in these areas. My point is that each and every initiative, in the pursuit of the development of our children, must incorporate an evaluation/ measurement component for a myriad of reasons, not the least of which, entails knowing objectively which efforts are producing the results desired and which fall short of the mark.

> RECOMMENDATION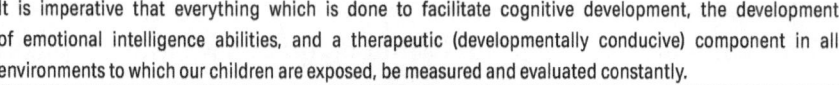
> It is imperative that everything which is done to facilitate cognitive development, the development of emotional intelligence abilities, and a therapeutic (developmentally conducive) component in all environments to which our children are exposed, be measured and evaluated constantly.

The importance of this recommendation is derived from the necessity to guide, by means of objective data, the efforts of the doers. The process of change must be dynamically responsive to quantitative and qualitative feedback. Do more of what works and what produces desired results most effectively. Eliminate or fix what does not work by understanding why the intervention did not produce the desired outcome. Fortunately, evaluation methods exist, one method is to solicit, for example, from those involved their subjective assessment as to how helpful and responsive to their needs is the environment in which they spent their time. This type of feedback is essential to move forward and to fight off stagnation for both staff and the individuals on whose behalf programs are initiated. When efforts are measured, everyone is served well and the morale of everyone is pervasively positive and, most importantly for staff, it brings greater meaning to their professional lives. Needless to say, the exponential beneficiaries of the recommended paradigm shift in our educational focus will be the majority of youths in each successive generation.

In conclusion, this chapter was all about actions conducive to development and the acquisition of abilities all which ultimately must start with how we treat our children. Very early in life, and before adults have the chance to inadvertently destroy children's sensitive sociability, children are acutely aware of that which we do and, if what we do promotes, the vision of the prophets this ultimately will forever change the course of our future. Children, indeed all of us, begin life as moral beings who are concerned about being and doing good. Granted, at first, we want to please who cares for us but we come to grow morally as a consequence of learning how to be with others and how to behave in their world. Whatever we learn is facilitated by what we see and hear. To date, what we have seen and heard has not been terribly conducive to our growth and development. As such, much has and continues to take place which diminishes and obstructs the development of our humanity. To quote psychoanalyst Carl Jung, " We all walk in shoes too small, diminished lives not in accord with our potential." Consequently, we have as a collective subjugated ourselves to the status quo and by omission, if nothing else, allowed the emergence of powerful and corrupt individuals in every generation. In our vision of the future, conditions will obstruct the emergence, especially the power of such corrupt individuals. They will always exists, unfortunately, but their power will be inconsequential when the world is comprised almost entirely of optimally emotionally intelligent and morally principled individuals. The next chapter deals with who will get us there.

CHAPTER EIGHT

WHO WILL BE THE AGENTS OF CHANGE

Grass Roots Doers and Those Who Don't

I began the introduction to Chapter Seven by referencing my facilitation of strategic plans. Each step in the process is of equal importance and requires equal attention and effort to address. So far, we have defined a vision or goal for the human species by using modern language to articulate the message of the prophets, messages which were virtually identical, regardless of the prophet and the time each lived. The next step was to identify and elaborate on the remedial and innovative objectives through which the vision will be achieved. It cannot be overstated that a goal, a vision or a mission, cannot be pursued directly. It only can be achieved through the completion of objectives. It is imperative that the operational definition of each objective be stated in an observable and measurable way. That will come at the hands of the implementers. My primary purpose is to sell the ideas and then to spur creativity by beginning the process of change. I hope it will take on a life of its own by morphing into forms, methods, and a language, all of which will resonate with the local agents of change until such time as everyone speaks the same way, shares the vision, and agrees with how to get there.

As with all initiatives, big or small, trivial or important, complex or simple, the challenge always is persuading people to action. More often than not, the best laid strategic plans die on the flip chart papers because the doing did not get done. The doing in such instances remained inert because of the people involved. Leadership was lacking. No one identified and assigning task completion responsibility to the appropriate people. Our crucially important task here is to identify rationally who or which group, makes most sense to be the harbingers of change?

As a prerequisite to talking about the doers I must elucidate the inherent assumption I am making. Specifically, if you have read this far, I hope that you are in agreement with the need to do something drastic and that you recognize that without circumventing the status quo, sooner than later, we will reach the point beyond which there is no return from our decline into extinction. I am assuming also that you are in agreement with the vision, as set out by the prophets and reiterated here along with the objectives through which it will be reached.

These are critically important assumptions because if you are reading this, you and whoever you can recruit are the initiators, agents of change. Nothing else matters much other than believing in and behaving as an agent of change.

Fortunately, the very survival of the human species rests

upon your shoulders. You will need, however, some assistance to begin. Just remember what Margaret Mead said: "Never doubt that a small group of thoughtful, committed individuals can change the world - it is the only thing that ever has".

So the next step, even before you complete reading this book is to start recruiting likely coconspirators to overthrow the status quo. Admittedly, this is a little bit of an overstatement but sometimes superlatives are necessarily to concretize the message. Once you have a small, committed group of individuals you then have to focus on influencing simultaneously a specific group of people, teachers, and the social institutions, educational systems in which they do their work. Teachers and the educational system are going to be our salvation. I say this fully cognizant that the profession and their administrators will be, for the most part, reluctant rescuers of the human species. However, there is no one else, individual or group, to whom we can look.

We certainly do not need more prophets. Those of us who can, get it, those of us who can't get it, will never get it. The task is to alter the intergenerational perpetuation of their family's respective legacies of not getting it. This requires working on the aforementioned objectives.

Before elaborating as to why the teaching profession must be the virtual saviours of the human species, albeit reluctant ones, we need to examine the major groups who cannot take on this task. This needs to be done to dissuade you from trying, thereby wasting your time with these groups. In addition to the profession of teaching, I can offer you only three other factions, ones which pervasively affect how human beings develop and, as a result, how the status quo is maintained. The first and most obvious faction is the nuclear and extended family. The second is organized, institutionalized religion, and the third is political ideologies which seek to control our behaviour for self-serving purposes. The media, in the various forms they take, are simply a tool, a very powerful tool, used by organized religion and political ideologies to achieve their respective self serving agenda, ie., the acquisition of power by maintaining the status quo.

So let us first dispense with the media. Do not look to the mass media for any constructive and substantive assistance to initiate change. There are small exceptions to this view but by and large be very mindful of what Chomsky has been showing us for decades about the media. They are profit-driven propagators of political and religious propaganda. Sensationalism sells their wares and there is nothing sensational about a systemic, plotted effort, generation by generation to develop optimally the full potential of all children. I do not think that the mass media are particularly concerned about the status quo being threatened. As a collective entity, the media are a chameleon able and willing to respond to the environment in which it operates. I am certain this chameleon will survive even when the vision for the human race is fully realized. I cannot imagine, however, what colour it will take, but I have no reservations about the fact that this chameleon will survive forever.

I implore you therefore, sidestep the media. This will not be too difficult to do because they will not come looking for you. Certainly they will not come looking for you on mass and those who do, out of passing curiosity soon will lose interest. To reiterate, do not waste your time or effort in trying to solicit their support of your endeavours. There is not much more to say about the media, so let us look to what reasonably can be expected from the family.

The family in the western world, as we know it, is a relatively new phenomenon. Despite what we would like to believe and what media image is portrayed to us for the most part, the family does not approximate the old television show Father Knows Best. It is closer to the patriarchical Archie Bunker led paradigm, All In The Family, where status quo maintenance is paramount and articulated as "it was good enough for me, it is good enough for my children". Said differently, the message is; Do not mess with the minds of my children, just teach them to read, write, count, and I will do the rest.

Lest you think of this as a gross and unfair generalization, reflect upon what was said in Parts One and Two. Reflect upon the importance of attachment and the various negative ways failure is subsequently manifested. A significant manifestation is addiction to all types of ingestible substances which has reached epidemic proportions. As well, there are other later life negative consequences to failed attachment such as personality disorders. For the most part, when marriages fail children remain properties to be argued over in protracted, adversarial custody and access battles. The same is true when a child welfare agency intervenes to protect a child at risk. In most instances the response of inept parents is an indignant: "Something of mine has been taken away and I want it back", instead of rectifying the risk conditions and demonstrating their abilities to control their dysfunctionalities. In contrast, most intact families are often under siege conditions for a variety of reasons not the least of which is financial. This also serves to compromise familial efforts to promote the optimal development of children. To reiterate, therefore, the themes conveyed in Parts One and Two, the malaise of the human condition starts and is perpetuated in families.

The siege conditions families must endure in the Third World, from my perspective are simply unimaginable and certainly explain the markedly prehistoric ways in which families continue to organize themselves to this day. For far too many families their primary, daily goal is physical survival. Much will have to happen in the First World before Third World countries can be relieved of the oppressive conditions which obstruct their moral and emotional development and before they can participate constructively in pursuit of the vision for the human race. We should all be mindful, however, that one of the greatest prophets was Mohammed, who is revered by much of the Third World. As discussed earlier, his message also was corrupted not unlike that of Jesus. Spurred on by the overwhelming dismal conditions in their lives, perhaps the change will come from them. After all, everyone anticipated the communist revolution to rise in England, much to the surprise and demise of the Russian Czar when it did not. They also probably are you.

Not all is dismal, however, when it comes to the family and the precipitation of change. There are many moral children in our schools who are high achievers, not so much because of their cognitive intelligence but because the family environment created by their parents freed them to do good rather than act out negatively the emotional turmoil of where they live. Pulitzer Prize winning author, Robert Coles, admirably examined and brought to our attention the development of kindness in our children. As young as six years, a child demonstrated to him a wise awareness that God does not interfere with the universe or the human condition. According to the youngster it is all up to us. I recommend strongly his 1997 publication: The Moral Intelligence of Children, not because it is consistent with this work and the social science on which it is based, but because he offers proof that some families will be supportive of the initiative which is required to achieve the vision of the prophets. They will identify themselves and will participate but probably not before the status quo protectors rally against efforts to promote the full development of our children.

I am careful here not to reiterate what has been said already about religion. I do believe, however, that the point cannot be overstated that religion is no ally to advancing the human condition. Therefore, do not look to any religion, especially any religious instructional events, to change their ways and be of assistance to you in initiating the change process. For the most part, the recommendations probably will be implemented first in non-denominational schools. I say this mindful of my early reference to the parochial school focus on family, parenting, and relationships. As said often before and as will be said again, while the parochial focus is necessary and conducive to change, it is not sufficient to break through the "gangism" which all religions advocate and which obstructs us from moving beyond the Stage Three perspective.

All writers, including myself, are in various states of dread, from time to time, that someone will beat us to publishing the same ideas we are taking so long to commit to text. The upside to this inevitability is, once again, the Cialdini-described phenomenon of social proof. If others are saying similar things, then our ideas are not so outlandish, indeed, they will be more acceptable than not. I welcome, therefore, the publication of Christopher Hitchens. It came out around the time I was writing Parts One and Two. Said more eloquently than I, he, too, has a dismal view of organized religion and predictably raised the ire of religious fundamentalists. In part, my ambition is to be characterized similarly by them as the purveyor of "sly distortions and grotesque errors that appear in every chapter". The more fervent the rhetoric of detractors, otherwise known as protectors of the status quo, the better I will consider the work I have done. Suffice it to say, once again, do not waste your time recruiting organized religion to the social movement I am advocating.

What about politicians? What about the state and the provincially elected officials in charge of education? Surely they will have no objection to being innovative, especially if some of the strategies have the potential of addressing school violence and the unacceptable troublesome behaviour of some of the children. Probably there will be, albeit a very few, who will support or even advocate for significant changes so that school systems in their jurisdiction will promote the cognitive moral and emotional intelligence of our children simultaneously with traditional academic topics. Their support will be invaluable. On the whole, however, the reality is that most politicians are short-sighted and concerned mostly with being re-elected. Born of this concern is the penchant to pander to the masses. Much has been said already about the masses so there is no reason to repeat it here. Suffice it to say that the masses engage in magical thinking, especially about children, and then have a strong preference for using force, coercion, punishment or any aversive measure to control the behaviour of troublesome youth. Remember the discussion about drugging our children with Ritalin or some other substance because they have a chemical disorder? The etiology and biochemistry of which is a mystery. A mystery which absolves the environment in which the children were raised and certainly the parenting they endured. So the masses demand zero tolerance, harsher treatment of juvenile offenders, and an almost exclusive focus on academic grades. On the one hand, parents often exclaim that their child's marks improved when the child was drugged with Ritalin. On the other hand these same parents are the first to take great pride in knowing that children are best potty trained or taught how to cross the street safely by the use of patient positive reward strategies. At some stage, perhaps when a child reaches puberty, as if to punish them for growing up, becoming sexual adults, the method of teaching by a system of rewards is abandoned by these very same knowledgeable parents. It is replaced by punishment. This makes absolutely no sense but there is a mass subscription to this pattern of reasoning and behaving. Moreover, most politicians are happy to join in, in order to garner the favour of the masses by passing harsher laws. Some politicians actually believe that something positive will come out of the punitive approach. Let me remind you of the earlier reference to John Eisenberg, who wrote so eloquently about the futility inherent in the escalating creation of more rules, especially in troubled times.

Garner whatever support you can but do not waste your time recruiting politicians to address the developmental needs of our children so that each successive generation will be better parents.

Do, however, find areas in which politicians can tinker for they love to tinker and some tinkering may be supportive of the developmental cause. For example, get political support for such apple pie and motherhood issues as training in nutrition, returning to physical education, and involvement in the community through volunteer activities. Such curriculum components do not seem to threaten the status quo and, therefore, are unlikely to be resisted. Fortunately, such activities enrich the experiences of children and, therefore, contribute to their optimal development in all spheres of their functioning.

Clearly I am not particularly politically astute, and at this time I am not interested in garnering the favour of the masses. Also, I am not concerned about being politically correct and dare to say things which will alienate many, probably some of whom are my friends and colleagues. There are many in this group, as in the general population, who believe that the troublesome behaviour of children and the need for them to be drugged is attributable to factors other than environments created by adults specifically their parents. Many subscribe to the "chemical imbalance" cause of children's misbehaviour. They are silent about the etiology of this "chemical imbalance", some hinting that it is genetic, and they are especially silent about the total absence of any physical markers of this chemical imbalance. They are just grateful that drugs decrease the acting out of their child. Would that they could instead seek relief from having to engage in mental gymnastics to abdicate parental responsibility for how their child developed. All they would have to say is that I did what I believed was the best because of what I experienced in my life. There is neither shame nor blame for not knowing better.

Most parents will be unable to accept responsibility for how their children turned out when there are problems. There is no merit in pursuing their consciousness raising because efforts would be better directed at preventing the problems from arising in the first place. To get there will require mobilizing the teaching profession, a feat which will be the responsibility of the few of you who have read this far because you accept the premises of this work.

Before we address the need to form an alliance with the teaching profession and its socially sanctioned institutions and the method of realizing this enterprise, the role of the so-called helping professions begs at least some discussion. Specifically, I am referring to the main three in the western world: Physicians, psychologists, and social workers. By now, it will make perfect sense to you when I label them each as nothing more than another form of "gangism". Despite rhetoric to the contrary, each of these professions is rabidly territorial and more concerned with the promotion of their respective discipline than advancement of the human condition. Each pursue, its self-promotion in idiosyncratic ways. Physicians especially gain much public favour by their well-practised medical model, whereby they take something out or put something in as a reaction to some malady. The operative term is "reaction" which is a much welcomed response in a time of crisis. I am eternally grateful to my friend Jim Martin, physician specialist in opthamology, for saving my sight in one eye after I had two spontaneous retinal tears. I am also grateful to the surgeon who repaired a painful hernia and to our family physician who administered to my two children when they fell ill with the various childhood diseases all children contract. Every one of you will have similar stories of gratitude, stories which serve to explain the near noble status afforded the medical profession. As technicians go, the medics have come a long way in a relatively short time. While they perform a vital service - and there are exceptional humanitarians among them - being a physician is no more or less a business than any other profession. Physician's training is very specific and as such their expertise is very sharply honed. In many respects, this is the profession where you want singularly focussed expertise. Realistically therefore, medicine will be an unlikely ally in the pursuit of the prophets' vision. More likely this profession, because of its conservative propensity and focus on moving forward only after much study and experimentation, is going to be obstructionistic. Obstructionistic not in a proactive way but in a characteristic reactive way if asked to comment or evaluate the proposed ways to achieving the vision for the human race. After all, and this is perhaps an unfair generalization, medicine's answer to the human malaise is to alter genes, to fix chemical imbalances or, when all else fails, to use various techniques to take stuff out or put stuff into our bodies. Before medicine can fully embrace preventative measures pertaining to both body and soul, much will have to be accomplished toward achieving our defined vision.

The profession of psychology has advanced greatly in recent times by the arrival of Dr. Phil on popular television. Single-handedly, he has given shape and form to an otherwise nebulous profession one which everyone knows about but would have great difficulty describing in a coherent way. Since the discipline degree is a Doctorate in Philosophy, the professional is first required to make a significant knowledge-building contribution in a unique area of concentration and then to disseminate the contribution through such measures as publications and/or teaching. What we know today about cognitive moral development and emotional intelligence largely can be attributed to this discipline. There, however, is an important distinction to be made between psychologists who are academics and those who are practitioners. First and foremost, practitioners also are business people, not unlike television's Dr. Phil. On the whole, they run successful private or institution based practices and help many suffering from a myriad of problems. This is aptly demonstrated during the commercial-filled one hour program of Dr. Phil. However, the services rendered by most psychologists also are reactive to an already well-manifested, troublesome dysfunctionality. Most, if not all, of what practising psychologists do therefore, also is reactive in nature. Seldom, if ever, are they consulted and paid for implementing preventative measures.

My consternation is with Lawrence Kohlberg and his colleagues. For the life of me, I do not understand why their work and the work of academics concerning emotional intelligence have not had a profound impact on the human condition. Clearly, I place great stock in their work and, for the most part, I am in great awe of their insight and efforts to shed light on the human condition. At best, I can attribute their popular obscurity to the politics of academia which work against the broad dissemination of ideas. First, and for the most part, it is all about publish or perish. This really means one must gain the favour of other academics. This axiom of survival in academia also serves to socialize even the wisest; some to specialization, and others to accepting the limited practical application of their work. After all, the protectors of the status quo are an insidious and formidable lot better to be avoided. than fought against in a protracted battle, so think many academics. Kohlberg's Just Community in the women's prison soon dissipated, despite its success, immediately after he and his colleagues left. My own experience in designing, implementing, and evaluating a similar prison based program was the same. As soon as I left, it was dismantled within months if not weeks, and there was not a trace of it ever having been there. Therefore, while you are unlikely to recruit from the discipline of psychology, in time you can count on specialists in the field of cognitive moral development and emotional intelligence, to be allies and advisors in pursuit of your vision.

Last but by no means the least is the profession of social work. Within this profession there is a shared self perception of an advocacy mandate. In fact, the advocacy function is so pervasive in the profession that it is generally recognized by the populous. Unfortunately, because of the genesis of the profession of social work, advocacy is mostly afforded to the poor, the visibly disadvantaged, and the clearly downtrodden amongst us. As such, there is a narrow focus on improving their lot in life. At best, some lip service is given to addressing the systemic conditions which create and perpetuate the problems in the first place. For example, there is little focus in the profession on preventative measures such as curtailing the intergenerational emergence of corrupt oppressors and the organizational structures in why they ply their trade.

The profession of social work, however, is very much involved, through child welfare services, in rescuing children from the maladaptive legacies into which they are destined by virtue of the family into which they were born. Social work also is the discipline which understands best the psychosocial nature of the human condition. That is to say, each and every one of us is a product of the sum total of our experiences, and our functioning at any given time is intricately linked to the past and the environmental conditions at the time. To a large extent, this psychosocial perspective explains the profession's penchant to be advocates for the disadvantaged; at times the profession's actions even verge on embracing preventative measures. I am guessing that it would not take too much to recruit, at least, some professional social workers, to participate in the recommended change process. Those involved in community organization especially would be helpful to the change implementation process. On the whole, however, as with psychology, the best that can be expected from the profession of social work is consultation, which should be welcomed and actively solicited.

There are other professions, such as economists, who were the initial social reformers, who, you might expect, may see the financial value of what is recommended in this book. Unfortunately, the profession has evolved in a very different direction from their past interest in the charitable treatment of dependency. As so aptly put by the economist John Galbraith, their current focus is on explaining what has happened, avoiding even explaining what is happening.

Realistically therefore, if the message of this work resonates with you, the work is up to you to do. Do not wait for someone else. The fact is that no one profession has started what needs to be done on the scale at which it needs to be done. There is no reason to believe that any one of the professions will step up and start a discernable focussed initiative today or in the foreseeable future. This is not meant to cast aspersions on any one group or the collective. This is meant to impress upon you the reality that it is up to you. If you ever wondered, what meaning is there to your life or if there should be more meaning to it, here is an opportunity to respond in a significant way.

The Role of the Teaching Profession

As the adage goes in public speaking, know your audience. In this matter, it is imperative that you recognize and accept that the teaching profession initially will be reluctant doers of the tasks required of them. They will be reluctant to expand their socialized role, of teaching children, to a specified standard, how to read, write, and do arithmetic. To illustrate this point, I would like to share with you some of my personal experiences. Whenever I talk, about my ideas concerning the teaching profession's role, with friends who are teachers, people I care very much about, each and every one of them is singularly negative. I believe their negativity is based on their co-opted, insidiously socialized status quo maintenance perspective, namely that it is challenging enough to teach our children the so called three Rs let alone have time left over to do any of this other 'stuff' about which I am talking. Sadly and almost without exception, they do not want to hear about any of this other stuff. Without curiosity, they are quick to reject something without really knowing anything about it. In many respects, I cannot fault them for their response because most of them have been or are under siege from the guardians of the status quo. From time to time, in various jurisdictions, teachers are threatened with the loss of their jobs if their students do not meet some locally set academic criteria. As reported by Levitt and Dubner, in their seminal book Freakonomics, some teachers have engaged, albeit under duress, in such regressive behaviour as cheating on behalf of their students to keep their own jobs.

Undeniably, the so called three Rs are necessary criteria to function in today's world but this, too, is far from sufficient to define the optimal development of our children. Moreover, the fact is that competently cared for (parented) children learn better than children who are the subject of a narrow academic focus and live in adverse environmental conditions. Most, if not all, teachers know this. However, they are unable to act on this crucially important knowledge because most times they are in a regressed, survival state due to the siege they have to endure from their employers.

While we all need to be compassionate to the plight of teachers in most places, we also need to be mindful of the reality that not only children, but we, too, learn better in a hospitable setting. In an environment of co-operation and in an environment in which the constructive creation of new meaning is encouraged, all types of learning and development take place. Armed with this knowledge, your small group of Margaret Meadeans, are ready to engage the primary allies in order to achieve what the prophets have told us we are capable of doing.

My first suggestion is to further your knowledge about development so that rather than appear as some zealot, you present as well-informed individual who promotes additions to curricula. It is far more constructive to validate what has gone on, since it is of significant value, and then add to it. This was the essence of the power tactics of Jesus, as so aptly described decades ago by psychotherapist Jay Haley. Always praise the past and then just add to it. To become better informed, it will be worth the cost to subscribe to the Journal of Moral Education and/or become a member of the Association For Moral Education. Both are accessible through the internet.

Next, you need to find like-minded individuals. That is to say, people who are interested and inclined to fix things, as opposed to only complain about them. Share your ideas, debate your ideas, especially the ideas being advanced in this book. When you have gained confidence in discussing the vision and what needs to occur to get there, become involved, hopefully with some allies or in the knowledge that allies are embarking on a similar journey in another jurisdiction. Heeding the sage observation of Margaret Mead, one of the best places to start is with your local Parent-Teacher Association, whatever form this may take. If you are a teacher become involved in curriculum development. While overcoming inertia always is challenging, once an object is in motion, like the proverbial locomotive, it quickly gathers speed to the point that it will take a great force to stop it. I am counting on exponential growth and that each new generation will embrace the human revolution rather than joining the rank and file of the status quo protectors.

At first glance, the preceding may well be regarded as too simplistic, some critics likely will judge it also to be naive. I fully expect such reactions and, for this very reason, decided to spend the entire last chapter on convincing you that great things can be accomplished if there is a vision, a plan, and individuals willing to act. All three elements are necessary. The reason for optimism is that now we understand the difference between self-serving corruption and what conditions have the potential of advancing the human condition as well as what cognitive developmental perspectives are conducive to it. Simply put, an exponentially growing population of post conventional principled thinkers, who also have excellent emotional intelligence, in short order will disrupt the status quo which benefit mostly a very few.

In defence of my optimism about the teaching profession, a few examples are warranted. Examples that reveal the profession's commitment to fostering the development of our children and to do so in innovative ways. Hopefully, I have made the point adequately that innovation is necessary since doing more of the same inevitably continues to produce more of the same results. What we clearly need is more than great readers, writers, and mathematicians. We need to produce, through our educational systems, young adults who also are morally mature, principled in thought and action, superiorly advanced in their emotional intelligence abilities, capable of wisely choosing life partners, able to recognize that procreation is a responsibility not a right, and that parenting is an onerous responsibility which requires well informed purposeful actions.

Since the Journal of Moral Education is not only alive and well but is flourishing, it means that there are educators out there who are actively engaged in promoting their student's development in various relevant content areas. For example, educators are addressing racism, sexism, classism, heterosexualism, citizenship, and critical thinking, to name just a few areas of foci. Of even greater significance, is that in some educational settings the above, and more, content areas are being addressed in a mileau, a mileau not unlike the correctional institution programs referenced before and not unlike the Just Community Approach to Moral Education, Lawrence Kohlberg and his colleagues initiated, prior to his death, as experimental programs in public high schools. These same programs, have been empirically demonstrated to be conducive to the development of socio-moral reasoning and action.

Then there is the innovative private school in Atlanta, in one of the city's poorest neighbourhoods, that uses novel ways of helping students learn. The innovations emanating from the passion for teaching by its staff. There also is innovation in the, Knowledge Is Power Program (KIPP), in the New York City South Bronx public school, started as an experimental program in the mid - 1990s. In one decade this place of learning has become one of the most desirable public schools to attend, in New York City. You may be astounded to know that central to the school program is long days of learning which end each night with the completion of much school home work. At KIPP there also is school on Saturday, and a markedly shortened summer vacation. The children spend fifty to sixty percent more time learning than children in traditional public schools. According to sociologist researches, Karl Alexander, "the only problem with school, for the kids who aren't achieving, is that there isn't enough of it". The KIPP school program is a living testament to this, every one of its students outperforming their comparative demographic, those who attend traditional school programs where the archaic belief prevails that "working students too hard can cause the mind injury". Remember, however, that there should be more to schooling than exceptional grades.

To conclude this chapter, it will be useful to reflect once more on the basic elements of a strategic plan. So far, we have a vision and objectives through which our vision will be achieved. Furthermore, we now have the doers who will work on the objectives. Last but by no means least, we now need a time-targeted, critical path, one which specifies actions. Not a linear path but a path which is comprised of staggered lines of activities which compress the total time required to achieve our vision.

CHAPTER NINE
THE CRITICAL PATH TO ACHIEVING OUR VISION

Isomorphism

In a strategic plan when a vision or goal is articulated, when the objectives through which the goal will be achieved are operationally stated, when responsibilities for task completion are assigned, the final step, as important as all the others, is the development of a time targeted critical path. The most important element of a critical path is that time lines for tasks are not configured linearly. That is to say, when task A is finished, task B starts and when B is complete, C can commence. To fully grasp this point, take a moment to draw one inch lines one after another and then randomly create a staggered line configuration of the same number of one inch lines, one below the other, as a critical path whereby starting on B does not depend on completing A, and starting on C does not depend on completing B. Some tasks can commence at the same time, whereas other tasks require partial completion of one or more other tasks before startup can occur. Figuratively, a linear line of twelve inches can be replaced with a staggered configuration, one which takes half the duration represented by the same number of one-inch, time lines. This is the essence of a critical path. To some, this may be stating the obvious but for most of us learning the difference between the two approaches always is hard earned.

The purpose of this chapter essentially is to demystify the method of accomplishing complex multifaceted tasks. The purpose of this chapter also is to convince you of the doability of the ideas being advanced and to help you recognize that when there is a buy-in, the creative juices of initial skeptics invariably are released. As a consultant to various organizations, I quickly learned this to be the first and most important task in any project. Once accomplished, those with far greater knowledge about the workings of the organization solved for themselves all the problems they said would obstruct the goal when it was first presented. Solving the obstacles is an essential part of the doing in any plan. Solving the obstacles also is necessary to maintain momentum, indeed to incrementally accelerate the process of achieving the goal.

A significant problem of the prophets was that they had a wonderful message but lacked a critical path to bring to fruition their respective, but incredibly similar goals. For the most part, each prophet underestimated the force required to diminish the corruptive influences of the status quo protectors. Unfortunately, this significant oversight prevails to this day. As the prophets so also the current socially conscious advocates such as Gore,

Suzuki, President Obama, and others who believe that people can be talked into behaving as conventional moral thinkers with better than average emotional intelligence. If the prophets could not talk people into behaving as such, there is no reason to believe anyone else can simply talk people into sustainably doing the right things.

Most, if not all of us, need to be habilitated before sustainable, adaptive functionalities can prevail. By now you will know habilitation means development of the full human potential.

There is a concept in the system's theory literature which conveys an interesting axiom, one which applies across all fields of study. The term is isomorphism. It refers to similar concepts, models, and laws which appear in widely different fields, independently and based upon totally different facts. As a result, there are many examples of identical principles being discovered several times because the researchers in one field are unaware that the theoretical structure required was already well-developed in some other field. The intent of general system theory, referenced earlier, is to avoid such unnecessary duplication of labour. In this spirit then, let us stop doing the same things expecting different results, one which have not been or will be forthcoming. Let us explore what there is to learn of relevance, to achieve our vision from other fields of endeavour.

I will offer two examples of monumental achievement, although there are many more. The first concerns the modern industrialization of Brazil, and the second, landing astronauts on the moon and then bringing them safely back to earth.

The reference for the first example is R. Buckminster Fuller's: Critical Path. It is a dense book which requires tenacious stamina to read, but the effort is well worth it. Fuller chronicles a myriad of cosmic and human events, many of which give cause for optimism. Most optimistic, for our purposes, is his involvement in the industrialization of Brazil. In exchange for allowing the United States to conduct extensive radio surveying over Brazil, in preparation for the Allied invasion of Europe, then President Vargas of Brazil demanded from President Franklin Roosevelt a well informed and far reaching plan for the industrialization of his country. Roosevelt's staff assigned the task to a US engineering company which had organized many of J. P. Morgan's foreign, electric power generating, private enterprises. J. P. Morgan saw this as an opportunity to unload his immense inventory of second-hand machinery. Vargas saw through this scheme and would have nothing to do with it. Vargas who was knowledgeable about the US involvement in the USSR five year plan strategy asked Roosevelt to have someone contact all the US engineers who were so involved and apply the practice wisdom they gained to the needs of Brazil. In response, the task was assigned to the engineering department of the USA's Board of Economic Warfare. Its head mechanical engineer was Buckminster Fuller. He interviewed thirty-two, high-ranking engineers in twenty-one corporations about their experiences in the USSR. He then discussed the application of their Russian experiences to the industrialization of Brazil with the same engineers. Based on his fact finding and discussions, Fuller then wrote a plan for Brazil and asked the group of engineers he interviewed for their comments on the written document. Just as Fuller was completing his plan, Vargas was deposed, and the document was not forwarded to the new political leader for very obvious reasons. Instead, one of the major US engineers he consulted took the "compendium" informally to Brazil's leading industrialists and powers behind the political scene. Fixing their fundamental flaw in the USSR, the strategic plan was launched in Brazil. The plan called for the division of environment and technical planning and required of university science and engineering graduates in Brazil that they complete two years of field work, (as opposed to in the USSR, where graduates were assigned to senior management positions). Fifty years later, the success rate of completion was calculated to be in excess of 80%.

By way of a brief digression, it is noteworthy that Fuller's plan for the whole world, what he coined "spaceship earth", was technological and economic in nature. While he envisioned a blending of the races as a function of exponential mobility afforded by various means of transportation, Fuller also failed to recognize the forces which mitigate development of the human potential. Curtailed by failed attachment, cognitive developmental perspective, and marginal emotional intelligence, history unequivocally demonstrates that even the technical brilliance of a Buckminster Fuller is woefully inadequate to advance the human condition beyond where it has been stuck since the beginning of recorded history. Nevertheless, mindful of the principle of isomorphism, there is much which is relevant to pursuing the vision for the human race from what occurred in Brazil as a result of Fuller's efforts.

To illustrate the point of isomorphism further, it will be useful to examine a universally familiar, human accomplishment known as the Apollo Project. This was the official name of the venture to land humans on the moon and then return them safely to earth. It is this project which is the quintessential, the very best example of what is meant by a critical path. First, it starts with the generation of an exhaustive list of all which has to be accomplished in order to achieve an operationally defined goal never reached before. The critical path of the Apollo Project identified some two million tasks which had to be successfully accomplished to reach its well-defined goal. A million of these tasks required technological performances, the design, production, and successful operation of which had never been done before. All was accomplished, and the goal of the Apollo Project was successfully reached, indeed more than once, in a relatively brief period of time. I would think it would be safe to say that the two million tasks were not linearly tackled one after the other. Much was done simultaneously to do it in such a short time.

To achieve the vision of the prophets, will require probably the successful completion of more than two million tasks. To generate, at this time, such a comprehensive list is an impossibility. To attempt to generate the list not only is not necessary at this time but would be tantamount to embracing, fully and willingly, a complete disconnect from reality. In brief, total insanity. Since we know where we want to arrive, it is sufficient to embark slowly on the journey which, like all journeys, always begins with the first step. Whether the first step is short or long, careful and steady or a hop, skip, and a jump is not relevant. It just needs to be taken.

The same can be said of the doing. The doing can be simple or ingenious, creative or mundane, inspired or plotting. It really does not matter as long as good direct discernable actions are initiated. Success will breed success, and the benefits will start to reveal themselves in an exponential way and will culminate in the vision being achieved in five generations. Slowly the numbers of those who will not tolerate the status quo, the corruption, the greed, and all that was examined in Part One of this work, will grow. At first, gradually but then gaining momentum.

In the remainder of this chapter, I present my idea of a macro critical path to achieve the visions of the prophets. The operative word is my. It is meant to be a starting point. It is meant to be a catalyst, to get your creativity activated. As long as your actions can be related logically to goal relevant objectives, they will be good. At this stage, we just need to start doing specific developmentally conducive things, joining forces with others doing similar things, and work toward creating a critical mass of action, which will reach a point beyond which regression cannot occur.

Action and Funding

As the consulting engineers to the former USSR pointed out to Buckminster Fuller the number one error they made was to separate their program into "economic" and "technical" categories. The economic category was supposed to come first insofar as through analysis the plan was to define technical requirements. Time proved this to be a static viewpoint, one which failed to take into consideration the dynamic elements of industrial engineering. In other words, accurate economic forecasts almost always were compromised by the dynamic and creative aspects inherent to manufacturing by means of technology. The experiences in Brazil are not too far off from the need to retool our social institutions, specifically those which teach. How will this be funded predictably is the first question of obstruction by the status quo protectors and virtually everyone else innately afraid of change. The answer is very simple: By gradually shifting resources from where they will be needed incrementally less.

Draw a triangle with the point facing the bottom of the page. Right next to it, draw a same size triangle with the point facing the top of the page. The top of the first triangle represents everything which is spent on trying to curtail and respond to the myriad of social problems, especially caused by the young against whom we continually legislate. It represents the war on drugs; the myriad of costs created by addiction; the cost of protecting children through child welfare agencies; the cost of prosecuting, assessing, supervising, institutionalizing delinquent children; the cost of providing a police presence in our schools; the costs of enforcing zero tolerance policies in our schools; in Canada, the cost of implementing and maintaining a gun registry; the cost of lost productivity due to physical illness traceable to early life adverse conditions; and the list can go on for several pages. You will recall from Part Two that the earlier the intervention, regardless of what needs attention, the better and less costly the results. Beyond a certain point of a problem's existence, society simply reacts in ways which are extremely costly without any hope of benefit, just to do something. Witness the rate of incarceration. The United States has the dubious honour of being the most inclined to invoke this mostly useless reaction.

The cost of reactive measures simply is enormous. The war on drugs and the cost of imprisonment alone amount to billions of dollars nationally. Internationally, the cost exponentially escalate. The point is, there is much to be allocated differently.

Now, think of the point of the triangle oriented to the top of the page as representing costs allocated to preventative measures. The comparative costs are astounding, not figuratively but literally. Compare the wage of a correctional officer with that of an early childhood educator, someone to whom many parents entrust their diapered toddlers from 7:00 in the morning until 7:00 at night, or later. The early childhood educator in most jurisdictions in the US and Canada earns a minimum wage. Many parents cannot even afford day care and leave their infants with grandparents or the kindly person down the block. Consider also how many schools incorporate and spend resources on curriculum other than reading, writing and arithmetic. How many elementary schools have empathy-training, ongoing courses on relationships, human sexuality, parenting, and other developmentally conducive curriculum, thankfully a few but not enough. Similarly, consider how much effort and resources are allocated to identifying worrisome new parents and then providing them with relevant, competent support. At the very best, some new mothers get a home visit from a nurse practitioner once, seldom more, the focus of which almost always is on the physical needs of the child. One, but ideally two years of regular support would go far to averting the costly and devastating later life negative consequences to formative stage adverse environmental conditions in a child's life.

The first, overriding critical path strategy, therefore, is to associate each habilitative initiative with an existing problem, on which the initiative will ameliorate and eventually prevent altogether. As the costs required by the actions to address the problem diminish, the savings then should be channelled into expanding the specific habilitative efforts responsible for the gains being made. The very same economic principle is applicable to the allocation of human resources. The economic and technical strategies are not to take financial and human resources out of the total system. The idea is to invest both gradually in very different ways.

This discussion requires some very concrete examples of a specific nature. It is one thing to say that fewer prisons and prison guards will be needed when the activation of the plan is well under way, and savings can be channelled into early childhood and elementary education. It is altogether different to illustrate the principle by something which can be done in a semester. The challenge, indeed the obstacle, is to start at a grass roots level. The adage, "you look after the pennies and the dollars will take care of themselves", probably applies. But then what are the examples of pennies? To orient you, I would like to recommend an extremely uplifting book by David Suzuki and Holly Dressel, Good News For A Change: How Everyday People Are Helping The Planet. The content is not on our topic but it certainly illustrates the integration of economic and technology with which the consulting engineers had difficulty in the USSR. The point Suzuki makes is that being environmentally responsible does not equate with fiscal responsibility. Moreover, the book chronicles the efforts of creative and courageous individuals who have discovered ways of supporting themselves without despoiling the planet. We need the same courage and creativity to unleash the human developmental potential by overcoming the millennia of obstacles created by the protectors of the status quo. Suzuki and Dressel identify people who probably are principled individuals. Motivated by their developmental perspective, they found solutions to environmental problems others could not be bothered to care about. While few such principled people are out there, the challenge is to marshal them and their efforts to get the proverbial ball rolling. For example, the courageous and creative people of Good News seldom conform to large constructs such as nation-states or global marketing groups. According to the authors, such people are nearly always locally based or else working in close contact with local people. Because the groups are diverse and in a state of constant flux, they are difficult to zero in on, difficult to curtail or stamp out. I believe the same will apply to our pursuit of the prophets' vision, because the focus will start where we live and where we will continue to live.

Another vivid example of a grass-roots initiative, one which has grown exponentially, is the transformation of many youth in Venezuela. It is called El Sistema and is now celebrating thirty years of making classical musicians out of half-a-million Venezuelan children. The program is said to have transformed the lives of innumerable underprivileged and at-risk youths in the process. The program's founder, alive today, is Jose Antonio Abreu. He articulates his vision to be "the fight of a poor and abandoned child against everything that opposes his full realization as a human being". This idea sounds very similar to the ideas of the historical prophets and, in my mind, makes Signor Abreu another modern prophet. Perhaps more so, because his message has not been corrupted but in fact has been actualized. It is still going strong.

Another brief digression is warranted, the impetus of which are my frequent references to the visions of the prophets. I am concerned that the protectors of the status quo will attack or otherwise dismiss these ideas as pie in the sky, naive rantings of some religious zealot or anti religious zealot who invokes religiosity for self-serving purpose. Nothing could be further from the truth. And there is nothing whatsoever wrong with being idealistic, hence my reference to the prophets. This contention is supported by Suzuki and Dressel as they report that the initiatives they describe all emanate from a consensus positive, "almost idyllic vision" generated by small groups of people. People who define for themselves how they want life to be, what they want, and how they went about getting there. It is noteworthy that the key ingredient to the successes described involved very little, if any self-sacrifice or the proverbial wearing of uncomfortable hair-shirts as a form of penance. Vision, creativity, and commitment rule the day for the people described by Suzuki and Dressel.

So then, let us consider some very doable examples starting with the problem of bullying. It is not necessary to describe here the myriad of problems created by this type of unacceptable behaviour, especially in our elementary schools. The typical response is to create rules against such behaviour and then to enforce the rules by various means most often through zero tolerance. There are quantifiable costs associated with responses which easily can be specified in any setting. A program which is specifically designed to prevent bullying in a particular setting can be designed by drawing on the various experiences of others and from what is reported in the social science literature. There is no reason to reinvent the wheel but there is a need to sell the preventative program to the powers that be. The sales pitch has to be custom-tailored and capable of immediately answering the economic obstacle. The path of least resistance, ie., the drawing upon the consulting experiences of the US engineers in the former USSR, is an interplay between economics and technology. Translated to be applicable to our example, this entails initially redirecting curtailment and enforcement resources to preventative efforts initiated where the need is the greatest. Those who focus on curtailing and enforcing rules against bullying, at first would spend only a little time implementing the prevention program. As the demand on their reactive tasks diminish, their preventive task involvement can increase proportionately. Remember, children are especially responsive to environmental conditions. Within a semester, in most settings, bullying can be eradicated, and the achievement made completely sustainable by diverting all curtailment and enforcement resources to efforts of prevention. No one loses one's job, and no new monies are required. Perhaps, my time frame of a semester is too optimistic, but the principle of dynamic interplay between economic and technical (intervention) factors is sound.

What about creating a drug free school environment?. No one disagrees with this objective. Indeed there are many schools which actively enforce this policy essentially by various curtailment measures such as a police presence and the use of sniffer-dogs to ferret out the presence of illegal substances in lockers and on the person of students. Once again, there are direct costs to doing these things. Costs which can be specified with little effort. There are, specific, preventive strategies to children bringing, selling, and using drugs in school. They are not well known, and they are not used widely in the educational system. They exist, however, and accomplish well the stated objective. Using the same strategy as before, the challenge is to divert initially some of the curtailment resources to preventative measures and especially to focus upon where the need is the greatest. Not to diminish the inherent challenges of doing so, local consensus, based on the ideal of a drug free school, will assuredly release the creativity of grass roots activists to turn the tide. When the preventative measures become incorporated into all aspects of the school's life and all resources previously assigned to enforcement are channelled to prevention, this initiative also will become sustainable at no extra cost or loss of job.

This is not entirely true, however, the drug-sniffing dogs will have to find work elsewhere.

A word about the comment no one loses one's job, is warranted before moving on with our discussion. Of course, the aptitude, personality configuration of those who are drawn to enforcement is different from those who are ideally suited to deliver habilitative/preventative measures. The comment therefore, at least in part, is figurative. More accurately, perhaps, the comment should be that the number of employees remain the same. Enforcement people eventually will be replaced by habilitative staff. It is conceivable that the aptitudes are transferable and that with facilitation, different knowledge and skill sets can be acquired. Many school-based police officers are assigned their roles precisely because they are deemed to have interpersonal skills and a predisposition to shun the punitive and favour the constructive reaction to transgressions. Each setting will define the specifics of what is required.

Addressing issues of personal safety and clarity of mind, a product of being drug free, along with other behavioural problems in the above described way, will go far toward creating an environment conducive to optimal learning and development. In a growth environment teaching and learning the three Rs become easier and requires fewer resources to be allocated to remedial efforts. The special, teaching resources then can be allocated to the implementation of a developmentally conducive curriculum at no extra, financial cost or additional, personnel allocations.

Expanding the Elementary and High School Curriculum

My intent here is to generate a list of developmentally conducive curriculum which will slowly be funded by the diversion of resources previously required to address behavioural problems and learning disabilities. From the habilitative initiatives, it is noteworthy that not only will students benefit from the gains but so also will teachers and administrators. In a better frame of mind, under less duress, it will be easier to persuade both teachers and administrators to introduce increasingly more new topics into their teaching agenda. These topics, most of which will be repeated throughout both elementary and high school grades, are specifically structured to address the developmental stage perspective of groups of children. For example, the topic of parenting is never too early to introduce as long as it is presented in a way which students can understand. There is much written about this, and there were earlier references made to the relevant literature. The information is there for use as well as the experiences of some teachers to draw upon.

The first phase in the critical path must address environmental conditions in schools and then, even before this task is complete, expand on the core curriculum. In addition to a parenting course at each grade, the following content also should be included at each grade: The dynamics of romantic- or-infatuation based attraction; elements of positive relationships; values versus principles; the art of thinking; problem solving life situations; finding meaning to what you do; empathy; conflict resolution; emotional intelligence; human sexuality; music and art appreciation; elements of basic home repair; creating and following personal and household budgets; informed consumerism; healthy living; the benefits of eating good and physical fitness; and planning your future. These subjects should suffice as a preliminary list to be expanded and elaborated upon over time as a function of experience and creativity. The list of topics should not be reduced, although many probably can be combined so that the curriculum requirement does not become overwhelming to students and teachers alike.

The critical path strategy, therefore, for the generation entering elementary school now, is that each and every one has extensive exposure to developmentally conducive topics every year. As the first generation of children in the new curriculum program develops, the content must deal with topics in increasingly more complex ways, always presented from a cognitive developmental perspective to which the group can relate.

In this plan, equal emphasis is placed on facilitating the development of cognitive and emotional intelligence and teaching reading, writing, and arithmetic. Whereas I would be pleased with average academic knowledge and skills preferring instead exceptional cognitive moral developmental and emotional intelligence abilities, the interplay between the foci predictably will positively effect on each other. The number of drop-outs in high school will decrease for this first cohort and the majority will seek post-secondary education and/or training. When this group advances to decision making status, it will become easier to sustain and improve on school-based habilitative efforts for their children. This cohort also will choose life-partners more wisely and will parent their offspring with greater competence, in part, because of their empathic nurturance abilities. They will relate to their partners and care for their children better than any generation previously.

Concomitant Strategies

Given the crucially important role which would be played by teachers in pursuit of the prophets' vision, the education and training of teachers also must be addressed. Currently, in most jurisdictions, aspiring teachers complete a baccalaureate program. It can be a three-or-four year endeavour, in no particular content area of study. Some take psychology, sociology, criminology, history, English, geography, and so on, and a very few pursue a combined degree that include principles of education. The goal is to attain the best possible marks because the competition for acceptance in teacher's college is fierce. The teacher's college program is one year long, in most jurisdictions and incorporates in this time frame some periods of practical experience learning.

The current process requires an extensive modification starting with a baccalaureate specialization, tailored specifically for aspiring teachers. A full, four-year program is needed, one which teaches knowledge required to promote the growth and development of children including under what conditions optimal learning takes place. There will be no difficulty filling the four year curriculum. The problem will be responding to the vast number of students applying. For starters, the following topics are advisable: theories of learning; group dynamics; human sexuality; cognitive development; emotional development; raising moral children; values and principles; emotional intelligence; elements of empathy; parenting; elements of various relationships; creativity; critical thinking; problem solving; overcoming weaknesses with existing strengths; the nature of behavioural dysfunctionalities in children and young adults; creating participatory democratic academic environments; engaging or forming educational alliances with the parents of children; evaluating educational relevant research reports; report writing; theories of socialization; elements of justice; art and music appreciation; healthy living; finding meaning to what you do; nature versus nurture; attachment; the development of pro social reasoning; elements of mutual aid; conflict resolution; mediation; restorative justice; the determining consequences of Early Years environmental factors and last but not least the activity of ethicing. I believe there are enough topics here to easily fill a four-year curriculum. Hopefully, additional courses would emanate from the creativity and enthusiasm of those who advocate this educational strategy. You also will have noted that the suggested list of courses is virtually void of pathology. The focus is on promoting optimal development and emotional intelligence. You will have noted also that the list of courses is knowledge-based, and this fact begs the question: Where will the aspiring teacher learn the techniques or skills of teaching?

I submit that skills training should occur in so-called teacher's colleges, technological institutes, in Canada community colleges or other such places of learning, where the emphasis is on skill acquisition. At this level, specialization can be made possible. There can be specializations in teaching pre-school, first-or-second half, elementary school grades, first-or-second half secondary school grades and sub-specializations in academic topics such as reading, writing, arithmetic, history, geography or any of the other sciences. Needless to say it would be at this level that aspiring teachers are taught the practicalities of any of the knowledge-based courses taken during their baccalaureate education. For example, it is one thing to know about group dynamics, it is completely something else to facilitate and manage them. Similarly, it is one thing to know about the design of a participatory democratic school milieu, it is something else altogether to actually implement, facilitate, and evaluate one. Ideally, aspiring teachers at this level will be taught by practice professors, people who have spent part of their careers actually teaching. In this model, the graduate teachers, regardless of age group they teach whether it be toddlers in diapers or the last year of high-school, science majors, are all treated and, most importantly paid equally.

Another brief digression is warranted to suggest the application of this model for other disciplines, particularly in the mental health field. For example, social workers and psychologists should fill their minds, as much as possible, with knowledge and advance their speciality to the doctorate level in universities. This is more than less what they are doing currently. Contrary to popular belief, however, they acquire very few, if any, practical skills. Whatever skills they acquire is done so in brief practicums or a year of internship during or after graduation. Some also acquire specialized clinical or technical skills required to conduct their independent research through which a doctorate in philosophy is earned. Even their research skills are very narrowly focussed in pursuit of their doctoral degree. A better model would be to attend a polytechnical institute after obtaining a graduate degree to learn clinical skills such as conducting specific kinds of assessments; scoring and interpreting specific kinds of standardized instruments; marriage/couples therapy; group and individual therapy; methods of intervention based on a specific theoretical model; designing and evaluating specific programs, and this list also could go on. Instructors in skills also should be from the field and should have gained their respective practice-wisdom from actually doing, or having done, for a significant part of their career, what they teach. Such instructors should be financially valued as much as their theory teaching counterparts and be afforded the same academic advantages such as tenure and full professorship.

Returning to the topic at hand, the issue of aptitude requires addressing. By aptitude I mean the configuration of personality factors empirically demonstrated to be associated with a predictably competent teacher. The same principle applies to the digression about mental health professionals. Out of misguided human rights concerns, screening for discipline relevant aptitude has been diluted and in many educational settings completely abandoned. Most of what matters now is: Do you have the marks we require and the funds to pay our academic fees? Not only is the general populous unaware of this but so also are many employers. When performance and other behavioural problems become manifest, the employers of professionals are incredulous and exclaim "but he is so smart". You will remember the earlier discussion, in which I said, that we have given far more credit to cognitive intelligence than is warranted. There are far more important factors, in the context of this discussion, the aptitude to learn specific knowledge, skills, and then to apply these with predictable competence.

I trust you agree that children who will be the product of this altered educational system will be increasingly different and that as changes in their development become integrated, each subsequent generation will be developmentally more advanced. I trust you agree that the difference will be a good one, one which will have a myriad of ramifications including: Support for all types of habilitative measures; growing unresponsiveness to efforts of seduction into consumerism; growing social and environmental responsibility; and most importantly, a growing intolerance of corruption, terrorism and tribalism, just to name a few outcomes we reasonably can expect.

What about those staggered time lines in a critical path which expedite a more timely completion of an undertaking? Initially, at least until the second or perhaps the third generation benefits from the proposed changes, deliberately developing staggered time lines will not be an issue. As noted earlier it will first be necessary to make our schools safe and drug free but then almost simultaneously also working on the introduction of the new curriculum. At first, only certain aspects of the new curriculum will be incorporated, but eventually, ways will be found to group them and ensure that there is a full parallel co-curriculum, one which focusses on the cognitive and emotional development of our children. Realistically, especially initially, the various forces of the status quo protectors naturally will create lengthy time frames. As such, it is probably wise to advocate for as much as possible, with the expectation that only a few initiatives will go forward. Moreover, initially, you may have to settle for a linear implementation of new initiatives. The point is that grass-roots precipitated changes will have to gain momentum before it will be advantageous to actively steer the educational, evolutionary process towards the vision by means of a well-formulated critical path.

It will be obvious that my thinking about change singularly concerns First World countries. This is true for at least the first two generations. The reason is that in First World countries some of this already is going on. In some First World countries more so than in others. It is always easier to add momentum and mass than to build or start something rolling. I am also of the belief that because of the self-serving exploitation of many by a very few, obstacles in Third World countries are formidable. Furthermore, in many places, educational systems are either so fragile or non existent as to afford no place to readily intervene. Nevertheless, I could be mistaken in this as Marx and Engels were about where the revolution of the poor working classes would occur. I think not, however, especially since it is difficult to engage people in talk about pursuing the optimum development of their children when their primary daily concern is one of survival. For change to commence in Third World countries, it will take at least the second generation products of the new initiatives to not tolerate the exploitation of others. Their intolerance will be expressed through definitive actions.

It is not difficult to imagine that the definitive actions of future generations will evolve into the active pursuit of the vision of the prophets. For example, future generations will not purchase the products of child labour, so-called blood diamonds or tolerate oppression and exploitation by demanding more for less, since consumerism gradually will be replaced by different emphasis in the pursuit of an informed life of quality and relevance. Once the majority of the First World develops a cognitive developmental perspective and emotional intelligence, neither of which can abide abuse and embrace a world view of co-operation, not unlike the prisoner's dilemma discussed earlier, this perspective and concomitant behaviours will become the new reality. The Third World will start their own purposeful pursuit of the prophets' vision but first their lives will have to be freed from struggling daily to survive.

When I first sketched the outline of this chapter, I intended to touch upon strategies for eliminating systemic obstacles to initiating the change process discussed so far. Clearly, I changed my mind about this as is revealed by the tone and focus I have taken. Nevertheless, the rationale of my strategy bares elaboration which includes some reiteration. The status quo protectors are far too skilled, have practised their obstructionism for far too long to be easily vanquished. Warring with them has been, is and will be a colossal waste of time. The best strategy is to go around them. This has been discussed, but the point cannot be overstated. Also, remember Buckminster Fuller's description of the Brazil experience. The success of the fifty-year plan is attributable not to official bureaucratic and/or political sanction. It is attributable to grass roots interests and initiatives. This is the same point which Suzuki and Dressel made in Good News. The successes they report were and are accomplished by small, local groups who work in close contact with local people. They are said to be committed to one place and have no plan to move away. How encouraging are their successes and how relevant to the action plan recommended here? I trust that you see them to be extremely so.

A final word of caution also is warranted. To emphasize the importance of caution, it will be useful to remember the discussion about the fate of doers as opposed to tale bearers. The tale bearers such as Chomsky are marginalised, the doers are assassinated.. As I am often reminded by my loved ones, assassinations are no longer literal. At least not most of the time. Today those who threaten the status quo are fiercely and relentlessly attacked until they slip into professional oblivion. While many courageously act on principle, few can persevere the forces of the status quo when tactics become dirty and beyond the individual's personal resources to take on. Witness the past actions of the tobacco industry and the story of Vitamin B-17 told by G. Edward Griffin. These two examples cogently illustrate the power of the status quo. While Griffin is too easily dismissed as a conspiracy theorist, the fact is that history reveals conspiracy to be a persuasive human tactic for gaining and holding onto power. He chronicles the war waged by the establishment medical profession and its agents against the renegades who point to science as revealing cancer to be a deficiency disease - like scurvy - aggravated by the lack of an essential food compound in our modern diet. According to the renegade group, the problem of cancer is not science but economics and the power agenda of those who dominate the medical and pharmaceutical profession. Griffin also talks of status quo and what can happen to someone who not only complains but actually does something about disrupting it.

The message, therefore, is that it will be prudent to stay below the radar as much as possible when you begin your locally developed initiative. It will be prudent also to stay clear of the media since there is no other entity so able and willing to sensationalise and find the negative aspects of a story, where there is none, especially in initiatives which have even the remotest possibility of threatening the status quo. The last thing you want to do is to raise the ire of establishment educators by doing measurably positive things which reveal their previous ideologically, one of narrowly based strategies obstructive to the development of principled reasoning and emotional intelligence. When the media first report your success, it will be done mostly in the context of vilifying the status quo protectors. Alternatively, the media will vilify you, accuse you of social engineering and endeavouring to inculcate our children with ideologies of co-operation, concern for the greatest good for the greatest number, and, worst, promoting principled thinking and concomitant behaviours. Just remember Chomsky's position described earlier, that the media deliberately and inadvertently are the primary propaganda machine of the status quo.

At least, initially avoid publicity and focus your energies on your group and the objectives you want to achieve. By the end of the first generation, and once the first cohort has experienced the changes, it will be less dangerous to gradually reveal yourself publicly. Other local groups will have been doing similar things and will have achieved similar results. When local groups unite, the coalition will become a formidable counter-force to the establishment, who will be weakened considerably by the loss of the previously discussed, inadvertent protectors of the status quo. As the first generation moves into the adult world, they, too, will be your allies, no longer willing to tolerate or be seduced by the forces described in Part One.

Admittedly, the preceding sounds too cynical. I prefer to call it realistic and cautious. My final prescriptive to you, who are contemplating taking on the challenge advocated in this work, is to be very careful, focussed, and single-minded on benefiting your community. When you accomplish this, the rest gradually will follow, revealing at each and every phase that we can change the course of human history and because we can, we must.

EPILOGUE

So there you have it! Now you have a working understanding of what has gone on and continues to have an adverse effect upon our world. You also have a working understanding of a particular explanation of why the world is in such a mess. The value of the explanation is that there are definable actions which come from it. Not only are the actions definable but they also are doable. Understanding why we need to do something makes the doing easier. Furthermore, the actual recommended strategies fortunately exist and there are experts out there who can deliver them or teach your local resources to deliver them. Unlike the Apollo Project, there is no need to invent a million new things to accomplish our goal, although probably there are a million things to do. Unlike the Apollo Project, to be the first at doing something, there already are numerous examples of innovative educational programs and schools, of the type recommended in this book. Most importantly there are principled individuals who have and continue to live among us. We just need to alter drastically the numerical configuration from a few, to this group becoming the majority.

The global financial crisis that came to light in the fall of 2008, which probably continues as you are reading this, underscores the need to advance the human condition in ways never before fully understood. Sooner than later, it will become apparent that financial bail outs, as all the other times before, do not produce sustainable changes. Sustainable changes, such as the vision of the prophets, the financial crisis hopefully will help us see, can only come when the majority of the professions, groups, indeed the majority of people globally, are comprised of morally mature, principled individuals, with superior emotional intelligence, the genesis of which are life long environmental conditions optimally conducive to all aspects of development. With such people, even flawed entities, such as the historically maligned legal profession, more recently seriously challenged for first place by the banking and financial investment sector, can become a service to people as opposed to the majority of people serving it.

I remain concerned, however, that I have not conveyed adequately the nature of our potential. Consequently, even here I am compelled to generate analogies which will resonate with most people. So here it goes: Think of the human potential being obstructed as a twelve cylinder Ferrari running on six pistons or a double-convection stainless steel oven with a six burner gas range used only to make scrambled eggs or a technologically advanced sewing machine without the array of threads to produce that of which it is capable or Wayne Gretzky without the support and facilitation of his father Walter or buildings such as the La Scala in Milan, Italy, without the operatic voices to perform in it or a mass of marble without Michelangelo to take away the extra pieces to reveal within the statue of David and finally your child without your empathic nurturance to develop his full potential.

I am, however, very comfortable in that I am not alone in exalting the full extent of the human potential. The primary message of every prophet essentially has been that. Whatever else they said, or someone else said they said, the message of every prophet in ancient times and now is that we are capable of far better than we have done so far. Unfortunately, the prophets of old and the current popular activists believe that reason will prevail, that reason will be sufficient. Only with some people, reason serves as both necessary and sufficient, the small group of you I am counting on. The majority has to develop the cognitive constructs before they can understand the reason advanced in this book or message of the prophets, let alone act on it. Moreover, those who can relate to the prophets' message, for the most part, are living principled lives, unless grave siege circumstances precipitate their regression. With each positive step forward, you can reasonably expect the diminishment of siege circumstances until such time as these negative occurrences become a rarity as opposed to the rule. The less we are under environmental siege the more rapidly changes will occur.

I am also compelled in these last pages to clarify my reference, indeed reliance, on the historical and current prophets to make my point. Since I believe that organized, institutionalized, and most religions in general have been key in obstructing the development of the human potential, I am probably an agnostic, although I do value tradition and ceremony for reasons mentioned before. The only benefit I can see to believing in some eternal force, a deity, from my perspective is a principled responsibility to use well what we have been given. Specifically, to use optimally the potential within us. To do so, however, we have to be able to recognize that we have not only the potential but also the responsibility to develop it. In lieu of our inability to recognize both, the prophets did it for us. Unfortunately, what they proposed and started to do were perceived to be dangerous to the status quo and their similar respective messages were quickly corrupted. Before we destroy ourselves and the planet afforded to us, it is time to stop this self-perpetuating stagnation and start on the journey to achieve the vision.

Throughout writing this work, I was constantly aware of what the critics probably would be saying. It was a real exercise in self-discipline to stay on track, namely to produce something for mass consumption. With this in mind, I channelled my energies to connect with as many people as possible rather than impressing a few academics or critics. I do not regret taking this course, although I do fear, that at times, I may have slipped into abstract unnecessary verbiage, using ten words where one would have been sufficient. I also fear perhaps not giving sufficient, accurate, and appropriate credit to my many sources. If there are commissions or omissions of this nature they were absolutely unintended, and I do beseech you to read for yourself, at least some of the sources I have recommended.

Last but not least, I want to share with you another trepidation throughout the evolution of the idea and then the writing of this book. My fear was that someone was going to pre-empt me, beat me to the punch, publish something similar if not exactly the same. Simultaneously, I harboured the fear that someone has already done all of this and that the ideas were tested and proven to be unattainable. If this has already happened, I have no awareness of it whatsoever. I am, however, acutely aware of several experiments, initiatives, and programs which are focussed on facilitating the development of young people and troubled adults. I have cited these and served them up to you as reasons for optimism and reasons to take action in your own communities. As such, even if some similar publication precedes the dissemination of this work, occurs simultaneously or shortly after, these events would be reasons to celebrate. My intent has not been to seek uniqueness, to go where no man has gone before, to discover or invent something absolutely unique and new. My intent has been to reach as many people as possible, to incite a focussed and increasingly sustainable action path which belongs to the people who are doing it. Success, to a large degree, will be determined neither by the vision nor the action plan being personified. Success will be determined by mass ownership of the various recommended initiatives and by responding to the question: Why are we doing these things? with a simple response: Because we can and because we can we must.

REFERENCES

PART ONE

CHAPTER ONE

Ball, Tim. Conversations from the Frontier Centre for Public Policy. **Frontier Centre for Public Policy**, Number 52, 2004. *While Dr. Ball has been a busy contributor in the popular press, he appears to not have published very much in professional peer-reviewed articles.*

Diamond, Jared.. **Collapse** Penguin Books:England, 2005.

Dunn, Seth Micropower: The next electrical era. **Worldwatch Paper** 151, Washington, D.C., Worldwatch Institute, July 2000.

Dunn, Seth Hydrogen futures: Toward a sustainable energy system. **Worldwatch Paper** 157, Washington, D.C., Worldwatch Institute, August 2001.

Griffin, Edward G. **A world without cancer:The story of vitamin B17**, American Media: Westlake Village, CA, 2007.

Hansen, J., et al., Target atmospheric CO^2 : Where should humanity aim? **Open Atmas. Sci. J.**, 2, 2003, 217-231.

Hansen J. Climate catastrophe. **New Science**, 195, No. 2614 (July 28), 2007, 30-34.

Hansen J. Defusing the global time bomb. **Scientific America**, 290, no. 3, 68-77, 2004, 68-77.

Homer-Dixon, Thomas **The up side of down.** Alfred A. Knopf: Canada, 2006.

Kasser, Tim **The high price of materialism.** Cambridge, MA: MIT Press, 2002.

Rifkin, Jeremy **The hydrogen economy.** Penguin Putman Inc.: New York, 2002.

Solow, Robert **The amateur: The new republic.** February, 1999.

Soros, George **Opensociety:Performing global capitalism.** New York: Public Affairs, 2000.

Suzuki, David **The David Suzuki reader: A lifetime of ideas from a leading activist and thinker.** Greystone Books: Vancouver, 2003.

von Bertalanffy, Ludwig **General system theory.** George Braziller: New York, 1968.

Whybrow, Peter **American mania: When more is not enough.** Norton: New York, 2005.

Wright, Ronald **A short history of progress.** House of Anans Press Inc.: Toronto, 2004.

CHAPTER TWO

Baigent, Michael, Leigh, Richard, and Lincoln, Henry, **The Holy Blood and The Holy Grail.** Arrow Books: U.K., 1996.

Bakan, Joel **The corporation: The pathological pursuit of profit and power.** Viking Press: Canada, 2004

REFERENCES

Chomsky, Noam, **9-11**, Seven Stories Press: New York, 2001.

Chomsky, Noam, **Class Warfare**. New Star Books: Vancouver, 1997.

Cole, Trevor Why good people do bad things: Are we living in an unethical era? **University of Toronto Magazine**, Winter 2005, Vol. 32, No. 2.

Druker, Peter F. **Concept of the corporation**. New York: John Day: New York, 1946.

Franken, Al **Lies and the lying liars who tell them**. A Plume Book: New York, 2004.

Hollis, James **Under saturn's shadow: The wounding and healing of men**. Inner City Books: Toronto, 1994.

Hollis, James **On this journey we call our life: Living the question**. Inner City Books: Toronto, 2003.

Kohlberg, Lawrence, Scharf, Peter Bureaucratic violence and conventional moral thinking. **American Journal of Orthopsychiatry**, 1972.

Moore, Michael **Stupid white men**. Regan Books: New York, 2001.

Moser, Bob The crusaders. **Rolling Stone**, issue 972, April 2005.

Nolan, Albert **Jesus before Christianity**. Orbis Books: New York, 1994.

Orwell, George **Animal farm**. Secker and Warburg: London, 1945.

CHAPTER THREE

Alexander, Bruce K. **Peaceful measures: Canada's way out of the war on drugs**. University of Toronto Press: Toronto, 1990.

Bork, Robert H. **Coercing virtue: The worldwide rule of judges**. Vintage Canada: Toronto, 2002.

Boyers, R. and Orrill, R. **R. D. Laing & anti-psychiatry.** Harper & Row: New York, 1971.

Caplan, Paula J. **They say you're crazy: How the world's most powerful psychiatrists decide who's normal.** Persus Books: Reading, Massachusetts, 1995.

Case, Roland **Understanding judicial reasoning: Controversies, concepts, and cases.** Thompson Educational Publishing Inc.: Toronto, 1997.

Cohen, M. And Davis, N. **Medication errors: Causes and preventions.** G.F. Stickley: Philadelphia,1981.

Conrad, Peter and Schneider, Joseph W. **Deviance and medicalization: From bedroom to sickness.** Temple University Press: Philadelphia, 1992.

Duncan, Barry L. and Miller, Scott D. **The heroic client.** Jossey-Bass: San Francisco, 2000.

Dworkin, Ronald **Taking rights seriously.** Harvard University Press: Cambridge, Massachusetts, 1977.

Eddy, Bill **High conflict people in legal disputes.** Janis publications: Canada, 2006.

Eisenberg, John A. **The limits of reason: Indeterminancy in law, education, and morality.** OISE Press: Toronto, 1992.

Hare, Robert **Without conscience: The disturbing world of the psychopaths among us.** Guildford Press: New York, 1993.

Hughes, Everett **Boys in white.** Transaction Publishers: New Jersey, 1961.

Leyton, Elliott **Hunting humans: The rise of the modern multiple murderer.** 2006.

Maté, Gabor **In the realm of hungry ghosts: Close encounters with addiction.** Alfred A. Knopf: Canada: 2008.

REFERENCES

Maté, Gabor **Scattered minds: A new look at the origins and healing of attention deficit disorder.** Vintage Canada: Toronto, 2000.

McBride Dabbs, James and Godwin Dabbs, Mary **Heroes, rogues and lovers: Testosterone and behaviour.** McGraw Hill: New York, 2000.

McCain, Margaret Norrie and Mustard, J. Frasier, **Early Years study.** Publications Ontario: Toronto, 1999.

Neef, M. And Neigel S. The adversary nature of the American legal system from a historical perspective. **New York Law Reform.**, 1974, 20:123-164.

Neufeld, Gordon and Maté, Gabor. **Hold on to your kids: Why parents need to matter more than peers.** Alfred A. Knopf: Canada, 2005.

Rawls, John **A theory of justice: Revised edition.** The Belknap Press of Harvard University Press: Cambridge, Massachusetts, 1999.

Read, J., Mosher, L.R. & Bentall, R.P., **Models of madness.** Routledge, Taylor and Francis Group: London, 2004.

Stone, M.H. **Personality disordered patients: Treatable and untreatable.** American Psychiatric Press: Washington, D.C., 2006.

Wright, Margaret M. **Judicial decision making in child sexual abuse cases.** University of British Columbia Press: British Columbia, 2007.

Young, Alan N. **Justice defiled: Perverts, potheads, serial killers and lawyers.** Key Porter Books: Toronto, 2003.

PART TWO

CHAPTER FOUR

Campbell, Joseph **Reflections on the art of living.** Selected and edited by Diane K. Osbon. Harper Perennial: New York, 1991.

Cummings, E.M., Davies, P.T. and Campbell, S.B. **Develpmental psychopathology and family process: Theory, research and clinical implications.** The Guildford Press: New York, 2000.

Doidge, Norman, **The brain that changes itself.** New York, New York: Viking, 2007.

Eisenberg, Nancy **The development of prosocial moral judgement and its correlates.** University Microfilms International: Ann Arbor, Michigan, 1979.

Gaarder, Jostein **Sophie's world: A novel about the history of philosophy.** Berkley Books: New York, 1996.

Goleman, Daniel **Emotional intelligence: Why it can matter more than IQ.** Bantam Books: New York, 1994.

Hendrix, H. **Getting the love you want: A guide for couples.** Harper: New York, 1990.

Keshavan, Matcheri S. and Murray, Robin M. **Neurodevelopment & adult psychopathy.** Cambridge University Press: Cambridge, U.K., 1997.

Kohlberg, L. **Stage and sequence: The cognitive develpmental approach to socialization.** Jn. Goslin, D.A. (ed.), Handbook of socialization theory and research. Rand McNally: Chicago, Il., 1969.

Kohlberg, L. **The psychology of moral development.** Harper Rowe: San Francisco, 1984.

McCain, Margaret Norrie and Mustard, J. Frasier, **Early years**

study. Publications Ontario: Ontario, Canada, 1999.

Milgram, S., Behavioural study of obedience. **Journal of Abnormal and Social Psychology,** 67, 1963, 371-78.

Polgar, A.T. **A structural-developmental analysis of levels of social reasoning in correctional volunteers.** University Microfilms International: Ann Arbor, Michigan, 1982.

Polgar, A. **Conducting parenting capacity assessments: A manual for mental health practioners.** Sandriam Publications: Hamilton, Ontario, 2002.

Randolph, E.M., **Broken hearts wounded minds: The psychological functioning of severely traumatized and behaviour problem children.** RFR Publications: Evergreen, CO, 2001.

Stein, Steven J. and Book, Howard E. **The E Q edge: Emotional intelligence and your success.** Stoddart Publishing: Toronto, Canada, 2000.

Tapp, June L. Developing senses of law and legal justice. **Journal of Social Issues.** Volume 27, Number 2, 1971.

CHAPTER FIVE

Cialdini, Robert B. **Influence: The psychology of persuasion.** Harper Collins Books: New York, 2007.

Marx, K. and Engels, F. **Manifesto of the communist party.** Progress Publishers: Moscow, 1969

Rest, Jim et al., Judging the important issues in moral dilemmas. **Developmental Psychology,** 10(4), 1974, 491-501. Warnock, Mary **Ethics since 1900.** Oxford University Press: New York, 1960.

CHAPTER SIX

Aronson, E. et al. **The jigsaw classroom.** Sage Publications: Beverly Hills, 1978.

Boyd, Dwight and Bogdan, Deanne Something clarified, nothing of value: A rhetorical critique of values classification. **Education Theory,** Vol. 34, No. 3, pp 287-300, 1984.

Coloroso, Barbara **Kids are worth it.** Summerville House Publishing: Toronto, 1994.

DeLeon, George **The therapeutic community.** Springer Publishing Company: New York, N.Y., 2000.

Diener, Ed and Suh, Eunkook eds., **Culture and subjective well-being.** Cambridge, MA: MIT Press, 2000.

Easterlin, Richard, Will raising the incomes of all increase the happiness of all? **Journal of Economic Behaviour and Organization,** 27, 1995, 35-217.

Griffin, Edward G. **The creature from Jekyll Island.** American Media: Westlake Village, CA, 2007.

Griffin, Edward G. **The capitalist conspiracy.** H.B. Patriots: Huntington Beach, CA, 1971.

King, M. L. **I Have a Dream.** Douglas Archives of American Public Address (http://douglass.speech.nwu) On May 26, 1999. Prepared by D. Oetting (http://nonce.com/oetting).

Lennon, John **Imagine**

Lickona, Thomas **Raising good children.** New York: Bantam Books, 1983.

Power, Clark The just community approach to moral education. **Journal of Moral Education,** Vol. 17, No. 3, pp 195-208, 1988.

Roots of Empathy www.rootsofempathy.org.

Rosenthal, Jeffrey S. **Struck by lightning: The curious world of probabilities.** Harper Collins Publishers Ltd: Toronto, 2005.

Sherif, M. et al. **Intergroup conflict and cooperation: The robbers cave experiment.** Norman, Oklahoma Institute of Intergroup Relations, 1961.

Stephan, W.G. School desegregation: An evaluation of predictions made in Brown v. Board of Education. **Psychological Bulletin,** 85, 1978, 217-30.

PART THREE

CHAPTER SEVEN

Kohlberg, L., Kauffman, K., Scharf, P., and Hickey, J. **The just community approach to corrections: A manual.** Moral Education Research Foundation: Harvard University, 1974.

CHAPTER EIGHT

Alexander, Karl L., Entwisle, Doris R., and Olson, Linda S. Schools, achievement, and inequality: A seasonal perspective. **Educational Evaluation and Policy Analysis,** 23, No. 2, 171-191, Summer 2001.

Coles, Robert **The moral intelligence of children.** Random House: New York, 1997.

Fryer, R. G. and Levitt, S. D. Understanding the black-white test score gap in the first two years of school. **The Review of Economics and Statistics,** 86, No. 2, 2004.

Haley, Jay **The power tactics of Jesus Christ: And other essays.** Avon Books: New York, 1969.

Hitchens, Christopher **God is not great: How religion poisons everything.** Twelve Books: New York, 2007.

Levitt, Steven D. and Dubner, Stephen J. **Freakonomics.** William Morrow: New York, 2005.

CHAPTER NINE

Fuller, Buckminster R. **Critical path.** St. Martins Press: New York, 1981.

Griffin, Edward G. **World without cancer: The story of vitamin B-17.** American Media, Nineteenth Printing: Westlake Village, CA, 2007.

Suzuki, David and Dressel, Holly **Good news for a change: How everyday people are helping the planet.** Greystone Books: New York, 2002.

ABOUT THE AUTHOR

Dr. Alexander T. Polgar, Ph.D. is a persistent and ever curious learner who has combined in a thirty-five year span several parallel careers grounded in a passionate pursuit to improve the individual and the collective human condition. He is a member of that unique group of individuals who believe that we are all human becomings, prevented from realizing our true and full developmental potential by obstacles of our own inadvertent complacency. From his perspective our wondrous technological achievements are mere hints of our greater capacity to live in cooperative and facilitative harmony among ourselves and with our environment. While living in this way is a formidable goal, he believes it not to be impossible and a pursuit which is worthy of a life long commitment. This commitment is reflected in his approach to his life's work. Instead of pursuing a singularly focussed career path to acquire expertise in one well defined area, he has combined many interests personally and professionally. To whatever he does he brings his artistic aptness and practice wisdom that is the product of his breadth and depth of adventuress exploration and discovery.

In his career of curious inquiry into the human condition Dr. Polgar has worked in many different clinical settings providing direct mental health services, as well as performing program design, implementation, and evaluation functions. He has taught empirical practice methodology at the graduate school level and conducted assessments for a variety of purposes.

As a management consultant in the private and public sectors Dr. Polgar's focus has always been innovative and grounded in optimizing individual as well as organizational wellness. For example, he was among the first to act on the scientifically validated importance of emotional intelligence as it pertains to individuals as well as the organizations in which they work.

Thirty-five years of accumulative, varied learning experiences, have culminated in Dr. Polgar embarking on a new career path for the second half of his life. His interest is to write about and teach that which touches in a meaningful way the greatest number of people. Even more importantly, through these efforts, his goal is to recruit an ever increasing number of allies in the quest to actualize our potential to become truly human.

www.ingramcontent.com/pod-product-compliance
Lightning Source LLC
Chambersburg PA
CBHW030849170426
43193CB00009BA/549